Unlocking THE 6 POWERS OF THE HEART
HAQQAIQ AL QALB

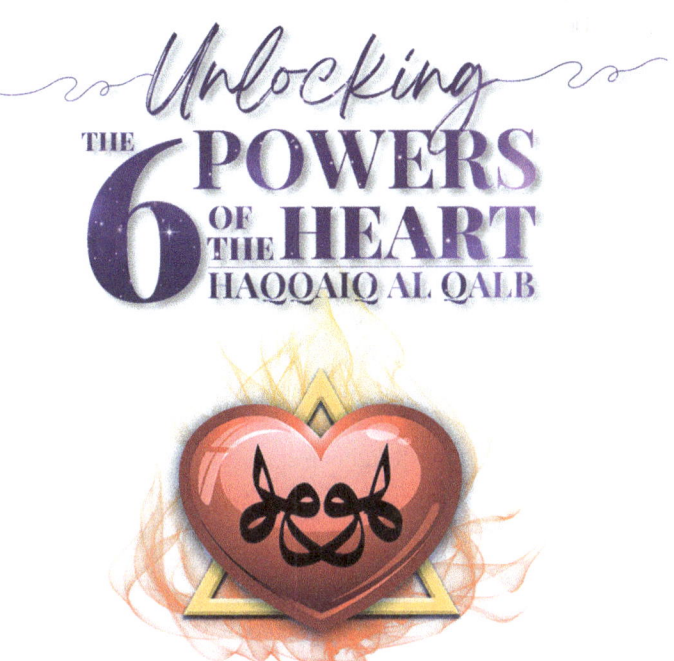

SHAYKH NURJAN MIRAHMADI

Shokran for your purchase of the book. May Allah ﷻ shower His Divine Blessings upon you and all your loved ones.

May He keep us all with the Love of Sayyidina Muhammad ﷺ

PUBLISHED BY THE
SUFI MEDITATION CENTRES SOCIETY

UNLOCKING THE 6 POWERS OF THE HEART
HAQQAIQ AL QALB

Copyright © 2023

by Shaykh Nurjan Mirahmadi

ISBN: 978-1-989602-06-5

Published and Distributed by:

Sufi Meditation Centers Society
3660 East Hastings St.
Vancouver, BC V5K 2A9 Canada
Tel: (604) 558-4455

NurMuhammad.com

First Edition: November 2023

TABLE OF CONTENTS

ABOUT THE AUTHOR

PROFILE

For the past two decades, Shaykh Nurjan Mirahmadi has worked hard to spread the true Islamic teachings of love, acceptance, respect, and peace throughout the world and opposes extremism in all its forms. An expert on Islamic spirituality, he has studied with some of the world's leading Islamic scholars of our time.

Shaykh Mirahmadi has also founded numerous educational and charitable organizations. He has travelled extensively throughout the world learning and teaching Islamic meditation and healing, understanding the channeling of Divine energy, discipline of the self, and the process of self-realization. He teaches these spiritual arts to groups around the world, regardless of religious denomination.

BACKGROUND

Shaykh Nurjan Mirahmadi studied Business Management at the University of Southern California. He then established and managed a successful healthcare company and imaging centers throughout Southern California. Having achieved business success at a remarkably young age, Shaykh Nurjan Mirahmadi shifted his focus from the private sector to the world of spirituality. In 1994 he pursued his religious studies and devoted himself to be of service to those in need. He combined his personal drive and financial talents to work for the less fortunate and founded an international relief organization, a spiritual healing center, and a religious social group for at risk youth.

In 1995, he became a protégé of Mawlana Shaykh Hisham Kabbani for in-depth studies in Islamic spirituality known as Sufism. He studied and accompanied Shaykh Kabbani on many tours and learned about Sufi practices around the world. Together with Shaykh Kabbani, he has established a number of other Islamic educational organizations and relief programs throughout the world.

Shaykh Nurjan Mirahmadi has received written authorization to be a Spiritual Guide from the World Leader of the Naqshbandi Islamic Sufi Order, Shaykh Muhammad Nazim al-Haqqani, as per the permission of the 41st Shaykh of the Golden Chain, Shaykh Muhammad Adil ar-Rabbani and Shaykh Hisham Kabbani. He is authorized to teach, guide, and counsel religious students around the world to Islamic Spirituality.

IJAZAS (AUTHORIZATION)

Shaykh Nurjan Mirahmadi has taught and travelled extensively throughout the world from Uzbekistan to Singapore, Thailand, Indonesia, Cyprus, Argentina, Peru, and North America. He teaches the spiritual sciences of Classical Islam, including meditation (*tafakkur*), subtle energy points (*lataif*), Islamic healing, the secrets of letters and numbers (*ilm huroof*), disciplining the self (*tarbiya*), and the process of self-realization (*ma'rifah*). He teaches the Muslim communities the prophetic ways of being kind, respectful and live in harmony with people. He emphasizes on good manners and respect, and often reminds his students that the spiritual journey begins from within and "You can't give what you don't have."

ACCOMPLISHMENTS

One of Shaykh Nurjan's greatest accomplishments has been the worldwide dissemination of the spiritual teachings of Classical Islam through his books and online presence. The Prophet Muhammad ﷺ has told us, "Speak to people according to their levels." In an era of social media, Shaykh Nurjan's ability to reach a new generation of spiritual seekers through the Internet has been remarkable. His NurMuhammad.com website alone has over 1,500 unique visitors each day, and since its inception has seen more than 200,000 downloads of the book *"Dailal Khairat"*, 1.5 Million free downloads of *Naqshbandi Muraqabah*, and another 700,000 downloads of the *Naqshbandi Book of Devotions (Awrad)*, as well as many more articles. His Facebook pages "Shaykh Nurjan Mirahmadi" and "Nur Muhammad" combined have over 1.1 million likes and followers. Furthermore, his YouTube Channel "The Muhammadan Way" has over 9 million views, and his Google page, "Shaykh Sayed Nurjan Mirahmadi" has over 2.7 million views.

Shaykh Nurjan Mirahmadi focuses on the worldwide social media presence working on ways to bring knowledge to all seekers around the world. In 2015 he launched an Online University, called *SimplyIman.org*, to spread these traditional Spiritual Islamic teachings even further and make it accessible to all seekers around the world.

For over 25 years Shaykh Nurjan has dedicated his life to spreading the true Islamic teachings of love, acceptance, respect, and peace. He has established several non-profit organizations and has founded numerous educational and charitable organizations.

YouTube Channels – Subscribe Today!

- **The Muhammadan Way** – a world leading Islamic media platform with over 9 million views, featuring a library of over 1,000 videos on various topics. Join the live broadcast of Mawlid and Zikr every Thursday, Friday, & Saturday, including interactive Question & Answer sessions.
- **Divine Love: Hub-E-Rasul** – based on the acclaimed TV series with over 27,000 views and 200 episodes.
- **Shaykh Talks** – video series of short, powerful talks focusing on Spiritual Reminders and Motivational Topics.

Muhammadan Way App (over 50,000 Users Worldwide) – a free comprehensive resource of Islamic information for all mobile devices. Created for both Muslims and non-Muslims, it provides users with a wealth of knowledge including access to books, supplications, prayer times, month-specific practices, a media library of audio and video files, an events calendar, and much more.

Social Media / Online Presence

- **Facebook (Shaykh Nurjan Mirahmadi)** with over 1.1 million followers.
- **NurMuhammad.com** – a comprehensive website containing many resources covering the deep realities of classical Islam.
- **SMC (sufimeditationcenter.com)** – an outreach organization that spreads teachings to the Western audience including concepts such as meditation and charity. It reaches out to other faiths to increase peace, love, and acceptance in the interfaith environment.

Fatima Zahra Helping Hand (muslimcharity.com) – a non-profit, volunteer-based organization that supports those less fortunate. Projects are thoughtfully designed to help those in hardship to gain support and better their lives. Through a blended approach of building strong partnerships and working with local volunteers, all initiatives are easily accessible by those who are in need.

Divine Love: Hub-E-Rasul TV Series – launched in May 2017, this weekly half-hour Islamic television show covers a wide range of topics, focusing on spreading Prophet Muhammad's ﷺ message that Islam is a religion based on peace, love, and acceptance. The show reaches the online community through social media and through its website **huberasul.net.**

Naqshbandi Islamic Center of Vancouver – this Center is a place for people of all faiths and beliefs to attend weekly *zikr* programs (circles of remembrance) three times a week (Thursdays, Fridays, and Saturdays). Shaykh Nurjan teaches above and beyond the principles of Islam including the deep realities of *maqam al-iman* (belief) and *maqam al-ihsan* (excellence of character).

Hub-E-Rasul ﷺ Conference – monthly Mawlid & Mehfil e Dhikr events are organized and held throughout the Lower Mainland. The aim is to revive the teachings of the Qur'an and *Sunnah* by celebrating holy events in true Islamic spirit (*Isra wal Mi'raj, Lailatul Bara'h, Lailatul Qadr, Mawlid an-Nabi* etc.)

Simply Iman Cloud University – an international online platform allowing people from around the world to pursue studies in various aspects of faith and spirituality from a classical Islamic perspective. Students have the opportunity to learn at their own pace and engage in an open dialogue with a teacher in real-time.

Ahle Sunnah wal Jama of BC – this organization is a resource for authentic content, books, and articles from the Qur'an & Sunnah from around the world. It works in collaboration with the well-known international organizations, Al Azhar University of Cairo, Dar al Ifta of Egypt and Islamic Supreme Council of North America.

Shaykh Nurjan's Published Books – titles are available at all major retailers and online at Amazon.

- A Timeless Reality – Ancient Wisdoms of the Soul & Meditation
- Insan al Kamil – The Universal Perfect Being ﷺ
- Rising Sun of the West
- YASEEN – Prophet ﷺ is the Walking Qur'an
- Divinely Praising Upon the Pearl of Creation
- In Pursuit of Angelic Power / Malakuti Taqat Ki Justuju May (Urdu Translation)
- Levels of the Heart – Lataif al Qalb
- Secret Realities of Hajj

Shaykh Nurjan's sincere mission is to globally spread the love of Sayyidina Muhammad ﷺ for our families and children. If you would like to be a shareholder in all these blessings, we invite you to support by any means possible. We hope to strengthen our efforts by joining our hands in raising the Honourable Flag of Sayyidina Muhammad ﷺ.

Special thanks to the Team for book design and layout and to all the Transcribers.

UNIVERSALLY RECOGNIZED SYMBOLS

The following Arabic and English symbols connote sacredness and are universally recognized by Muslims:

The symbol ﷻ represents *Azza wa Jal*, a high form of praise reserved for God alone, which is customarily recited after reading or pronouncing the common name Allah, and any of the ninety-nine Islamic Holy Names of God.

The symbol ﷺ represents *sall Allahu 'alayhi wa salaam* (God's blessings and greetings of peace be upon the Prophet), which is customarily recited after reading or pronouncing the holy name of the Prophet Muhammad ﷺ. It commonly appears as *pbuh* (Peace and Blessings be Upon Him) in English translations.

The symbol ؑ represents *'alayhi 's-salam* (peace be upon him/her), which is customarily recited after reading or pronouncing the sanctified names of prophets, Prophet Muhammad's ﷺ family members, and the angels.

The symbol ؓ represents *radi-allahu 'anh/'anha* (may God be pleased with him/her), which is customarily recited after reading or pronouncing the holy names of Prophet Muhammad's ﷺ Companions.

The symbol ق represents *qaddas-allahu sirrah* (may God sanctify his or her secret), which is customarily recited after reading or pronouncing the name of a saint.

Introduction to the
Six Powers of the Heart

Follow the Rightly Guided Companions Who Are Eternal Stars

Alhamdulillah, that we talked about the six powers of the heart and the depth of that reality and the ocean of guidance and becoming a star. This is all from the holy *Hadith* that this *haqqaiq* (reality) – every *haqqaiq* Prophet ﷺ giving from his holy *Hadith* – everything

opens from these realities. That when Sayyidina Muhammad ﷺ described that, 'Follow my companions. Any of my companions, they are like stars on a dark night.'

أَصْحَابِيْ كَالنُّجُــومْ بِأَيِّهِمْ اَقْتَدَيْتِمْ اَهْتَدَيْتِمْ

"Ashabi kan Nujoom, bi ayyihim aqta daytum ahta daytum."

"My companions are like stars. Whoever among them you follow, you will be rightly guided." Prophet Muhammad (pbuh)

It means opened for us the reality of *najm* and a star. That through the darkness of ignorance and the night describes the oceans of ignorance. That, 'If you want to follow *Khulafa e Rasihdin al Mahdiyeen wal Kamilin* (The Perfected and Rightly Guided Muhammadan Representatives), that my *Sahabi* – my companions – those who

1

accompanied me with their heart, with their actions, and with their deeds, they're like stars. I've made them into stars, *najm*. They are eternal lights.' It means that now that we reached a point of understanding and sciences and all these realities, that this was an *isharah* (sign) and a guidance for us that take the way of light and become something eternal.

The Eternal Stars Always Shine On Creation

That you live a life of service and the ultimate service. That's why when we live a life of service – giving food, donating, serving, being of service with my skill, with my ability, with my *rizq* (sustenance) – anything that I have, I put in the way of Allah ﷻ. And this is still just *dunya* (material world) so that Allah ﷻ accept that *dunya* and say that, 'I will grant you an eternal service.' Eternal service is when Allah ﷻ ignite the soul of the believer. That your soul to become an eternal reality of guidance because guidance and *Rashidin* (rightly guided), and *sifat ar-Rashid* (attribute of rightly guided) is guidance.

That when Allah ﷻ open the soul for guidance then that's the concept of the star within the dark nights. That, 'Your light will always guide.' When Allah ﷻ open for a servant to be an eternal star, then they have always been an eternal star. Whatever form they take in this material world and how many times they appear within this material world, it doesn't take away from the reality of who their star.

So, for those who contemplate, contemplate. It means that's a deep reality. That Allah ﷻ says that, 'You...' – because Allah ﷻ has no time – that, 'Your soul is from My eternal stars and you'll always shine within My creation. Whatever physicality I put you with within time and in dimensions, your *ruh*, your soul, is always that *najm*.' That's why

Prophet ﷺ was giving that *isharah* (sign) that, 'My *Sahabi*, any one of them you follow, they're stars on a dark night.' That was enough for that opening to open within the heart of *awliyaullah* (saints), that seek to be of an eternal service.

The Star of Sulaiman ؈ Symbolizes the Six Powers of the Heart

When you give from the physical world, serve with the physical world, then enter into a station of guidance in which you're trying to be of service to Allah's ﷻ creation and guiding them towards realities. Allah ﷻ give the true gift of guidance in which your soul reaches these six powers. That's why the six – the three points up, three points down; you become *Najm e*

Sulaiman ؈ (Star of Solomon) in which the whole kingdom will be given to that soul and has access. That soul has access to the entire kingdom of Allah ﷻ.

Prophet Solomon ؈ Was Granted From Sayyidina Muhammad's ﷺ Kingdom

That's what Sayyidina Sulaiman ؈ represented in Qur'an. That if the kingdom… Allah ﷻ can give the kingdom to whomever He likes.

قُلِ اللَّهُمَّ مَالِكَ الْمُلْكِ تُؤْتِي الْمُلْكَ مَنْ تَشَاءُ وَتَنْزِعُ الْمُلْكَ مِمَّنْ تَشَاءُ, وَتُعِزُّ مَنْ تَشَاءُ وَتُذِلُّ مَنْ تَشَاءُ بِيَدِكَ الْخَيْرُ . إِنَّكَ عَلَى كُلِّ شَيْئٍ قَدِيرٌ سُوْرَةُ أَلِ عِمْرَان ﴿٢٦﴾

3:26 – "Qulillahumma Malikul mulki, tu'til mulka man tashaau wa tanzi'ul mulka mimman tasha'u, wa tu'izzu man tasha'u, wa tudhillu man tasha'u, bi yadikal khayr, innaka 'ala kulli shay'in qadir." (Surat Ali 'Imran)

"Say: O Allah, Master of the Kingdom, You give the Kingdom to whom You will, and You Take away the Kingdom from whom You will, You honor whom You will and You humble whom You will; in Your hand is [all] the good, Indeed, You are over all things Powerful."
(Family of Imran, 3:26)

This kingdom of Sayyidina Muhammad ﷺ and its immensity can't be imagined. Allah ﷻ is describing, 'That soul that is in submission lived a life of *taslim* (submission). I'm going to give to it to inherit that kingdom. As a result, that soul will become a star in My heavens.' That star that Prophet ﷺ described will be giving guidance eternally. So that anyone who's lost on the Earth, they look up and they can receive even physical guidance. They can get the co-ordinance of where they are and how they're lost on this world. Spiritually, that *tajalli* (manifestation) of that star is continuously dressing them.

1. Haqiqatul Juzba (Reality of Magnetism)

Heavenly Guides are the Power Source That Magnetize Us Through Madad

That's why the depth of *Haqiqatul Juzba* (Reality of Magentism). The first that we talk about is like an eternal circle. The depth of *juzba* (attraction) is not something that has a limit. If the servant doesn't learn how to connect and how to magnetize themselves, how to take their body and to become magnetized with a charge. The coiling, we said in school,

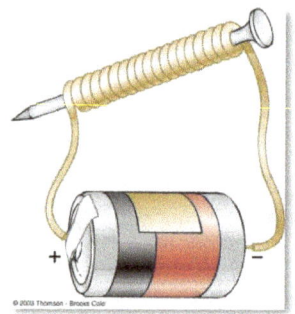

everyone is taught that you get a rod, a metal rod, and the rod has no magnetic connection. As soon as you take an electrical coil and you coil it and wrap it all the way around the rod. Then connect to a power source, and you're actually magnetizing the metal. So, when you take that coil and you touch it, it begins to attract all of the paper clips in the school experiments that we did in school. It means becoming magnetized and coiling. Well, that's the same concept of understanding the *madad* (support) and the meditation.

When you sit for meditation that, '*Ya Rabbi*, I want to open the heavenly kingdom within my being.' As soon as you learned the *madad* (support), the *madad* and the shaykhs are the power source. They are the battery of Allah 🕌 that is accessible for creation. They don't take from the trees and the air and the atmosphere. They're taking from Allah's 🕌 servants who are custodians of a Divinely Power, a Divinely Grace. That's why we distinguish between these sci-fi movies where they're taking from the forest, they're taking from electromagnetic energy of the Earth. No, they're not taking. That's a limited source of energy and that's not a clean energy from the heavens. But Allah 🕌 has on this Earth, *"Ittaqollah, wa kono ma'as sadiqeen,"* 'Have consciousness. Be conscious and obedient servant of Allah 🕌 and keep the company of God's truthful servants.'

يَا أَيُّهَا الَّذِينَ آمَنُوا اتَّقُوا اللَّهَ وَكُونُوا مَعَ الصَّادِقِينَ ﴿١١٩﴾

9:119 – "Ya ayyuhal ladheena amanoo ittaqollaha wa kono ma'as sadiqeen." (Surat At-Tawbah)

"O you who have believed, have consciousness of Allah and be with those who are truthful/Pious/sincere (in words and deed)."
(The Repentance, 9:119)

Awliya Hold the Covenant of Allah ﷻ and are Custodians of Heavenly Light

For those truthful servants, they contain the covenant of Allah ﷻ. The covenant of Allah ﷻ and that which Sayyidina Musa ﷺ was carrying

with angels. The covenant of Allah ﷻ is the holy heart of *insan* (human being). That if that heart opened to the Divinely Kingdom, 'Thy Kingdom come, thy will be done on Earth as it is in heaven.' It means their heart became the Kingdom of God. As a result, they hold the covenant and the contract of God within their heart. As a result, they are the custodians of that light.

Make Your Madad to Connect With Awliya's Encrypted Light

When you learn to be with them, eat with them, pray with them, accompany them through these modalities in which Allah ﷻ has offered and opened, then you begin to learn how to connect to them. As a result of connecting to them, they contain an energy source that's not available anywhere. It's an encrypted light. So, only now we're understanding coding. There are places that you can get information from and that you may have access to and there are other sources that are highly encrypted and you don't have access to. That's one of the encrypted sources. So that *shaitan* (satan) is not taking that light. *Shaitan* is not using and abusing that light, that it's through an encrypted source.

That's why then the *madad.* As soon as they make the connection, they learn how to make the connection, they study the way of how to make the connection. They begin to open with the permission of Allah ﷻ, the permission of Sayyidina Muhammad ﷺ and the permission of these *awliya* (saints), *"Ulil amre minkum"* (those in authority among you).

...أَطِيعُوا اللَّهَ وَأَطِيعُوا الرَّسُولَ وَأُوْلِي الْأَمْرِ مِنْكُمْ... ﴿٥٩﴾

4:59 – "...Atiullaha wa atiur Rasula wa Ulil amre minkum..."
(Surat An-Nisa)

...Obey Allah, Obey the Messenger, and those in authority among you..." (The Women, 4:59)

That they carry *"Izzatullah* (Allah's ﷻ Might and Magnificence), *'izzatur Rasul* (honour of the Messenger), *wal 'izzatul mumineen* (honour of the believers)." They carry the *'Izzat* (Might) of Allah ﷻ, the power of Allah ﷻ is moving within them. As a result, this encrypted code, encrypted light begin to enter within their reality. And that is the reality of becoming magnetized.

...وَلِلَّهِ الْعِزَّةُ وَلِرَسُولِهِ وَلِلْمُؤْمِنِينَ ... ﴿٨﴾

63:8 – "...Wa Lillahil 'izzatu wa li Rasooli hi wa lil Mumineen..."
(Surat Al-Munafiqoon)

"...And to Allah belongs [all] honor, and to His messenger, and to the
believers..." (The Hypocrites, 63:8)

The Sufi Alchemy is to Turn Hearts Into Gold for the Divinely Presence

Everything about them is going from
silver to gold and that's what we talked
last night. That is the alchemy. The way
of alchemy and the Sufi alchemy, the
path of alchemy was not to take the silver
of the material world and turn it to gold.
What they want from the physical world?
What are you going to do with gold like
Qaroon [also known as Croesus] and
holding treasures of gold going
nowhere?

The real purpose of making gold was to turn people's hearts into gold,
something precious for the Divinely Presence. To take that which is of
a regular metal, iron metal, dirty copper metal, or steel within people and
to make it into something of value to the Divinely Presence, to make
their hearts like gold. As a result of the heart being gold and precious, it
can contain Divinely grace and emanations that begin to dress it. We've
described before how can God's grace dress a heart that's like
styrofoam? As soon as that energy comes, it melts and dissipates
everything. So, the heart has to be turned into a golden vessel for the
Divinely Presence, clean and purified.

Training in Juzba Leads to a Magnetic Character

As a result of their training in *juzba*, becoming magnetic, becoming magnetized and filled with energies, they become a magnet. Because anything that's connecting with a magnet is being magnetized. That's what the reality of when we say, '*Juzba*, you have a *juzba*. You have a magnetic character where people are attracted to you, your speech and your light.' They want to be around magnetic people because the charge of that person is a very positive charge. As a result, they take away the negativities of other people.

Allah ﷻ Put a Certain Juzba in the Shaykh That Attracts Students

One – this magnet in dealing with students is that it immediately puts a charge and the students which are of a negative charge are directed and guided towards that magnet. So, this is not of their own doing. This is not the way to force people to follow you and keep putting out things that, 'You have to follow me!' They can't follow if they're not feeling an attraction within their heart because this is not business and this is not the physical world. The physical world, you say, 'Follow' and your advice on financial issues and every mind is listening to you.

But this, in dealing with the people of the heart, if their heart has no connection with you, you cannot force them to follow you. The heart has no feeling for that person because they're not understanding that Allah ﷻ is in charge of this *juzba*. Allah ﷻ is putting this charge of this student who became a shaykh and is now trained. Allah ﷻ puts the charge within that individual [shaykh], and they merely do the work that they've been guided to do and Allah ﷻ is in charge of who will be coming to you.

Shaykhs Spread the Divine's Message and Allah ﷻ Sends the Students

That's why they don't seek out people. They seek out openings. So, it means for an example for us to understand – they open a door to a channel, for example. They immediately begin to do what Allah ﷻ guided them to do of their teaching, their style of teaching. The rest is for Allah ﷻ. He's going to determine which of these 'paper clips,' if we want to understand, will be attracted to that magnet.

Not that the shaykh can go out and grab people and force people to listen to them. It's just they provide and they keep praying for an opening, '*Ya Rabbi*, granting us an opening through that door.' As soon as that door opens, they do what they've been trained to do. And Allah ﷻ begins to send the attraction of people who will be attracted to that magnet, to the flavour of that magnet, and the teachings of that magnet. That's the reality of how the shaykh has a *juzba* on Earth.

They teach what they need to teach. That's why they need the modalities; they need the books, they need the videos, they need the postings. They need the social media to get the message of what Allah 🕌 want them to disseminate. The rest is from Allah 🕌 who's going to come, who's going to be attracted. That's why they don't go out and put out ads in the paper that, 'You have to follow, you have to do this,' because it's not in their hands. They merely put the ad out of, 'This is the teachings,' and then from the thousand that listen, fifty of them are attracted to that teacher.

There is Magnetism Between the Teacher and His Students

People begin to levitate and move towards that reality. That's not even within their own hand and their own minds. If you read the comments on the videos that are being posted, they say, 'I'm a Christian and I believe in my book but I'm attracted to what you're saying.' That is the *juzba*. It's not that we got on the phone and we forced this guy, 'Please, can you please watch my video? You have to watch my video.' No. The *juzba* is that his heart, regardless of what his brain has studied, his heart is in God's Hand. God is the one whom controls the heart and says, 'Listen to this magnet.' If you listen, you feel an attraction from heart to heart.

There are even video comments that, 'I don't even understand an hour of what you were talking about because of your Arabic phonics and the words that you use from Arabic to English words.' So, unfortunately a lot of our words may be lost in translations. But he says, 'I didn't understand it but I was crying the whole time watching it.'

Because again this is a system through the heart. The mouth is saying things for entertainment for people but the energy that's being moved through heart to heart, that is the *haqqaiq* and the reality. That is the grace of the Divine that moves through the heart of the one speaking to the ones whom listening through their heart system. That is the reality of the *juzba* and magnetism for the connection between the teacher and the student.

The Danger of Jealousy to Those With Immense Juzba Like Imam Hussain ﷺ

Now between the teacher and his teachers, that is now the *juzba* of how they connect. So imagine again if they didn't train on this step, that's why you find a lot of people angry, 'Oh, they don't listen to me. People don't follow me, they only follow you.' How many times they become jealous and they would try to destroy these types of people. So, the history of Islam was deep into that. They wanted to kill Imam Hussain ﷺ because he had immense *juzba*. They said, 'As long as you're on this Earth, people want to take your hand and not our hand. So better we take you from this Earth and get rid of this problem.'

This was again the immensity of the jealousy of *juzba* and what Allah ﷻ put within the heart of a servant. That Allah ﷻ put that connection, Allah ﷻ put that energy, Allah ﷻ put that magnetism. As a result, people are attracted to that reality. The one whom doesn't study that way, because those holy souls were given that *juzba*, the other ones are being trained in the way of that *juzba*. If they don't train for the magnetism, then there's nothing that is in their heart emanating for people to be attracted to.

2. Haqiqatul Faiz
(Reality of Downpouring Emanation)

The Juzba of the Shaykh Attracts the Nazar and Faiz of His Shaykhs

Now even more dangerous is the system between the shaykh to his shaykhs. It's that when he's been trained in *juzba*, been trained in magnetism. As soon as he makes his connection, the energy frequency is going to their reality. In the spiritual world, there's no

tiring, there's no being tired. Their souls can be in infinite number of places in an instant. As soon as they're trained and they make their connection, they prepare themself for the speech they're supposed to give, the association they're supposed to attend.

Immediately, their *juzba* goes to attract their shaykhs. Their shaykh, the shaykh, the shaykh, the shaykh, all the way to *Sahabi Kiram* (Honoured Companions of Prophet ﷺ), *Ahlul Baytin Nabi* ﷺ (Holy Family of the Prophet ﷺ), all the way to the presence of Sayyidina Muhammad ﷺ. Their magnet goes on for the heavens and as a result is attracting the *nazar* (gaze) of the holy ones.

As a result of their magnet attracting the *nazar* of holy ones, they begin to receive the *nazar* upon themselves. So we can understand the immensity of *juzba*. So when the shaykh is trained, he turns his energy on and immediately the frequency goes out and attracts then the higher heavens' attraction. So, the shaykhs at the heavens are now picking the signal up of that shaykh and they begin to send the *faiz* (downpouring blessings) upon that shaykh.

Without that, the shaykh can speak nothing. There's nothing to say, nothing to talk about. He's not attracted the connection to the heavens so as a result, he's useless to anybody on Earth. This is the difference between real and fake. Real and fake. Fake connects to nothing above. Nothing in the heavens is connecting to that shaykh. Nothing is with a *juzba* connected to them and nothing sending a *faiz* to them.

Awliya Seek the Nazar of Prophet ﷺ Which is the Power Station

We said the next *haqqaiq* is the *faiz* (downpouring emanation). That once you connect with the big souls of the *tariqah* (spiritual path), and all the Holy Companions and *Ahlul Bayt* (Holy Family of Prophet ﷺ), all the way to the presence of Holy Sayyidina Muhammad ﷺ. This magnetic connection is from

ishq and love in their heart. When they connect, what happens? What we say *"unzur halana"* (gaze upon my condition). That's why Allah ﷻ clarified this connection. That, all you who want to be connecting, 'Don't say listen to me, but say *unzur halana*.'

يَا أَيُّهَا الَّذِينَ آمَنُوا لَا تَقُولُوا رَاعِنَا وَقُولُوا انظُرْنَا وَاسْمَعُوا ...﴿١٠٤﴾

2:104 – "Yaa ayyuhal ladheena aamano, laa taqolo ra'yina wa qolu unzurna wasma'o..." (Surat Al-Baqarah)

"O you who believe! Do not say (to Prophet Muhammad (pbuh)) ra'yena, listen to us, and say Unzurna (gaze upon us) and you listen (to him (pbuh)..." (The Cow, 2:104)

It means don't ask Prophet ﷺ to listen to you because he is *"sam'ina wa ata'na"* ﷺ. His ears and the *sifat* (attribute) of hearing is only for the Divinely Presence. He listens to nobody but Allah ﷻ.

$$\text{سَمِعْنَا وَأَطَعْنَا غُفْرَانَكَ رَبَّنَا وَاِلَيْكَ الْمَصِيْرُ ﴿٢٨٥﴾}$$

2:285 – *"Sam'ina wa ata'na, ghufranaka Rabbana wa ilaykal masir."*
(Surat Al-Baqarah)

"...We hear, and we obey: (We seek) Thy forgiveness, our Lord, and to Thee is the end of all journeys." (The Cow, 2:285)

But in that holy verse Allah ﷻ is giving the secret of the *nazar* of Prophet ﷺ – *"unzur halana"* – 'just please keep your gaze upon me.' Why? Because that's the holy power station. If the power station of Prophet's ﷺ *nazar* immediately falls upon that soul, then imagine all the *nazars* are following. Because if it was worth the gaze of Prophet ﷺ, imagine then how much the *Ahlul Bayt* ﷺ love, how much *Sahabi* love, how much *awliyaullah* love and are in service to that *nazar* that immediately, it attracts all the *nazar* upon that soul of that servant. As a result of the immensity of the *nazar* upon that shaykh's soul, that's what he has of a food to give to his students that are also connecting with him.

Shaykh's Magnet Connects to Heaven and Becomes Loaded With Energies

We see from the heavenly power, the shaykh is an intermediary on Earth and then all the students that are learning how to make the connection. So the magnet goes up first to the heavens, connects, the *faiz* begins to dress the emanation,  the talks, the inspirations. As a result, that shaykh becomes *"fulkil mashhoon* – a loaded ship." Their soul is loaded with energies and knowledges. The minute they begin to disseminate that, then all those whom learn how to connect they begin to receive the *faiz* of that shaykh.

وَآيَةٌ لَّهُمْ أَنَّا حَمَلْنَا ذُرِّيَّتَهُمْ فِي الْفُلْكِ الْمَشْحُونِ ﴿٤١﴾

36:41 – "Wa ayatul lahum anna hamalna dhurriyyatahum fil fulkil mashhooni." (Surat YaSeen)

"And a sign for them is that we have carried their atoms/forefathers in the loaded ship." (YaSeen, 36:41)

Our Love and Connection to the Shaykh is Due to the Muhammadan Faiz in Them

That is the *haqqaiq* that they are asking to train. So when we train with the connection, it is the whole way. It's not a part of the way, it's the only way. If you didn't train in *juzba*, you don't have a connection up and as a result, nobody wants to connect with you down because there's nothing in you. You're not a magnet. You're a piece of metal. Nobody can connect with metal other than you put a rope and you force people and tie them to you by force. So because this connection is not by force, nobody is imprisoned and confined to a camp or a farm, where we all have to live together by force.

This is a connection based on *ishq* and *muhabbat* – love, love and respect. That through love and respect, the hearts are connected. Wherever they are on this Earth people are connected, interested in that level of teaching, that guidance. As a result, that *juzba* is there, and that *juzba* is in existence because of the *faiz* and the *juzba* above. That they have the *nazar* (gaze) of Sayyidina Muhammad ﷺ. This is the *daleel* and the proof of why people are connected to them, and why people are interested in their teachings. They can't force people to, but because the *faiz* of Prophet ﷺ emanates through them. As a result, it emanates to the people and people are attracted. The personality is less important and is not important. What's important is the *faiz* of Prophet ﷺ is flowing through them and the knowledges are flowing through them.

Shaykh's Connection to Prophet ﷺ is Delicate and Requires Taqwa

If they should do something wrong and inappropriate against the way of Sayyidina Muhammad ﷺ, their *faiz* will be cut. As a result, you see many of the students will run and it will be gone. They have no more connection with that person. So what  keeps us is not a physical rope but this spiritual rope of *faiz* and connection, and that's through a *muhabbat* and through the love and through the connection to the heart of Sayyidina Muhammad ﷺ. Because it's a delicate connection.

That's why everything they do is always with *istighfar* (seeking forgiveness), asking forgiveness if they've done anything to upset the reality of Sayyidina Muhammad ﷺ. As a result, there is a reality of their *taqwa* (consciousness). They're continuously in that engagement and in that connection that, 'If I'm doing anything wrong forgive me, guide me.'

"Shahidan" (witness), for them is a different level than what we described before. They are in direct communication with that light. *"Shahidan"* that Allah ﷻ is describing, 'He's witnessing you. You know that because you're connecting with him.' This is the level of the shaykh

to that reality, *"Shahidan." "Mubashshiran"* – he ﷺ is happy, he's sending his *faiz* to you. *"Wa Nazeeran"* – he'll begin to describe, 'I'm not happy with that action that you're doing. You do it anymore and this connection cuts.' So that's *taqwa*.

$$\text{يَا أَيُّهَا النَّبِيُّ إِنَّا أَرْسَلْنَاكَ شَاهِدًا وَمُبَشِّرًا وَنَذِيرًا ﴿٤٥﴾ وَدَاعِيًا إِلَى اللَّهِ بِإِذْنِهِ}$$
$$\text{وَسِرَاجًا مُّنِيرًا ﴿٤٦﴾}$$

33:45-46 – "Ya ayyuhan Nabiyu inna arsalnaka Shahidan wa Mubashshiran wa Nazeera. (45) Wa daiyan ila Allahi`bi-idhnihi wa Sirajan Muneera. (46)" (Surat Al-Ahzab)

"O Prophet, indeed We have sent you as a Witness and a Bearer of Glad Tidings and a Warner. (45) And the one who invites to Allah, by His permission, and as an illuminating lamp spreading light."
(The Combined Forces, 33:45-46)

Faiz and Heavenly Connection are Life Support for Awliya

That for them is their real *taqwa*. The real *taqwa*! Not the *imam* (religious leader) at the mosque saying, 'Taqwa is this, *taqwa* is this,' but he's behind six feet of metal and never seen or felt anything. That's not *taqwa*! Real *taqwa* is when you're in their presence and they're guiding you. And they're telling you your whole life and your life support is this *faiz* and this connection. For if they cut you, you die and wither away in an instant. Only way you're surviving on this Earth because they dressed you from that reality, they blessed you from that reality. You taste, breathe, eat, and drink from that reality. As a result, you're being fed from that reality. It's like you're now from a foreign land. You're on a spaceship walking on an Earth that's not yours. You have a mask and you breathe from the *faiz* of Sayyidina Muhammad ﷺ. Can you imagine for one minute that to be cut? How they have absolutely become nothing. They become lost, they become scattered. That nothing for them would be of any importance anymore.

So, everything has to be governed with that reality that *"ilahi anta maqsudi wa radhaaka matloob* – I'm begging your forgiveness and seeking your satisfaction."* That you are consistently content with me and that forgive me for all the wrongs and any direction that I'm going incorrectly.

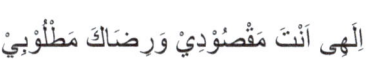

"Ilahi anta maqsudi wa radhaaka matloob."

"My God, You are my aim, and Your Satisfaction is what I seek."

Because nobody's perfect but we sought a path of perfection. That's how they live their lives and that is what's important for them. If they do it, they receive the *faiz*. They receive the satisfaction and the *rida* of Sayyidina Muhammad ﷺ is upon them, dressing them, blessing them. Then these *faiz* and knowledges dissipate out towards the students that are connecting. That's the reality of the *juzba* and the reality of the *faiz* and downpouring and emanations and dressings and blessings.

3. Haqiqatul Tawajjuh
(Reality of Directing to Divinely Face)

Haqiqatul Tawajjuh is a New Level of Understanding to Be Nothing

Haqiqatul Tawajjuh (Reality of Directing to Divinely Face) is in that same reality. That when they learned to connect and they made their connection. They went deep into their connection, they ask from everything that is not perishing that, 'Dress me from your dress, that I'm nothing.' They began to take a deeper path into annihilating themselves that, 'I'm nothing, I'm nothing, I'm nothing.' Then we put out some of the 40 rules from Rumi ﷺ and they had nice explanations. 'For if you're nothing, why are you to be upset about anything?' When someone insults you, aggravates you, bothers you, why to be upset? If you took a path in which to be nothing, who's upset? Your *nafs* (ego) or the soul? So then that had to become real.

Then this *Haqiqatul Tawajjuh*, the reality of the face and connecting with the face. Saying it in English is much easier for me. Is that the reality to connect with the face is in a new level in which to really understand you're nothing. That's why then through touring and accompanying the shaykhs and it was complete oceans of humiliation. One test after another humiliating, humiliating, humiliating in front of people, in front of crowds of people, in private, all the time, all the time. Why? Was to crush the self.

So the shaykh who's been trained – that's why you don't go into an area and say, 'Okay you're a shaykh, you're a shaykh, you're a shaykh.' No, they don't have *juzba*, they don't have *faiz*, and they don't have any connection with the *tawajjuh*. They don't have a connection with the face. So, this process of annihilating was only through the crushing in which that reality of yourself doesn't exist.

Humiliation Crushes Our Ego and Increases Our Spiritual Connection

So Allah going to make it real. For every time they crushed and humiliated, it wasn't your soul that was humiliated; it was your ego. So if you run to the defence of the ego, then you're giving the ego its life support. Then your process of dying becomes that much harder. It means they want you, they're asking you, Sayyidina Abu Bakr as Siddiq is asking you, *mawt qablil mawt* (death of desires before physical death)? Do you want death before death? Or you're going to sit and play with your ego for the next 25 years?' You have a process to learn.

So, then humiliation would come; a big test would come and you connect with your *muraqabah* (spiritual connection), you connect with your connection. And they tell you, 'Your soul has not been insulted' because if your soul was attacked, it was an attack against Allah and his *Rasul* (Messenger) . But your soul wasn't attacked. What you feel is the pain and the sting of a humiliation towards your *nafs* (ego). You stay quiet, you stay quiet, and you stay quiet because you want the *nafs* to die.

You want the *nafs* to be nothing but that requires a very strong connection. As they are beating the *nafs*, the connection must be increasing. Because if they beat the *nafs* (ego) and you have no connection, then that's just not going to happen. Those are the people who continuously are arguing and fighting back.

But the process of connecting is every time they're hurt by the *nafs*, they connect and the connection becomes stronger. Then the shaykh begins to open a very strong connection to his *ruhaniyat* (spirituality) and to his soul. This is by permission of Prophet ﷺ. It's not the shaykh. When we say that, 'The shaykh is connecting and opening from his soul,' it's not him saying, 'Okay here soul, go to him.' It's Allah ﷻ allowing the soul of that shaykh to draw closer to the student. And Allah ﷻ giving the *isharah* to Prophet ﷺ.

When Prophet ﷺ feels it's necessary and okay and signed for it, says, 'Now the soul of that shaykh, the soul of his shaykh,' known to the shaykh or not, 'will draw closer to the student in which the student can begin to connect with his face.'

7 Divinely Essences Dress the Soul Through Tawajjuh

As a result, they see the *wajh* (holy face). They see the face of the shaykh and they receive the emanation from the face of the shaykh. So every time the shaykh's face appears to them. And we're not talking about a dream where you saw the shaykh, he didn't have a turban, he didn't have a beard – those are all imperfections in your own character. This is through live *muraqabah* that they're connecting live. They're not sleeping. It's not hallucinating. They're in a connection. As a result of the connection, they know how they've been tested in life so it's not imagination. That the face of the shaykh begins to appear in their meditation and begins to dress them.

He dresses them from seven essences. This dress is then a continuous dress upon them. From *As-Sami* (All Hearing), *Al Basir* (All Seeing) begin to dress for them the ability to hear, the ability to see. *Alim* (All Knower), *Al Qadir* (All Powerful) begin to dress from Allah's ﷻ ancient knowledges, Allah's ﷻ ancient oceans of power. *Nur* (The Light), *Al Hay* (The Ever-living) begin to dress them with *nur* and light from Allah's ﷻ Divinely and oceans of *al-Hayat* (Ever-living). It means these seven essences are continuously dressing their soul from face to face. No longer a *tajalli* (manifestation) only dressing their soul on the body,

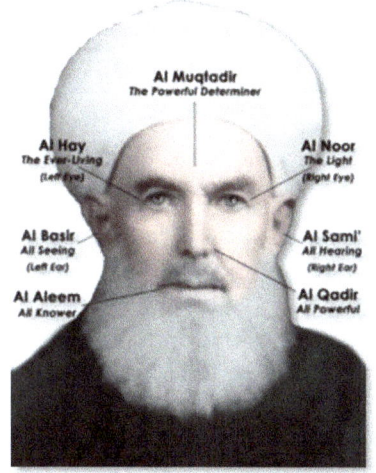

but from the face is dressing their face, until their face becomes a perfected face that receives that *tajalli*. That is the reality of the reality of the face and *tawajjuh* (directing to Divinely Face).

4. Haqiqatul Tawassul (Reality of Conveyance)

Awliya Whom Are Connected to the Holy Face Emanate Throughout the Earth

As a result of the *tawajjuh* and the connection with the face, then what's the next obvious opening? It's the *tawassul* (conveyance) because if your face is connecting, it means your mobile connection is very strong. That your face is connecting to that ocean of power. It's receiving emanation from them. So,

these shaykhs who have reached these levels – if other shaykhs are like satellites – these are like global positioning shaykhs. Their souls are immense and they receive heavenly co-ordinance upon their face. As a result, their *tajalli* is dressing many, many *awliyaullah* all on a different scale because they reach from the face. So, if you imagine a big radar station and some are connecting their radar from lower levels. Those whom are receiving from this reality of *tawajjuh* means that they receive the connection from their face. From their face, it begin to emanate throughout the Earth to all the different levels of *awliya* and they connect from lower levels of their body but not from face. So, the face to face *awliya* are very limited covering this Earth.

Awliya Use an Encrypted Line of Communication to Convey Prayers

As a result, *Haqiqatul Tawassul* (Reality of Intercession), the ability to convey what Allah ﷻ wants conveyed. So, it doesn't mean that you email him that, 'I want this, this, this, this. Now use this and make the connection.' But those are realities for the soul in which Allah ﷻ, when it comes to the soul that, 'Convey such and such *du'a* (supplication) for such and such condition, for such and such.' Whatever Allah ﷻ wants, that soul when it begins to convey, it's conveying from the authority of their face to the connection of the face in which Allah ﷻ has established them. As a result, the *tawajjuh* and the *tawassul*, it has the ability to convey that reality.

Then Allah ﷻ perfected their line of communication. What's being conveyed to the shaykh is a very highly encrypted reality. What the shaykh has is a reality to convey back again on an encrypted signal at a very high level of conveyance. So then that becomes, that's why people seek out these *awliya* for *du'as*. It doesn't mean everything you ask is going to be granted but know that it has been requested.

When the request is something that Allah ﷻ put within their heart that, 'I'm happy that servant asked that from you and I'm granting you to make the full communication.' At that time, they'll be guided in which to fully ask with their authority that such and such has to be requested. That has to come from the permission of Allah ﷻ, through permission of Sayyidina Muhammad ﷺ, through the permission of their shaykhs.

Be Humble in Your Approach and Keep the Fellowship of Love

Allah ﷻ looks for a sign of humility in people. When people say, 'Allah ﷻ can answer directly,' of course, Allah ﷻ could do everything directly. He could throw me and you off of this Earth and do everything Himself but that wasn't this Earth's game. The game on this Earth was a path of humility. Allah ﷻ wants to see, 'Are you a humble servant?' Because if you're not humble and you begin to become arrogant, why would God grant arrogance? Why would [He] grant a character to build arrogance?

God wants us to keep the fellowship of love. That we said the Lord of the Rings [movie], in some of these marketing understandings, Allah ﷻ wants the fellowship of love. That keep the company of like-minded, like-hearted people. Allah ﷻ loves the *jama'ah* (congregation). We pray in *jama'ah*, we don't pray by ourselves where Allah ﷻ just answer all our prayers. Allah ﷻ loves for us to come together and then build character, test each other, and seek humility. That when the servant even has an ability themself to ask directly but then they are humble, say, 'Please, oh pray for me, oh I'm nothing, I'm nothing, I'm nothing' because Allah ﷻ loves humility. 'Be humble when you approach Me.

Don't, don't have the character of arrogance,' because that is from the characteristics of *shaitan*. So always to show ourselves as nothing, that we're no one. To seek a path through humility in which to pray for us and *inshAllah*, Allah ﷻ be happy and pleased with us. That becomes the characteristic in which Allah ﷻ is happy with.

5. Haqiqatut Tayy
(Reality of Folding Time and Space)

Haqiqatut Tayy ul Lisan and the Speed of the Tongue

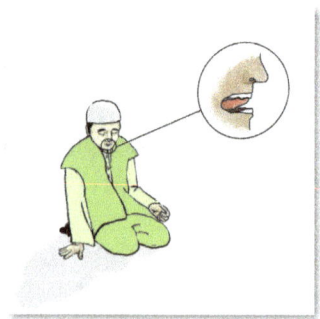

Haqiqatut Tayy, Haqiqatut Tayy. That first *tayy* and first reality of speed and movement is through the tongue, *Haqiqatut Tayy ul Lisan* (Reality of Speed of Recitation). That there's a power within the tongue when the servant locks their tongue to the roof of their mouth. When they're in their *muraqabah* and their meditation, they enter into a position of what we call 'sealed.' So they meditate, immediately lock the tongue to the palate of the mouth and when they connect their heart, this *Tayy ul Lisan* begin to open an enormous amount of speed in their *zikr* (Divine remembrance). So, many people will ask that, 'How you people do the *zikr* so fast? How can you do so many things so fast?' It's a bit Allah ﷻ has to open this reality. So that in their *zikrs*, their meditation, their connections are coming that they can begin through their heart to make very large amounts of *zikr* in very short amount of times.

So their *zikr* is like speed of light, *"Allah Allah Allah Allah Allah Allah Allah Allah Allah Allah Allah Allah Allah,"* [Shaykh recites very fast] very conscious, but very fast it's moving. Even their recitations of *surahs* (chapters) like speed of light versus speed of tongue, *"Allah, Allah, Allah"* [Shaykh recites using tongue slowly] like that. But  saying *"Allah"* moving through their heart through a light. Allah 🕌 opened for them that reality through their seclusions because they're given very long and big *awrads* (daily practices) to recite. They can't be achieved just by normal means. So, then these realities open for those whom seclude themselves. They do their *zikr* and make their connection.

Spiritual Practices Can Be Dangerous Without a Connection to a Shaykh

Again, don't say, 'I make a lot of *zikr* and these things are not opening.' Because if you make a lot of *zikr* and a lot of different *wazifas* (spiritual practices) without a connection, you can go mad! Just sitting and reciting a whole bunch of things in the thousands and thousands but yet you don't have a connection. You don't have a security built with you that you're connected to a shaykh, or shaykhs or to the *tariqah*, then that can be very dangerous. Just because you're opening a power that you don't know how to control, you don't know how to contain, and you don't know what it's attracting as a counter. Every light opens up a counter from *shaitan*.

It means when the shaykhs build the person they're building them with all of the resources, all of their protections. So that every step they're being guarded and being built. So, you don't just sort of build yourself with an enormous amount of practices without making the foundation which is the *muraqabah*. So, *Haqiqatut Tayy ul Lisan* is that when Allah ﷻ opens the speed in which they can recite and do their *wazifas* and when they meditate and recite the speed in which it's reciting through their heart.

Allah ﷻ Can Fold the Earth Like a Scroll (Holy Qur'an, 21:104)

Then *Haqiqatut Tayy ul Badan* (Reality of Moving through Time and Space with the Body). That the movement through space and time and we described that in the talks on the Mandela Effect. That again I heard the CERN will be opening again in March (2022). So that, again *shaitan* is going to be using this system and opening. But the *Haqiqatut Tayy ul Badan* is a system in which Allah ﷻ can...this Earth is like an 'A' [point 1] 'B' [point 2] 'C,' [point 3]. At any time, Allah ﷻ can fold 'A' and 'C,' from point 'A' fold over to point 'C' and cross over the 'B.' So, it means that Allah ﷻ

described, 'The Earth are like scrolls.' At any time, He can fold them.

يَوْمَ نَطْوِي السَّمَاءَ كَطَيِّ السِّجِلِّ لِلْكُتُبِ ۚ كَمَا بَدَأْنَا أَوَّلَ خَلْقٍ نُّعِيدُهُ ۚ وَعْدًا عَلَيْنَا ۚ إِنَّا كُنَّا فَاعِلِينَ ﴿١٠٤﴾

21:104 – "Yawma natwee asSama a katayyi assijelli lilKutubi, kama bada anaa awwala khalqin nu'iduhu, wa'dan 'alayna, inna kunna fa'ileen." (Surat Al-Anbiya)

"The Day when We will fold/roll up the heaven like the folding/scroll rolled up of sheets of book (completed). We produced the first creation, so shall We produce a new one: a promise We have undertaken: truly shall We fulfil it." (The Prophets, 21:104)

Saints Move Through Space With the Power of "Bismillah"

So with power of *"Bismillahir Rahmanir Raheem"* the servant can move from one point to the next point and that's through their spiritual ability.

بِسْمِ اللَّهِ الرَّحْمَـٰنِ الرَّحِيمِ ﴿١﴾

1:1 – "Bismillaahir Rahmaanir Raheem." (Surat Al-Fatiha)

"In the Name of Allah, the Most Beneficent, the Most Merciful." (The Opener, 1:1)

That their soul is governing their physicality with all of these energies and practices. Because this is now the reality of moving towards *irshad* and guidance. So, these are the last stages and the most difficult stages. That the servant accomplished the *mawt qablil mawt* (death of desires before physical death). Their soul is governing their reality and as a result of that reality, their soul can move. They can move from location to location with their soul.

As a result of the last days and the advent of all these mobile phones, that's not being used. Because of the closeness to the proximity of *dajjal* (man of deceit) and miracles and conveying of bizarre events, that's not necessary. Allah 🕉, if needed, can make a shaykh appear in many places at the same time. But their need to move from point A to point C is being held for the time of Sayyidina Mahdi 🕉 at which point that would be open. Allah 🕉 will make their movements and all them who have been trained in that reality, their movement with *"Bismillahir Rahmanir Raheem."* They merely step and where Allah 🕉 want them to appear they will be appearing.

6. Haqiqatul Irshad (Reality of Guidance)

The Six Powers of the Heart Must Dress the Guide to Reach a Star Reality

As a result of that movement and the power that Allah 🕉 gives within their tongue and the ability for their heart to convey their *zikrs*, Allah 🕉 begin to open *Haqiqatul Irshad* (Reality of Guidance). *Irshad* means that 'been given the secrets of guidance.' That's what Prophet ﷺ described, 'My companions are like stars.' So, this was all the way of becoming a star. So that these six powers have to dress the heart and bless the heart so that they can reach towards their star reality. We said 'a star is born.'

أَصْحَابِيْ كَالنُّجُــومْ بِأَيِّهِمْ اَقْتَدَيْتِمْ اَهْتَدَيْتِمْ

"Ashabi kan Nujoom, bi ayyihim aqta daytum ahta daytum."

"My companions are like stars. Whoever among them you follow, you will be rightly guided." Prophet Muhammad (pbuh)

Ijazah of Irshad (Certificate of Guidance) Dresses Them as a Star of Guidance

That as soon as Allah ﷻ dress them and now want to give the servant *irshad* and guidance. At that time, they receive an *ijazah* (authorization) of guidance that, 'You have been given the reality of *irshad*.' As a result, it manifests with an *ijazah* of guidance. As a result of that, the certificate of guidance, the reality of *irshad* means then Allah ﷻ is dressing them from these powers, blessing them with these powers. That their guidance is with the heart that been lit and dressed with these realities. That with this reality of *juzba*, the reality of their connection and their *faiz*. The reality of their face connecting. The reality of the ability to convey their *zikr*, the ability to convey large amounts of *zikrs* in short period of time. All of these is that Allah ﷻ perfect them as a star with the star of guidance.

31

Real Guides Inherit the Face and Senses of the Prophetic Reality

Then as a result, they become from the dress of the Companions, the Companions ﷺ dress them, the *Ahlul Bayt* ﷺ dress them and they

become *Rashidin, Mahdiyeen wa Kamilin* (The Perfected and Rightly Guided Muhammadan Saints). That Allah ﷻ dress them *sifat Ar-Rashid* that, 'My reality of guidance dressing upon you, blessing upon you. That your face dressed upon this reality, that you inherit the face of the Prophetic reality.'

That's what we started at the beginning of the whole understanding that the prophets ﷺ of Allah ﷻ, why they became prophets. What was the power of their prophecy is that their ears from the Holy *Hadith al Qudsi* that, 'You do your *fard* (obligatory) and now you did all the voluntary acts of love, I became your hearing. I became your seeing. I became the breath in which you breathe, the tongue in which you speak, the hands in which you touch, the feet in which you move. That your heart and what you ask is *kun faya koon*, so much so you are *Rabbaniyoon* (Lordly Souls).' It means that this is a star.

عَنْ أَبِي هُرَيْرَةَ رَضِيَّ اللهُ عَنْهُ قَالَ، قَالَ رَسُولُ اللهِ ﷺ : إِنَّ اللهَ تَعَالَى قَالَ:" ...وَمَا
تَقَرُّبِ إِلَيَّ عَبْدِي بِشَيْءٍ أَحُبَّ إِلَيَّ مِمَّا افْتَرَضْتُ عَلَيْهِ. وَلَا يَزَالُ عَبْدِي يَتَقَرَّبُ إِلَيَّ
بِالنَّوَافِلِ حَتَّى أُحِبَّهُ، فَإِذَا أَحْبَبْتُهُ كُنْتَ سَمْعَهُ الَّذِي يَسْمَعُ بِهِ، وَبَصَرَهُ الَّذِي يُبْصِرُ بِهِ،
وَيَدَهُ الَّتِي يَبْطِشُ بِهَا، وَرِجْلَهُ الَّتِي يَمْشِي بِهَا. وَلَئِنْ سَأَلَنِي لَأُعْطِيَنَّهُ، ... "
[حَدِيثْ اَلْقُدْسِي – اَلمَصْدَرْ: صَحِيحُ الْبُخَارِي – رقم:٦٥٠٢]

'An Abi Hurairah (ra) qala, Qala Rasulullahi ﷺ : *InnAllaha ta'ala
qala: "…Wa maa taqarrubi ilayya 'abdi be shayin ahubba ilayya
memma iftaradhtu 'alayhi. Wa la yazaalu 'abdi yataqarrabu ilayya
binnawafile hatta uhebbahu, fa iza ahbabtuhu kunta Sam'ahul lazi
yasma'u behi, wa Basarahul lazi yubsiru behi, wa Yadahul lati yabteshu
beha, wa Rejlahul lati yamshi beha. Wa la in sa alani la a'teyannahu,
…" [Hadith al Qudsi, Sahih al Bukhari, Raqam: 6502)*

*Narrated by Abu Hurairah (ra) that: the Messenger of Allah (pbuh)
said that: Allah the Almighty said: "… My servant does not draw near
to Me with anything more loved by Me than the religious duties I have
obligated upon him. My servant continues to draw near to Me with
voluntary acts of worship so that I shall love him. When I love him, I am
his hearing with which he hears, his seeing with which he sees, his hand
with which he strikes, and his foot with which he walks. Were he to ask
(something) of Me, I would surely give it to him, …"
[Holy Hadith, Authentic by al-Bukhari, #6502]*

33

Like Prophets, Awliya Have Eternal Guidance

That's the reality of a star and that it represents Allah's ﷻ eternal kingdom. 'That I accepted all of your minor service and now I granted for you an eternal service' because their star is now eternally of service. Their body dies but their service never ends. Their guidance is guiding this kingdom for eternity. That they have always guided the kingdoms for eternity and all the prophets ﷺ of Allah ﷻ. It means the immensity of their light and the immensity of that reality is only Allah ﷻ knows. We pray that Allah ﷻ dress us and bless us from the immensity of these realities. That as we draw closer to the last days and the presence of Sayyidina Mahdi ﷺ that these realities begin to unfold very quickly within the hearts of those servants in which whom Allah ﷻ guides and brings to that reality.

Subhana rabbika rabbal 'izzati 'amma yasifoon, wa salaamun 'alal mursaleen, walhamdulillahi rabbil 'aalameen. Bi hurmati Muhammad al-Mustafa wa bi siri Surat al-Fatiha.

First Power

Haqiqatul Juzba

Reality of Magnetism

Building a Magnetic Character

Allah's ﷻ Love Guides Us to Sayyidina Muhammad ﷺ

The secret of Naqshbandi Shaykhs flows through love, not intelligence – not *'aqel*, not your head. It's through *muhabbat* (love) and *ishq*. Through the love of the way, the love of Sayyidina Muhammad ﷺ, love of Allah ﷻ supreme. That Allah ﷻ, when He accepts that love, He guides us to whom He loves. Can Allah ﷻ love somebody and they not be guided to Sayyidina Muhammad ﷺ? No. It means Allah ﷻ don't love you. If you're not guided, that's a secret. When Allah ﷻ loves you, He guides you to what He loves. This is love. Because for love, you give everything. You give the best of what you have – that's *ishq* (love). That's the reality of *ishq*, that's the generosity of *ishq*. So, if we are not guided to this, then Allah's ﷻ love has not yet reached that servant.

Allah ﷻ Grants Love Within the Heart, Not the Head

But *alhamdulillah*, there's time. There's time in this life, time in the grave, time in the Day of Resurrection. But a sign of Allah's ﷻ love for His servant is He grants them a love within their heart. If that love is sincere,

when Allah ﷻ loves them, He gives them from what He loves. That's the love of Sayyidina Muhammad ﷺ. Only through that *ishq* and *muhabbat* – it's not '*aqel* (intellect), it's not memorizing, it's not doing things that you've memorized and taught by your head, but it's only by the heart because love resides within the *qalb* (heart).

"Qalb al mu'min baitullah."

قَالَ رَسُولُ اللهِ ﷺ، قَالَ اللهُ عَزَّ وَجَلَّ: " قَلْبَ الْمُؤْمِنِ بَيْتُ الرَّبِ. " [حَدِيثٌ أَلْقُدْسِي]

Qala Rasulallahi ﷺ, Qala Allah (AJ): "Qalb al mu'min baytur rabb." *[Hadith al Qudsi]*

The Messenger of Allah (pbuh) said, that Allah (AJ) said: "The heart of the believer is the House of the Lord." (Holy Hadith)

Be Vigilant With Your Heart

Not the *maqhz* of *mu'min* (believer), not the brain of *mu'min*. But Allah ﷻ draws our attention that, 'My house and My *ishq*, My Divinely lights will reside within your heart. As a result, make your heart My home. Clean it, wash it, circumambulate.'

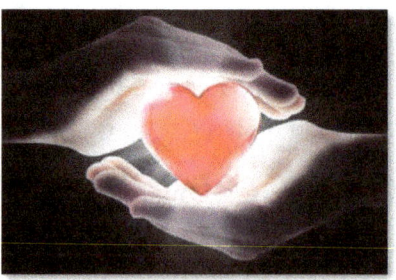

...أَن طَهِّرَا بَيْتِيَ لِلطَّائِفِينَ وَالْعَاكِفِينَ وَالرُّكَّعِ السُّجُودِ ﴿١٢٥﴾

2:125 – "...An Tahhir baytee liTayifeena, wal 'Aakifeena, wa ruka'is sujood." (Surat Al-Baqarah)

"...Purify/Sanctify My House for those who perform tawwaf (circumambulation) and those who seclude themselves for devotion, and bow and prostrate [in prayer]." (The Cow, 2:125)

Make circumambulation and *tawwaf* is that the whole focus of our existence is continuous *qalb, wuquf ul-qalb* – the vigilance of my heart. That, '*Ya Rabbi*, don't let something enter into my heart to disturb Your Divinely light.' Because there can't be, no man is made with two hearts. No man, woman; here's in reference to creation that – that is only one heart and that heart has to have the *ishq* of Allah ﷻ. When Allah ﷻ accepts that love as sincere and a clean love, He guides to whom He loves and He sends them to the love of Sayyidina Muhammad ﷺ.

مَّا جَعَلَ اللَّـهُ لِرَجُلٍ مِّن قَلْبَيْنِ فِي جَوْفِهِ ۚ ... ﴿٤﴾

33:4 – "Ma ja'ala Allahu lirajulin min Qalbayni fee jawfihi..." (Surat Al-Ahzab)

"Allah has not made for a man two hearts in his interior..." (The Combined Forces, 33:4)

Sunnah is to Adhere to Qur'an, Love Ahlul Bayt ◌, and Follow the Holy Companions

When Sayyidina Muhammad ﷺ loves the servant and accepted their love. So it's like a little litmus test for ourselves. 'Oh, if Allah ﷻ loves Me, He will guide me to the love of Sayyidina Muhammad ﷺ.' When we keep practicing and practicing and practicing, and if our love is sincere and true for Sayyidina Muhammad ﷺ, then Sayyidina Muhammad ﷺ loves us and guides us to what He loves which is Qur'an, his *sunnah* (traditions of Prophet Muhammad ﷺ), his *Ahlul Bayt* (Holy Family of Prophet ﷺ), his companions. So, that's a sign of the love of Sayyidina Muhammad ﷺ that, 'Dearest to me is the word of Allah ﷻ.'

عَنْ ابْنِ عَبَّاسٍ قَالَ، قَالَ رَسُولُ اللَّهِ ﷺ: " أَحِبُّوا اللَّهَ لِمَا يَغْذُوكُمْ مِنْ نِعَمِهِ وَأَحِبُّونِي بِحُبِّ اللَّهِ وَأَحِبُّوا أَهْلَ بَيْتِي بِحُبِّي."
[سنن الترمذي كتاب المناقب باب مناقب أهل بيت ٣٧٨٩]

'An Ibni 'Abass qala, Qala Rasulullahi ﷺ: "Ahibu Allah lima yaghdukum min nia'mih wa-ahibuni bihubi Allah wa-ahibu ahla bayti bihubi."

Ibn Abbas reported: The Messenger of Allah (pbuh) said, "Love Allah for the blessings by which He nourishes you, love me for the love of Allah, and love the people of my house for the love of me."
[Sunan al-Tirmidhi 3789]

So, they have a reverence and a respect, a love for Holy Qur'an that can't be imagined. That Qur'an for them is the source of guidance, the source of lights, the source of Divinely words of Allah ﷻ that can't be imagined. That the reverence for it is something that can't be understood and that they know it's guiding their every movement back into that Divinely Presence. As a result, Prophet ﷺ begins to dress them with the love that was of his love for his family.

So then they should have a love for *Ahlul Bayt* ﵌, a reverence and a respect for *Ahlul Bayt* ﵌ and the family of Sayyidina Muhammad ﷺ, and a love for his holy companions that, 'They accompanied me. They fought for me. They had a love and an *ishq* and lived and died for me. How could you not love them?' That, that is the *sunnah* of Sayyidina Muhammad ﷺ – to adhere to the Qur'an, to love the *Ahlul Bayt* ﵌ and to follow the holy companions of Sayyidina Muhammad ﷺ. That is all the sign of *ishq* and love and *muhabbat*.

Prophet ﷺ Guides Us to Ulul Amr, the Real Ashiqeen and Followers of His Way

Alhamdulillah, the people of the path, they understood that their whole life was this *ishq*, this love and their heart is that – how to make my heart the house of Allah ﷻ? There are six powers within the heart. That in the Levels of the heart and the book on the 'Levels of the Heart', that these are the necessary tools that one must have on this path. That to have the understanding of

tafakkur and contemplation and that this *tafakkur* and contemplation is based on building the energy within the heart. So, *Haqiqatul Juzba* (Reality of Attraction) is the first reality.

That we just described this whole path of love, that this is a sign that when Allah ﷻ loves, He dresses. He dresses with the light of Sayyidina Muhammad ﷺ. Prophet ﷺ dresses with the light of his holy family, his holy companions, lights of Qur'an, most supreme, and then the guidance of *awliyaullah* (saints) whom adhere and hold to that reality. They are called *Ulul Amr*, the People of the *Amr* (command). They are the real *'ulama* (scholars), the real followers and *'ashiqeen* (lovers) and *muhibbin* (lovers of the way) of Sayyidina Muhammad ﷺ. Prophet ﷺ guides us to that.

Purify Your Heart and Allah ﷻ Will Dress It With the Six Powers

Then they teach us that if that's what you want, purify your heart and make it the house of Allah ﷻ. In that house of Allah ﷻ, Allah ﷻ will dress the heart of the believer with these six powers. It means that the first power Allah ﷻ will

dress the believer – *Haqiqatul Juzba, Haqiqatul Faiz* and blessings and downpouring. *Haqiqatul Juzba* is magnetism and magnetic attraction.

Haqiqatul Faiz is the blessings and downpouring – that how your heart will be attracting these blessings and downpourings and emanating from the holy heart. *Haqiqatul Tawajjuh* – and the reality of focusing upon the Divinely Face. *Haqiqatul Tawassul* – which is the power of conveyance and intercession. *Haqiqatut Tayy* – and the folding of time and space; first by *lisan*, by tongue and then by the *badan* and body of moving through space and time. That space and time is irrelevant on the path. Then *Haqiqatul Irshad* (Reality of Guidance) and this is the *ijazah* (permission) for guidance.

The Six Pointed Star of Prophet ﷺ Opens the Heart of Holy Qur'an: Surah 36, YaSeen

That if the heart has been dressed by these six powers and that's why we show the heart and Divinely heart is the star of Sayyidina Sulaiman ﷺ which is the star of Sayyidina Muhammad ﷺ. Three points are up and three points are down and that these six points have to be brought into a reality and into submission. Each point and angle on this triangle is 60 degrees. We don't have 60, we have six with a *nuqt* (dot). So three points up is 18 and then three points down is 18. So then the whole when it reaches *kamil* and perfection – 18 and 18 is the 36.

That's why then the heart of Qur'an has from the reality of this number 36 (Chapter 36, Surat YaSeen). That Allah ﷻ is dressing the perfected heart in this world that understood these 6-6-6 up and the 6-6-6 down and perfected all of these sixes because these are six sixes – 6 x 6 = 36. So, that opens then that reality of the reality of the heart of Holy Qur'an which is the heart of Sayyidina Muhammad ﷺ and *Faiz ul Qur'an, Manzil ul Qur'an* (where the Holy Qur'an emanates) – that all these powers of Holy Qur'an are emanating from that reality.

External Scholars Bring People by Force, Internal Ones Inherit Prophetic Light

Haqiqatul Juzba and how to attain attraction. It means that the world that not studying these realities, they want people to be attracted to them by force. They put out something and hope that people will be attracted to them. They put out their titles and hope that people will be

attracted to them. They mandate their titles, 'I'm the representative of the North Pole and that you have to all follow me, even Eskimos and the seals.'

So, these are people whom want to force their will upon creation instead of having been trained on the reality of guidance because the end result of Allah ﷻ making His home within the heart of the servant is they inherit the realities or the lights of *risalat* (prophecy).

عَنْ أَبِي الدَّرْدَاءِ رَضِيَ اللَّهُ عَنْهُ قَالَ ، قَالَ رَسُولُ اللَّهِ ﷺ : " اَلْعُلَمَاءِ وَرَثَةُ الْأَنْبِيَاءِ."
[رِيَاضْ اَلصَّالِحِينْ: ١٣٨٨]

'An Abi Darda (ra) qala, qala Rasulullahi ﷺ: "Al 'Ulama ye warathatul Anbiya."

Narrated by Abi Darda (ra) that the Messenger of Allah (pbuh) said: "My scholars are the inheritors of the prophets." [Riyad As Saliheen)

Because there is no prophet after Sayyidina Muhammad ﷺ but what then Prophet ﷺ describe of his *awliya* (saints)? Because this is a description of these holy companions. *Ahlul Bayt* ﷺ are all under the same. *Ahlul Bayt* ﷺ, we love them because they're immense *awliya. Sahabi Kiram* (Honourable Companions of Prophet ﷺ), they have the highest reality of *awliyaullah* that can't be achieved because they accompanied Sayyidina Muhammad ﷺ, all *awliya.* Then *awliya* that are *awliya.* Why? Because they inherit the *risalat.*

Allah ﷻ Overtakes All Faculties of Awliya's Heart in Which He Resides

They inherit the good characteristics in which Allah ﷻ loves from the creation of prophecy. That's what makes them to be dressed by that light because Allah ﷻ resides within their heart. Allah ﷻ resides within their ears, their eyes, their hands, their feet. So much so, that their tongue and breath all under Divinely lights and that they walk and move with the power of Allah ﷻ and from what they want and their will matches Allah ﷻ and they say, *"Kun faya koon"* (Be and it is) and because it's the Will of Allah ﷻ, it's emanating from them.

عَنْ أَبِي هُرَيْرَةَ رَضِيَّ اللهُ عَنْهُ قَالَ، قَالَ رَسُولُ اللهِ ﷺ : إِنَّ اللهَ تَعَالَى قَالَ:"... وَلَا يَزَالُ عَبْدِي يَتَقَرَّبُ إِلَيَّ بِالنَّوَافِلِ حَتَّى أُحِبَّهُ، فَإِذَا أَحْبَبْتُهُ كُنْت سَمْعَهُ الَّذِي يَسْمَعُ بِهِ، وَبَصَرَهُ الَّذِي يُبْصِرُ بِهِ، وَيَدَهُ الَّتِي يَبْطِشُ بِهَا، وَرِجْلَهُ الَّتِي يَمْشِي بِهَا، وَلَئِنْ سَأَلَنِي لَأُعْطِيَنَّهُ، ... " [حَدِيثٌ اَلْقُدْسِي – اَلْمَصْدَرْ: صَحِيحُ الْبُخَارِي – رقم:٦٥٠٢]

'An Abi Hurairah (ra) qala, Qala Rasulullahi ﷺ *: InnAllaha ta'ala qala: " ...wa la yazaalu 'Abdi yataqarrabu ilayya bin nawafile hatta ahebahu, fa idha ahbabtuhu kunta Sam'ahul ladhi yasma'u behi, wa Basarahul ladhi yubsiru behi, wa Yadahul lati yabTeshu beha, wa Rejlahul lati yamshi beha, wa la in sa alani la a'Teyannahu, ..."*
[Hadith Qudsi, Sahih al Bukhari, Raqam: 6502)

Narrated by Abu Hurairah (ra) that: the Messenger of Allah ﷺ *said that: Allah the Almighty said: ..".My servant continues to draw near to Me with voluntary acts of worship so that I shall love him. When I love him, I am his hearing with which he hears, his seeing with which he sees, his hand with which he strikes and his foot with which he walks. Were he to ask [something] of Me, I would surely give it to him..."*
[Holy Hadith, Authentic by al-Bukhari, #6502]

إِنَّمَا أَمْرُهُ إِذَا أَرَادَ شَيْئًا أَن يَقُولَ لَهُ كُن فَيَكُونُ ﴿٨٢﴾

36:82 – "Innama AmruHu idha Arada shay an, an yaqola lahu kun faya koon." (Surat YaSeen)

"His Command is when He Wills/Intends a thing, He says to it, "Be," and it is!" (YaSeen, 36:82)

Awliya Inherit From All Other Prophets

That's why the holy *hadith* of Sayyidina Muhammad ﷺ described, 'My *'ulama* who are *awliya* are *Warith ul anbiya* (inheritor of prophets) from *Bani Israel*,' which is all prophets ﷺ.

قَالَ النَّبِيُّ ﷺ " عُلَمَاءُ أُمَّتِي كَأَنْبِيَاءِ بَنِي إِسْرَائِيلِ."
[عَوَالِي اَلْلَآلِي جُزْء ٤ / صفحة ٧٧، الحديث ٦٧]

Qala An Nabi ﷺ: *"'Ulama o Ummati ka Anbiya ye Bani Israel."*
['Awali Allaali, Juz' 4, Safha 77, Al Hadith 67]

The Prophet (pbuh) said: "The scholars of my nation are like the prophets of Bani Israel."
['Awali Allaali, Volume 4, Page 77, Hadith #67]

There's no prophet that wasn't from *Bani Israel* (Children of Israel) up to that time. Prophecy before that was of the different caliber. So, all the prophets ﷺ of Allah ﷻ is what Sayyidina Muhammad ﷺ is coding is that, 'My *'ulama* are like prophets of *Bani Israel'* because there's no coming to the even threshold of Sayyidina Muhammad ﷺ. So, they're inheriting from these qualities of prophecy because Allah ﷻ resides within the heart of that servant.

The Inner Devil is More Dangerous Than the Outer One

So *Haqiqatul Juzba*, and they took a path in which to meditate, contemplate. We described in the nights before – they don't fight devils outside. They're not yelling at people. They're not screaming at people. They're not trying to correct people because they don't care about that. They spent their life fighting the devil within them. Every desire that comes, they check that desire. Every pulse within their heart – anything that  affects them, anything that agitates them – they understood the devil within is more dangerous than the devil out.

47

Those Who Focus On the Outer Form Choose External Understandings

This is the Matrix now. Either the servant is willing to take that path. So there are two pills; you're *zahiri* (external understanding) or you're

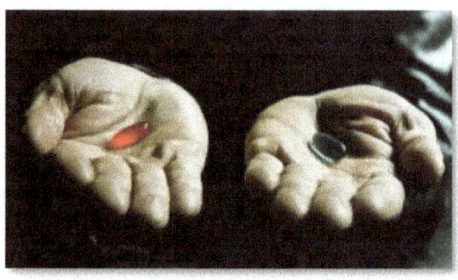

internal. They offered the shaykhs. There's a famous one now in Pakistan. His shaykh offered for him, 'You want internal knowledges or you want to be famous amongst people as an external *'alim*

(scholar)?' He said, 'External.' So, he took that pill.

It means he's now excluded from internal knowledges and realities. Everything they do; they sit 10,000 people, they give a *hadith*, they translate a *hadith* and everybody, "*Subhanallah, subhanAllah, subhanAllah, subhanAllah.*" It's just the translation services and they teach the *usool* (principles) and external understandings of Islam.

Those Who Take a Life of Inner Purity Choose Internal Understandings

But when they take the pill for internal, the path is completely different. The path and Allah ﷻ guide them to the *shuyukh* of that reality. Those *shuyukh*, they don't sit outside and speak of external matters. That's not their job. They are the shaykhs of internal reality. They're from a different pill. When you take that path and Allah ﷻ destines a servant to take that path, that's not the external.

So, then their internal path is not fighting external devils, correcting everything wrong, 'This is a this, this is a that. Write this against them.' That no, their internal path is that their own devil has to be fought. That what is their devil doing within them? What desire he's tempting them with? What understanding he's tempting them with? Everything within them is that they raised their sword for Allah ﷻ and they went in and they took in the inner battle against the demons. They

took in all of these inner fights. As a result of the inner battle, Allah ﷻ subdues that devil.

The Inner Path Has Immense Testing

Haqiqatul Juzba is magnetism. It's how to make the connection inside. It's not by forcing people to love you, forcing people to follow you, put out all of your claims of whatever you have. That doesn't make people to be attracted to you. You cannot force anyone to be attracted to you. This has to come from Allah ﷻ.

So, when the servant took his inner path and began the process of unplugging which is a difficult path. That's why many *'ulama* (scholars) have no interest in that. Many people who want to be shaykhs or scholars have no interest in being tested and crushed and tested and crushed because it's like that Matrix movie. They are fighting all day long from every direction, every type of humiliation, every type of difficulty, every type of testing and remain patient, remain calm, and keep surrendering.

Your Inner Connection is in the World of Light, Not the World of Form

As a result of the servant who went inside and began to dress and battle their inner demons and take away all of these characteristics, then they learned on how to connect their lifeline was how to connect in the World of Light, not the World of Form. They connect in the World of Light. No matter how much they know the shaykh, how much they accompanied the shaykh, their real connection with the shaykh was in the World of Light because that is the – and we have all the other talks on that on the meditation – that is the source of Allah's 󠀀 satellite reflecting.

As soon as they close their eyes and began their connection, connection because the connection and the battle, they go together. As soon as you connect, you think that the devil is going to leave you alone on the outside? Every type of testing begins to come. So then the servant has to be sincere for their inner struggle. When they fight, they fight, they fight, and they make their connection and they build that connection, that is the reality of *juzba* (attraction) that will be coming to them. They connect with the shaykh.

The Awliya are Moons Reflecting the Sun's Light

As a result of connecting with the shaykh, this light from the shaykh is dressing upon them. Because the shaykh is nobody. He's not claiming that he's the sun, but Allah ﷻ later teaches, 'No, he's one of my small moons and he does what he does correctly. He faces the sun and as a result, he reflects on to you whatever you're in need of.' Because if you try to stare at the sun, it takes your eyesight away. But go out on a dark night and stare all you want at the moon and no problem because Allah ﷻ wanted it that way for *ihtiram* (respect). That, 'Who are you to stare at My sun? It takes your eyesight and make you blind. But stare at the moon all you want. That's why I created that moon.'

Shaitan Tries to Take Your Lights When You Make a Magnetic Connection

So, it means that the *turuqs* (spiritual paths) come to teach that when we took a path in which to connect, connect, connect. 'Dress me. Send your *faiz* (downpouring blessings) upon me.' Then as soon as these lights come, it's a soccer game. As soon as *shaitan* is watching on the side that, 'Look he just got dressed by this light, take it away by the end of…' In five minutes of his meditation is finished *shaitan* make the person to become angry, scream and yell and immediately, all the lights have been taken away from that servant. That is the straight and that is the severe battle that they understood. Every time these *faiz* and lights are coming, *shaitan* is going to be trying to take that away.

Iron is Essential for Energy, Purify It to Negate Shaitan's Influence

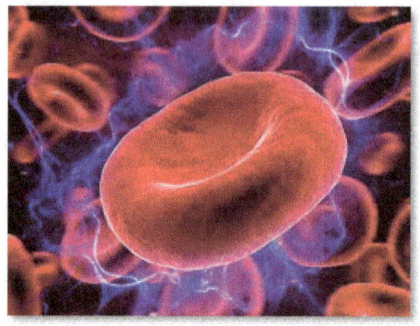

If they can successfully battle, battle the inner demon, bring that light in because the inner demon is burning by these lights. They bring these lights, bring these lights, dress themself with *faiz*, dress themself because the *Haqiqatul Faiz* (Reality of Downpouring Emanation) is that and the *Haqiqatul Juzba* is that they're building their magnetic connection with the shaykh. The light and the energy that coming upon them is dressing the iron of their body. The *juzba* is magnetism, the iron core of *insan* (human being). The iron core of *insan* is essential for their energy.

So, then they purified their blood because the iron runs in the blood. *Shaitan* runs in the blood.

عَنْ أَنَسٍ قَالَ، قَالَ رَسُولُ اللهِ ﷺ: " إِنَّ الشَّيْطَانَ يَجْرِي مِنَ الْإِنْسَانِ مَجْرَى اَلدَّمِ." [المَصْدَرْ: صَحِيحْ مُسْلِمْ ٢١٧٤]

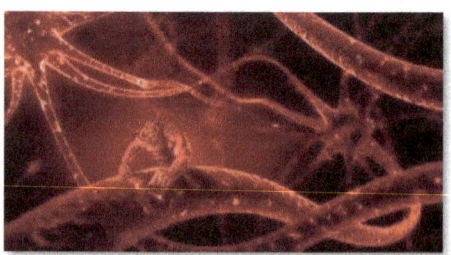

'An Anasin Qala Rasulallahi ﷺ: "Innash Shaitana yajri minal Insani majra addami." [Sahih Muslim 2174]

Narrated by 'An Anas (ra) that the Messenger of Allah (pbuh) said, "Satan circulates/flows through the human being as blood circulates/flow in the body." [Authentic by Muslim 2174]

So, the inner battle is what you eat, what you drink, how you meditate, how you bring this energy, how to purify the blood, how to push down the satanic power trying to run within the body system – then the *juzba* of light. As soon as you meditate and they reflect these lights upon your body, if your blood and your cleaning of your internal reality is cleaning, then these lights and energies begin to attach themself onto the body of that person.

The Secret of Guidance is in Your Iron

The iron of their body is carrying all of the charges and energy that they carry and that opens the reality of the reality of iron. Iron and *hadid* is a secret of guidance. So, Allah ﷻ put iron within all His creation for guidance. So you say, 'How the bird doesn't have a mobile phone or GPS or Siri and how do they find everything?'

It's the iron within their body and the electromagnetic field of this Earth is sending a signal. Because of their iron and they're tuned in with their energy, they can tell by the signal that they read within the Earth what their co-ordinance and where they're supposed to go and Allah ﷻ gave that iron to all creatures. The oceans are filled with whales; that how they find their guidance, how the dolphin finds its guidance. The secret of guidance is in the iron.

Shaitan Weaponizes Iron for Destruction of the Earth

What *shaitan* did? He came and manipulated iron and iron is not found on Earth but sent from the heavens upon the Earth. The Earth can't even produce an atom of iron. That's the same weapon in which *shaitan*

took iron and made atomic bombs from it. To explode the iron because it holds so much power in one atom of iron that *shaitan* made that to be the weapon of mass destruction upon this Earth.

﴿...وَأَنزَلْنَا الْحَدِيدَ فِيهِ بَأْسٌ شَدِيدٌ وَمَنَافِعُ لِلنَّاسِ ﴿٢٥﴾

57:25 – "...Wa anzalnal hadeeda feehi baasun shadeedun wa manaafi'u linnaasi..." (Surat Al-Hadid)

"...And We sent down iron, in which is (material for) great military might as well as many benefits for mankind..." (The Iron, 57:25)

With Purified Iron You Become Magnetized and Receive Shaykh's Faiz

But the reality of iron is in the *juzba* and opening the *juzba* of *insan* (human being). How to purify the iron, how to bring the energy of *insan* upon themselves, purifying that energy, purifying that

perfection. As a result, they begin to emanate energy all around them because the energy comes and this *juzba* comes to their heart, their iron has been purified, their character is continuously trying to purify. They have a strong built connection with the shaykh. As a result, the *faiz* of the shaykh is dressing the servant. *Haqiqatul Juzba* means that your iron is good. You've purified your inner reality and that you learned how to make a connection, right? As a result of the connection, you're now receiving the *faiz*. You're receiving the emanation, beatific and Divinely emanations.

So, if I take a metal and I put it towards the paper clips, nothing is attracted to it. That's why external scholars, they get very jealous of internal scholars because they wonder, 'How come the people are attracted to this person? Why are they attracted? He doesn't even know anything. What's this, what's that?' Because it's just a piece of metal. They're trying to put it to other paper clips and there's no attraction at all. But if the metal and the iron becomes magnetized and there's a charge within that iron, immediately that magnetized metal, as soon as it points out, it attracts all the paper clips.

Zikr of the Heart is Stamped on Every Blood Cell

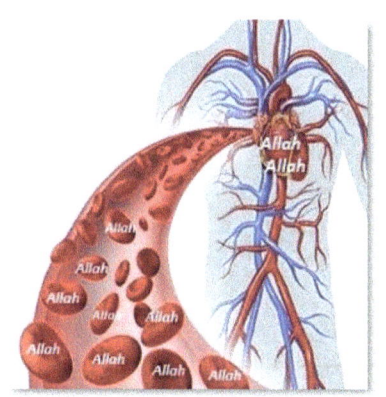

So, imagine then the magnetism and the magnetized heart of the servant in which continuously cleaning and continuously washing, making all the iron within the body to be clean. That iron is stamped by *zikrullah* (remembrance of Allah) because the blood, the breath, all of that is stamping that blood into their heart. All of that is being dressed upon that cell of the blood, the iron of the body.

They're emanating energy, they're emanating lights. As a result of emanating and shining these lights, people are attracted to them and that is the attraction and the reality of *juzba*. People log on, people are attracted. People want to take their guidance from that reality. That's a dress that only Allah ﷻ can begin to open through these knowledges. That they sat, they meditate, they clean, they purify, they understood, 'I have to purify the iron within my body.'

Cupping Purifies the Blood Within the Body

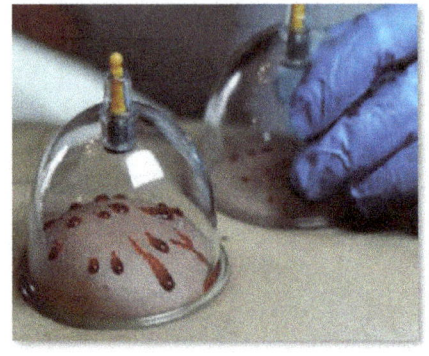

That's also the reality of *hijama* (cupping). Why they purify and clean their body? Why Prophet ﷺ required *hijama*? It was to purify the blood. Why do men especially have to do? Because there's no more war and they have no more blood loss. They especially have to clean themselves, not women because they have their own cycle of cleaning, but it's the men that are required. That, that *hijama* is for their spiritual vision and cleanliness of the blood and the iron within their body.

It means all of these realities were to perfect the reality of *juzba* and that when Allah ﷻ wants to dress their heart with *juzba*, it means then they have a magnetism, a magnanimous character in which people are attracted to that reality and the energy emanating from them. People say that, 'We can feel that positive energy' because it's radiating from that blessing.

Subhana rabbika rabbal 'izzati 'amma yasifoon, wa salaamun 'alal mursaleen, walhamdulillahi rabbil 'aalameen. Bi hurmati Muhammad al-Mustafa wa bi siri Surat al-Fatiha.

Reality of Magnetism in the Body

Muraqabah Builds Your Magnetic Character

What does it mean to feel a magnetic attraction, like an energy, pulsating in your body? Well, *alhamdulillah*, that is the teaching of magnetism. That's the whole teaching of the *muraqabah* (spiritual connection) and magnetic character. We were talking today on the same subject that the *tafakkur* (contemplation) and the immense depth of *tafakkur*. The shaykh won't go into it until people start to do it. When the people do it, based on how they're asking questions, then they can go deeper into these realities.

The Student Must Surrender Their Will to Achieve Realities

It's not just basic you meditate; it's basically trying to reprogram. So, we gave an example today [Shaykh asks an audience member for a TV remote]. We say 'slave' and 'master' but that's maybe a ruder understanding but this is a tech-knowledge; this is not us saying these things. There's a slave unit and there's a master unit in technology [Shaykh holds up two TV remotes]. The *adab* (manners) is the shaykh and the student.

That every student has their own buttons in life; what they want to do, their own will in life, and how they want to operate themself. *Tafakkur* and contemplation is that, 'I'm surrendering. I give up, *ya Rabbi*. I did life the way I wanted to and most likely, I probably ruined everything. I didn't achieve what I need to achieve. There's not that much time left for me to keep playing around like this. I want to achieve Your realities.'

Then this remote [referring to the student] has to be emptied. This technology has to become emptied, 'I don't want to program any more buttons. I don't want what I think. I don't want, what I have as an understanding.' So, once this  empties and takes a path of, 'I'm nothing, I'm nothing, I'm nothing. I'm going to sit and just admit to myself my nothingness.' What happens then, Allah ﷻ says then, 'Train with this master unit [referring to the shaykh].'

Shaykh Reprograms the Student and Transforms His Knowledge

 This master unit is capable of reprogramming this one [student], right? This master remote [shaykh] can program this [student] remote. Have you ever done that at home? Where you have to change with the infrared signal and there's a light coming from this [master unit/shaykh] that programs into this and then transforms all the knowledge of this remote [slave unit/student] so that now it can change the TV channels.

So, anybody who has a little bit of tech background understands. This master remote [shaykh] can completely change this remote [student] and begin to send its energy, send its lights, send all of its programming onto that unit and to train it. That's just the sample of its understanding.

Purity of the Blood Depends on the Quality of Our Breath

When they sit for energy, the shaykh is already of a magnetic character. That they have an energy, they've trained themselves on how to produce that energy. As a result of their energy and their energy field is based on the 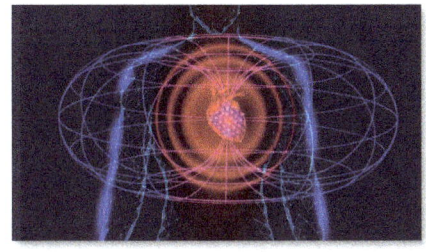 quality of the iron on their blood. So, they took a life in which to purify their blood, purify their iron, purify with *zikr* (Divine remembrance), purify their breath that comes in.

 The sanctity and the purity of the blood is… now we go backwards that, 'I want pure blood.' Say, 'Okay, I want pure blood.' How are you going to have pure blood? It's going to be rooted in your breath. How you breathe in is going to be the first dress and *tajjali* (manifestation) of the blood that you're going to be using in your body. So, I'm going to smoke and contaminate the blood and then contaminate my iron? No! I'm going to be near somebody who smokes or any type of inhalant that's going to come in and affect the purity of my breath? No!

Our Spiritual Practices Clean and Stamp Our Blood

When I understood those things then when I breathe, I bring in an energy. I begin to purify this blood, purify this energy. Then I'm a person from *zikrullah* (remembrance of Allah) and I have my *zikrs*, my *awrads*

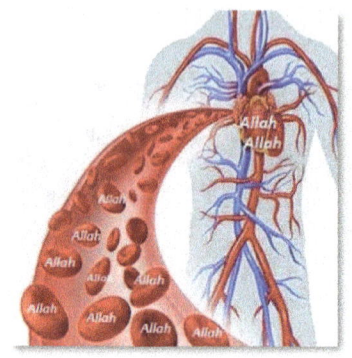

(daily practices) and everything that I'm supposed to recite. So, when I sit and meditate and I'm breathing in and I make, *"Allah,"* that breath purifies the blood, purifies the iron, cleans the iron, and the iron moves. The breath and the blood moves into the heart and the heart stamps, stamps that reality, *"Allah."*

Now that iron on the body is not just any type of satanic energy, negative energy, bad energies that are moving. Because any energy will be attached to that iron because the metal is conductive of that electricity and that *qudra* (power), *nazma* (energy field) or whatever type of energy they're trying to collect from this world. So, it's the *zikr*, the breathing, all of the purification processes.

Charging the Iron of Blood Results in Magnetism

Then they begin to charge their energy. So, what happens then if you charge your energy, charge your energy? You become magnetic and that's what they call magnetism. You have the ability to attract people with energy. The energy that you are putting out, your magnetism is very strong.

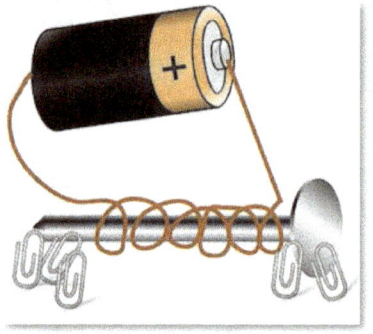

In school they gave us all the test where you take the battery, you put a coil and you try to magnetize the paper clips. Because anything with a magnetic charge, it will attract other metals. It will attract the metal. So, it means the iron in other people are attracted to the energy the shaykh is producing. The shaykh merely puts out the energy from the heart by *"'Izzatullah, 'izzatur Rasul wa 'izzatul mu'mineen"* and the energy field of your iron on your body is being pulled and drawn into their presence.

وَلِلَّهِ الْعِزَّةُ وَلِرَسُولِهِ وَلِلْمُؤْمِنِينَ ﴿٨﴾

63:8 – "...Wa Lillahil 'izzatu wa li Rasooli hi wa lil Mumineena.."
(Surat Al-Munafiqoon)

"...And to Allah belongs [all] honor, and to His Messenger, and to the
believers.." (The Hypocrites, 63:8)

Shaykh's Magnetic Character Draws People to the Love of Prophet ﷺ

It doesn't need to be physical, it can be just through watching the videos. As soon as you watch the video, the sound and the energy that is being produced is moving into the home. It begins to vibrate on the person's blood, on their iron of their blood specific and then resonate within their heart. So yes, then definitely magnetism and the magnetic character of the shaykh is what draws more and more power. As Prophet ﷺ gives more *qudra*, more power onto the heart [of the Shaykh] then that magnetism draws more people to it. That's what we call then the reality of magnetism.

By the reality of that magnetism, Allah ﷻ has drawn you to the love of Sayyidina Muhammad ﷺ. If you don't have that magnetism, there is no way that you can love that reality. That was then the talk that we gave on this magnetic character. When Allah ﷻ loves

61

you, He puts your frequency to the love of Sayyidina Muhammad ﷺ, that your heart is attracted to that reality. Your heart is beginning to move towards that reality. Nothing will satisfy you but to be in the presence of that reality. It means now the magnetic pull towards Prophet ﷺ is immensely strong.

Shaitan Reverses Our Polarity Through Bad Character

What's *shaitan's* (satan) role in magnetism? To reverse your polarity, right? So, if you're attracted, there's an attraction. When you studied about magnets, how you can reverse the polarity of the magnet? By hitting it. So, then *shaitan* comes and makes a *fitna* (confusion) in your life and hit your magnet. It means fighting, bad character, is a hit from *shaitan*. Why he's doing that? So that to reverse your polarity to that person and then to be unattracted to them. So, that happens in life. That happens with loved ones. That happens to everything. That one day you're attracted to something and *shaitan* hit it, hit it, hit it and then the polarity of that changes and now you're repelled from that person. You don't want anything to do with them.

But imagine then if that's with the heavens and that's the immense danger of the heavens. That this magnet of the heavens requires good character. As long as we keep our good character, we are drawn to the reality of Prophet ﷺ. When *shaitan* hits us with bad character, he's trying to reverse our polarity so that, 'Oh, you know, I don't think it's important anymore for me to ask Prophet ﷺ. I'm going to ask Allah ﷻ directly.' That's a big danger because then their whole system in the polarity of their reality is moving away from the *haqqaiq* (realities) and that's all that *shaitan* wants.

The Shaykhs are the Magnetic Reflection of Prophet ﷺ

 That's the whole safeguarding of life. So, our life is to build the energy, perfect that energy, build that frequency and that magnetism. That is the draw to the reality of the shaykh because they're the magnetic reflection of Sayyidina Muhammad ﷺ. If they lose that draw, everybody runs away from them because they're no longer feeling the magnetic charge. That's why their actions have to be 100% correct for the love of Sayyidina Muhammad ﷺ.

Subhana rabbika rabbal 'izzati 'amma yasifoon, wa salaamun 'alal mursaleen, walhamdulillahi rabbil 'aalameen. Bi hurmati Muhammad al-Mustafa wa bi siri Surat al-Fatiha.

The Reality of Divine Love at the Atomic Level

Divine Love is the Secret to All Creation

We talked before about the reality of gravity and *ishq* (love). That, what draws something from its pure

Divine reality is *ishq* – it's a Divine love. When we talk about love, people are thinking from a physical. When Allah ﷻ is describing that, 'All this creation was created in love.' That Prophet ﷺ was describing

that, 'Allah ﷻ created this creation from this *ishq* and this love.' 'I was a hidden treasure wanting to be known,' the secret of *Al Wadood* (The Most Loving).

قَالَ رَسُولَ اللَّهِ ﷺ، قَالَ اللَّهُ عَزَّ وَجَلَّ: " كُنْت كَنْزاً مخفيا فَأَحْبَبْت أَنْ أُعْرَفَ؛ فَخَلَقْت خَلْقاً فَعَرَّفْتهمْ بِي فَعَرَفُونِي ."

[حَدِيثْ اَلْقُدْسِي – بِحَارْ اَلْأَنْوَارْ، اَلْعَلَامَةُ اَلْمَجْلِسِيْ، جُزْء ٨٤، صَفْحَة ١٩٩]

Qala Rasulallahi ﷺ, Qala Allah ﷻ: "Kuntu kanzan makhfiyya, fa ahbabtu an a'rafa, fa khalaqtu khalqan, fa 'arraftahum bi fa 'arafonee."
[Hadith al Qudsi – Behar al Anwar, Al 'Alama al Majlisi, Juz' 84, Safha 199]

The Messenger of Allah (pbuh) said, that Allah (AJ) said: "I was a hidden Treasure then I desired to be known, so I created a creation to which I made Myself known; then they knew Me."
[Holy Hadith – Bihar al Anwar, by Al 'Alama al Majlisi, Volume 84, Page 199]

Allah ﷻ Put Divine Love in the Atomic Reality of Creation

That *ishq* and that love – we said the inside controls the outside. The inner reality is what's important. When *awliyaullah* (saints) come and teach us in our lives from these realities of Sayyidina Muhammad ﷺ, it's always in reference to *malakut* (heavenly realm) and the soul and light. For Allah ﷻ doesn't care for *dunya* (material world), like the wing of a mosquito. So, to understand when Allah ﷻ is describing *ishq* and love, it's not from the physical. So it has the immense, immense reality of the soul.

That, what draws the moon in its orbit, what keeps the Earth in its orbit. What keeps all of creation on top of the Earth and not floating away is that Allah ﷻ put in within its atomic reality this 'Divine Love.' That when Allah ﷻ saying, 'I created everything  from love,' it means that the real essence, not just the expression, 'I created with love.' It's the electrons – they are given a love for the power that's within the nucleus and the center.

Electrons are Attracted to the Positivity of the Nucleus

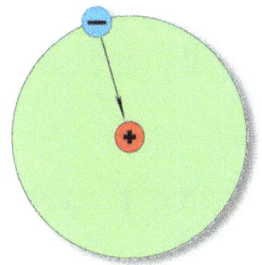

The center is positive and everything else is less than positive, so you would call that 'negative.' So you put the 'e' and a line from the 'e' to the center, which we would call the 'positive' and 'The Powerful,' the 'Divinely Presence' – that which is powerful and eternal and pure.

When Allah ﷻ wants to create its essence and its light, forget about the physical because the essence and the light is what's important. He put within that 'e' and that electron that, 'You are by your nature weak, and you are not independent. You are dependent.' Within its *zaat* and its essence, it has the love for the nucleus. It is attracted to the positivity.

So, then Allah ﷻ gives that attraction. So, the image that we have of the mass attraction, what we would call the 'circumambulation,' centrifugal force that spins it. Then as a result, the rise that begins to lift. We have it on the articles for the *sama'* and

the whirling, the *haqqaiqs* (realities) that *awliya* (saints) were teaching. Each of these *awliya* were given a way and an understanding to bring out that reality.

Our Positivity Depends on Our Proximity to the Divine Source

They are teaching the core of this love when Allah ﷻ is describing that, 'I wanted to be known.' The essence of this love, it's in the core of our *wujud* (existence), our being, and our essence. That these electrons and our reality is in its negativity, because it's not perfect. That's why the only perfection for Allah ﷻ is Sayyidina Muhammad ﷺ. That's why *"Qaaba qawsayni aw adna"* (a distance of two bow lengths or nearer).

$$فَكَانَ قَابَ قَوْسَيْنِ أَوْ أَدْنَىٰ ﴿٩﴾$$

53:9 – "Fakana qaaba qawsayni aw adna." (Surat An-Najm)

"And was at a distance of two bow lengths or nearer [to the Divine Presence]." (The Star, 53:9)

Because perfection is your proximity to the Divine source and power.

Anything less than that proximity is of a lesser positive charge. So as you go out, out, out – of course, then you become negative in comparison to the positive. So, it means the Muhammadan light and reality is right there at the center. The center of that is the power and the *qudra* (power) of Allah ﷻ – that makes the nucleus.

Sama' (Whirling) is to Reach Divine Love Within the Heart

Allah ﷻ put within us, because of our weakness and less than perfect, is the desire and the love for that perfection. As a result, it is with all its being attracted to the nucleus; not the ego and not the form is of any importance. That

when Allah ﷻ created this reality in truth and its reality is based on this Divine love. Because of the electron's love for the nucleus and the pure love, it begins to move. Because the magnetic force is so powerful, it doesn't stay because it's not connecting. It begins the centrifugal movement. That was the reality of the *sama.'* They were imitating the movement of *ishq* and love. Until they could reach that Divine love within their heart, they would not stop the whirling understanding. It means they would imitate the electron.

Whirl Around Your Heart Which is the Center of Your Universe

That was one way that Sayyidina Jalaluddin (Rumi) ق was teaching his students the same *haqqaiq* (realities). They were all teaching the same, whether they were standing and doing the *hadrah* (presence) or they were spinning and doing the *sama'* (whirling). Or whether they were sitting and doing the meditation, it was all the same *haqqaiq* taught in different ways. So that the students who wanted to understand the way of the *sama'* and whirl, they would whirl around their heart. The center of their universe is their left foot, their heart. That they reach to the heavens with their right hand and that they give back to creation with their left hand. And as a result, they become a vehicle of perfection.

The *sama'* was imitating the electrons and that the heart was the nucleus and that you have to rotate around the heart. Actual *dunya* (material world), the *shaitan* (satan) is trying to make people rotate away from their heart and make their heart follow them. But I have to whirl around my heart. I have to make my body to follow my heart under Allah's جل جلاله command. But not take my heart to follow my body where it doesn't want to go.

Whirling is an Inheritance From Sayyidina Abu Bakr as Siddiq ؑ

That was the teaching of the *sama'*. All of the rituals in that teaching were based on that *haqqaiq*, which *alhamdulillah*, Naqshbandiya hold that reality because it's from Sayyidina Abu Bakr as Siddiq ؑ. So, Sayyidina Jalaluddin ق was teaching the *sama'*; its *haqqaiq* is from Sayyidina Abu Bakr as Siddiq ؑ. When he (Abu Bakr as Siddiq ؑ) heard the *Hadith* of Sayyidina Muhammad ﷺ that he described that, 'You will be with whom you love.'

عَنْ أَنَسٍ رَضِيَ اللَّهُ عَنْهُ: ... فَقَالَ (رَسُولُ اللهِ ﷺ): " أَنْتَ مَعَ مَنْ أَحْبَبْتَ. "
[الْمَصْدَرْ: مُسْلِمْ: ٧٥٢٠]

'An Anasin (ra): ... Faqala (Rasulallahi) ﷺ: *"Anta ma'a man ahbabta."*

Narrated Anas ibn Malik (ra) that …the Messenger of Allah (pbuh) said: "You will be with whom you love." [Source: Muslim 7520]

As a result of the immensity of that *Hadith*, Sayyidina Abu Bakr as Siddiq ؑ got up, held his *jubba* (Islamic robe) and then whirled in the reality of the *jubba*. Out of his happiness that a confirmation and the fear that, 'Maybe my *'amal* (action) is not enough.' But Allah ﷻ is granting for us, 'No, no, you'll be with whom you love, regardless of your *'amal* and the perfection of its *'amal*, the state of that *'amal*. Imagine if the *Siddiq al-Mutlaq*, the Perfected Truthful Servant of Allah ﷻ was worried, imagine everybody else in creation.

That's why that *Hadith* is so powerful for us now. That if we were going to come with our actions, then that would be very difficult. But we are coming from this love that, '*Ya Rabbi*, grant us love and let our love to show. Let our actions of love to show and don't judge our love,' because love can't be judged. That let us to compete in love to everybody to do better and more. As a result, with that love that *Hadith* is our power, 'You'll be with whom you love.' So our love is for Sayyidina Muhammad ﷺ, *inshaAllah*.

Love and Attraction are the Core of Spinning

You make your electrons spin faster by more love and reading *Dalail ul Khairat* (book of praising on Prophet ﷺ). If we're understanding the variables, there's three – attraction, centrifugal force, and rise. So what was the core? The attraction. Without the attraction there's no spinning, there's just walking barely. So how do I increase my attraction for the love of Prophet ﷺ? That was the state of faith, 'Ya Umar, you have to love me more than you love yourself.'

وَعَنْ عُمَرَ عَلَيْهِ السَّلَامُ قَالَ: فَوَجَدْتُ نَفْسِي أَقُولُ: وَاللهِ يَا رَسُولَ اللهِ، إِنِّي أُحِبُّكَ! فَقَالَ لَهُ اَلنَّبِيِّ ﷺ: " أَكْثَرَ مِنْ أَهْلِكَ يَا عُمَرُ؟ " قُلْتُ: نَعَمْ. قَالَ ﷺ: " أَكْثَرَ مِنْ مَالِكَ يَا عُمَرُ؟ " قُلْتُ: نَعَمْ. قَالَ ﷺ: " أَكْثَرَ مِنْ نَفْسِكَ يَا عُمَرُ؟ " قَالَ: لَا.

فَقَالَ اَلنَّبِيِّ ﷺ: " لَا يَا عُمَرُ، لَا يَكْمُلُ إِيمَانُكَ حَتَّى أَكُونَ أَحَبَّ إِلَيْكَ مِنْ نَفْسِكَ."

يَقُولُ عُمَرُ: فَخَرَجْتُ فَفَكَّرْتُ. ثُمَّ عُدْتُ أَهْتَفُ بِهَا: وَاللهِ يَا رَسُولَ اللهِ لَأَنْتَ أَحَبُّ إِلَيَّ مِنْ نَفْسِي. فَقَالَ اَلنَّبِيِّ ﷺ: " اَلْآنَ يَا عُمَرُ اَلْآنَ "
[صَحِيحُ الْبُخَارِيِّ، الْمَجْلَدُ الرَّابِعُ، رَقْمُ الْحَدِيثِ ٥٩٤]

Wa 'an 'Umar (as) qala: "Fawajadtu nafsi aqoolo: Wallahi ya Rasulullahi, inni uhibbuka!

Faqala lahu anNabiyu 🌸: *"Akthara min ahlika ya 'Umar?" Qultu: Na'am. Qala* 🌸: *"Akthara min malika ya 'Umar?", Qultu: Na'am. Qala* 🌸: *"Akthara min nafsika ya 'Umar?", Qala: La.*

Faqala anNabiyu 🌸: *"La ya 'Umar, la yakmulu imanoka hatta akuna ahabba ilayka min nafsika." Yaqoolo 'Umar (as): Fakhrajtu fafakkartu. Thumma 'udtu ahtafu biha: Wallahi ya Rasulullahi la anta ahabbu ilayya min nafsi. Faqala anNabiyu* 🌸: *"Alan ya 'Umar, alan."*
[Sahih al-Bukhari, al-Majladu al-Rabi'o, Raqm al-Hadith 594]

Narrated by Sayyidina 'Umar (as) that he said: "I found myself saying, 'By Allah, O Messenger of Allah, I love you!' The Prophet (pbuh) said to him, 'Is it more than your love for your family, O 'Umar?' I said, 'Yes.' He (pbuh) said, 'Is it more than your love for your wealth, O 'Umar?' I said, 'Yes.' He said, 'Is it more than your love for yourself, O 'Umar?' He said, 'No.'

The Prophet (pbuh), said, 'No, O 'Umar, your faith will not be complete until I become more beloved to you than your own self.' 'Umar said: So I went out and thought. Then I returned and shouted, 'By Allah, O Messenger of Allah, you are more beloved to me than myself.' The Prophet (pbuh) said, 'Now, O 'Umar, now [you got it].'
[Sahih al-Bukhari, Volume 4, Hadith #594]

It means that when you love the reality more than you love yourself, you're directing all your energy in that direction. The *salawats* (praises upon Prophet Muhammad 🌸), the *zikr*, the attendance, the *Mawlid* (celebration of the birthday of Prophet 🌸). Go and give food for the love of Prophet 🌸, do

good deeds, be of service. Whatever you can do to put your entire being in that direction, then that love is moving towards Prophet ﷺ.

He ﷺ takes that love and then begins to send back an immense amount of love and *khushiya*. That's why, we're saying '*Rasulul Kareem* (The Most Generous Messenger)' – he is one that whom if you even gave a smile to that reality Prophet ﷺ would go out of his way to give back a smile. Immense love and generosity that Allah ﷻ was astonished, *"Khuluqal 'azheem,"* because Allah ﷻ created that reality that, 'You are of a magnificent character.'

$$\text{وَإِنَّكَ لَعَلَىٰ خُلُقٍ عَظِيمٍ ﴿٤﴾}$$

68:4 – "Wa innaka la'ala khuluqin 'azheem." (Surat Al-Qalam)

"Truly, You (O Muhammad!) are of a magnificent character."
(The Pen, 68:4)

Increase the Spin of Your Electrons With Salawats

This is a love that never wasted and never harmed. Nobody was harmed by this love for the reality of Sayyidina Muhammad ﷺ. So that's the core. If we build that love and we do the *Dalail ul Khairat*, we do the recitations, the *salawats*. That's why you do five thousand, ten thousand, twenty thousand *salawats* a day, so that what? Because you're building an immense love.

Immense love then creates what? Immense centrifugal force. So the more love you have and you can't get in, you're spinning even faster, faster, faster, faster, faster and now your rise is very strong. That's why many people may see these *'ashiqeen* (lovers of Prophet ﷺ) very tall in their dream. They distinguish that they are very big nature. Not that they're tall physically only but because I see them so big in their *ishq* and their love for the Divinely Presence, *inshaAllah*.

Electrons Vanish and Reappear With Immense Love

That which is spinning, is spinning so fast because of its immense *ishq*, its immense love. Then there *awliya* came and described that in their

spin, in the spin of their *wujud* and their atomic reality, their atoms would disappear. Where it would go and then how it would reappear? How long was it gone in that World of Light and came back? It means the

immensities of these realities. Only then later science understood when they were observing electrons that they would vanish at times. The electron would be under observation, vanish, and then reappear.

It means the spin and the love is so great. Because what causes the speed of the spin? It's the love – the attraction of the electron to the center. When Allah ﷻ increases the love, it means the *himmah* and the *zeal* to want to approach. If there's no *himmah* (zeal), 'Yeah, I don't care about that. I don't need to get it right now.' But when Allah ﷻ in the World of Light for the soul which is pure, because the *nafs* (ego) is what will pull the body not to understand and not allow the body to follow its own reality. Everyone's soul is created by this reality.

Atoms Spin Fast Creating Holograms

Everyone's soul has this love and it's spinning so fast. As a result it begins the rise. So it's attracted, it spins, and then it rises. That's why, 'This life is but an illusion.'

وَمَا الْحَيَاةُ الدُّنْيَا إِلَّا مَتَاعُ الْغُرُور ﴿١٨٥﴾...

3:185 – "...Wa ma al hayaatud dunyaaa illaa mataa'ul ghuroor."
(Surat Ali 'Imran)

"...And what is the life of this world except the enjoyment of deception/delusion." (The Family of Imran, 3:185)

The hologram of this Earth and everything around us – the wood, the floor, the pillows – everything is in a hologram. Because it's just atoms that spin fast. You see when something's spinning very fast, if you try to touch it, it feels solid because it's spinning so fast. If you slowed the spin, then you would hit here [at your hand], put your finger in and then when it would come again it would hit you. But when it spins faster than your movement, you can't get any closer because it keeps rubbing you and it gives the appearance of something solid.

That's why Allah ﷻ in Qur'an says, 'This *dunya's* (material world) an illusion. I'm making it to spin, because I put within its essence *ishq* and love.' Because what does it matter? The planet are the same atoms. You are the same atoms, the plant is the same atoms, the ant is the same atoms. So, it means they all have the same structure of an atom – a nucleus and electrons. Its atomic reality is all spinning. So, everything is created by that love and appearing now because of *ishq* and *muhabbat* (love).

Allah ﷻ Ordered the Electrons of All Creation to Come and Follow Prophet ﷺ

What is in the center is Allah's ﷻ Divine love. *"Qul in kuntum"* this is why quantum reality, *"kuntum."* That Allah ﷻ addressing in an ancient time, in an ancient light to the reality of Prophet ﷺ. He's not addressing a few people on Earth that, 'Oh you want, you want this, you want that. I don't care.' Allah ﷻ is addressing a *haqqaiq* from an ancient reality, *"Qul in kuntum tuhibbon Allah."* It means that, 'Your *wujud,* and tell everything in that World of Light, if they want the Divinely Presence and the nucleus, *Fattabi'uni.'* That, 'Come! That they must be coming to your reality.' As a result, all the order came for everything in existence, all of its electrons to come. Right?

قُلْ إِنْ كُنْتُمْ تُحِبُّونَ اللَّـهَ فَاتَّبِعُونِيْ يُحْبِبْكُمُ اللَّـهُ ... ﴿٣١﴾

3:31 – "Qul in kuntum tuhibbon Allaha fattabi'uni, yuhbibkumullahu..." (Surat Ali 'Imran)

"Say, [O Muhammad], "If you should love Allah, then follow me, [so] Allah will love you ..." (Family of Imran, 3:31)

He's not giving a direction for me and you, our physical bodies, and our ego says, 'I don't accept this. I accept this.' This was an ancient command of how Allah ﷻ formulated creation. That He commanded to the light, *"Qul in kuntum tuhibbon Allaha*

fattabi'uni" because the center and the nucleus is the Muhammadan *haqqaiq*. Allah's ﷻ command and *isharah* (sign) to all the lesser light which are the electrons, *'Fattabi'uni* – you are commanded by your essence to come and follow.' So by that command in the World of Light, there is *"sam'ina wa ata'na,"* we heard and we obeyed.

$$سَمِعْنَا وَأَطَعْنَا غُفْرَانَكَ رَبَّنَا وَإِلَيْكَ الْمَصِيْرُ ﴿٢٨٥﴾$$

2:285 – *"Sam'ina wa ata'na, ghufranaka Rabbana wa ilaykal masir."* (Surat Al-Baqarah)

"…We hear, and we obey: (We seek) Thy forgiveness, our Lord, and to Thee is the end of all journeys." (The Cow, 2:285)

There is a Distance Even Between Sayyidina Muhammad ﷺ and Allah ﷻ

As a result, the electrons of all these light are moving towards that nucleus. Then Allah ﷻ, 'Not so close.' There is a distance, *bayna* (between). There is like a *pardeh* (veil) and a distance between you and

this reality (Prophet Muhammad ﷺ). That reality is in distance to its Creator, *"Qaaba qawsayni aw adna."* Even the reality of that nucleus keeps a distance as an *adab* (manners) from Allah's ﷻ *'Izzah* (Honour) and Might. By the *adab* and following the understanding of *"Qaaba qawsayni aw adna"* because even the light of Prophet ﷺ, we never say, 'It collides with Allah ﷻ.' As a result, *"Qaaba qawsayni aw adna"* means 'Two bow lengths or nearer.' That with what type of power this attraction Allah ﷻ put into the Muhammadan light to move towards Allah ﷻ, in which it wants to completely collide and become one, but its *adab* is not *Wahdatul Wujud* (Oneness in Existence).

فَكَانَ قَابَ قَوْسَيْنِ أَوْ أَدْنَىٰ ﴿٩﴾

53:9 – "Fakana qaaba qawsayni aw adna." (Surat An-Najm)

"And was at a distance of two bow lengths or nearer [to the Divine Presence]." (The Star, 53:9)

That's the reality and the power of *Naqshbandiya tul 'Aliya* (The Most Distinguished Naqshbandi Order). That *Naqshbandiya tul 'Aliya* kept the *adab* and the *haqqaiq* in which Allah 🕮 showed to their *awliya*, the Muhammadan reality. For if you take out the Muhammadan reality, then you are a creation thinking you became one with Allah 🕮. That's why so many of them talked about becoming one with Allah 🕮, becoming one with Allah 🕮, *astaghfirullah*.

How can you become one with Allah 🕮 when all their teaching is that between you and Allah 🕮 is Sayyidina Muhammad ﷺ? That you're no one to be one with Allah 🕮. If you take out the Muhammadan *haqqaiq* and the shaykh doesn't teach the Muhammadan *haqqaiq*, which other *turuqs* (spiritual paths) may have fallen into that understanding? Then they thought themself approaching the proximity of Allah 🕮 and not knowing themself who they are and where they are.

Nobody Can Reach a Full Muhammadan Dress

It means that there is no way into that reality. That reality is *"Muhammadun Rasulallah* ﷺ.*"* Its inner core is making the *tawwaf* (circumambulation) around Allah 🕮. As a result of that *ishq* and that *muhabbat*, everything is drawn towards the Muhammadan *haqqaiq*. Then all the electrons are coming and Allah 🕮 keep them like a *"Qaaba qawsayni"* – is a distance from Prophet ﷺ. That even their essence wants to collide into the inner core of Prophet ﷺ and Allah ﷻ keep even their reality at a distance. Nobody reaches a full Muhammadan dress. There's only one *"Muhammadun Rasulallah* ﷺ.*"*

Otherwise, they would all reach into the complete *fana* (annihilation), but Allah ﷻ keep their light even that at an *ihtiram* (respect) and a distance. Your knowledge can only encompass what Prophet ﷺ wants to bestow. So, even to their Muhammadan dress there is an *adab* (manners) and a distance into that. That's a strong force that Allah ﷻ pulls all reality towards it. And at the same time, Allah ﷻ then push another force that, 'You cannot become one with it.' That becomes the core atomic force inside our essence and our atomic reality. As a result, everything is spinning.

Angels are the Manifestation of Pure Love

All the lights within paradises – as soon as they manifest, they have a spin because those lights that you see, they are of an atomic reality. So, they're spinning in their origin with an immense pure light and love. That's why the heavens is pure and purified. Because the angelic reality, they are in a  complete *ishq* and spinning. Their spin and their rotation, their *'ibadat* (worshipness) is complete and clean, with no *nafs*, no *mulk*, no *dunya*, no worldly form. As a result, that's why the heavens is pure and purified. That they are in a complete love. Their attraction and their manifestation is the manifestation of pure love. That's our core reality.

Nafs and Satan Create a Barrier Between Soul and Physicality

Then all the physicality and the physicality has a barrier between the soul, which we call the 'ego' the *'nafs'* and the 'devil.' As a result of that barrier, it blocks the physicality from understanding its own reality and its own soul. That's the purpose of that *nafs* and devil – to apply a negative force so that conveyance of love is not connecting.

So, we described that Prophet ﷺ is making *tawwaf* around Allah ﷻ, all creation is making *tawwaf* around Sayyidina Muhammad ﷺ. In their core love and their essence of their soul, all the heavens are in that manifestation. That's why we deem the heavens to be beatific and pure. It's just radiating pure love. Then the physical and the physical world of *insan* (mankind) and the physical manifestation of these creatures is that their physicality is making *tawwaf* around their soul.

But Allah ﷻ allowed their *nafs* and a *shaitan* (satan) to get in between that. So that the *nafs* and *shaitan* is blocking their soul from their physicality. As a result, their physicality is not sensing complete what the soul wants to communicate to it, what it wants to give it from its Divinely love. The physicality deems itself something by itself self-sufficient. It forgot it even had a core that radiates power. It comes to the Earth and because of the *nafs* and the *shaitan* that blocking it, it deems itself self-sufficient. Throughout the Qur'an, Allah ﷻ describes, 'You feel yourself. The arrogant ones, they feel themself to be self-sufficient.' [They say] 'Nobody can touch us from the wealth we have, the money we have, the power we have, the companies we have.'

وَكَانَ لَهُ ثَمَرٌ فَقَالَ لِصَاحِبِهِ وَهُوَ يُحَاوِرُهُ أَنَا أَكْثَرُ مِنكَ مَالًا وَأَعَزُّ نَفَرًا ﴿٣٤﴾
وَدَخَلَ جَنَّتَهُ وَهُوَ ظَالِمٌ لِّنَفْسِهِ قَالَ مَا أَظُنُّ أَن تَبِيدَ هَٰذِهِ أَبَدًا ﴿٣٥﴾

18:34-35 – " Wa kaana lahoo samarun faqaala lisaahibihee wa huwa yuhaawiruhoo ana aksaru minka maalanw wa a'azzu nafaraa. (34) Wa dakhala jannatahoo wa huwa zaalimul linafsihee qaala maaa azunnu an tabeeda haaziheee abadaa. (35) (Surat Al-Kahf)

And he had produce/fruit and he said to his companion, "I am greater than you in wealth and mightier in (numbers of) men/(manpower). And he went into his garden, while he was oppressor to his soul/wronged himself. He said: I do not think that this will ever perish."
(The Cave, 18:34-35)

Our Soul is Still ON Even When the Body Collapses

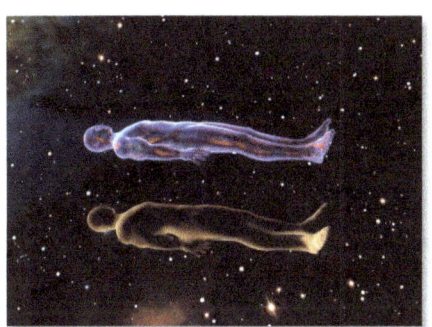

They forgot that Allah ﷻ controls their inner battery, their inner existence. It means if Allah ﷻ turned the love OFF, this entire creation, if He turned just OFF on humans, they collapse into nothing and the form collapses. He can keep the *ishq* and the love for the soul ON and collapse all the physicalities. The physicalities will collapse and the souls would be there. That is the reality of the grave, because when they go into the grave, the energy of the soul is still ON, not the energy of the body. So, the reality of *mawt* (death) is what's happening. The soul is there. That's why there are two beings coming, the physicality and the soul.

That's why Prophet ﷺ is describing, 'Be careful,' because now there are two entities, one you're not familiar with. The body that you're washing, there is a living soul right next to it that's going to complain about how you treat that body. It senses and it feels. That was the *isharah* (sign) that wash with warm water, do things correctly, speak politely in that presence. That soul has a feeling and it's attached to that understanding of the body. So that we would understand that our soul is feeling.

The Body of Eternal Souls Never Deteriorate Due to Love

That the grave is the great shutting-off. That Allah ﷻ begin to shut-off the attraction on the physicality. As a result, it's no longer in a rise, manifesting. You even see when you deal with those whom passed away, their physicality actually begins to wither away. They lose their size right away, all of their body is beginning to evaporate. All of their rise is beginning to go down because Allah ﷻ gave its command that, 'Now their *ishq*, their spin, their life, the existence and manifestation is  OFF.' If Allah ﷻ cut this attraction of the physicality, it's off. There's no more spinning. As a result, the rise begins to collapse. You open and the body deteriorated and there is nothing left of these atoms, this body. It became dust.

Except those whom Allah ﷻ grant them a *Hayat* (Ever-living) – that they are eternal souls. Their eternal soul is powered and their eternal soul is even eternally powering that physicality. Their physicality is in a continuous state of *ishq* and love. Allah ﷻ never pulled the love from their physicality and they don't deteriorate. Their physicality has a freshness within the grave years after because the power of the soul. It is such a powerful reality dressing that physicality that its power is still dressing Allah's ﷻ *ishq* on the body, Allah's ﷻ centrifugal power on the body, and Allah's 🕊 rise on the body. So, it's still in a state of manifestation because of its perfection of *ishq* and love.

The Sun Sends Gravitational Command to the Earth and the Moon

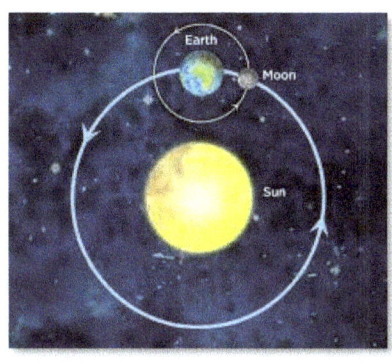

It means that we pray that Allah 🕊 give us more and more understanding. This is an understanding towards the understanding of gravity that, that which holds you onto the Earth. They want to explain things as a scientist, but more important is understanding through this Divinely light. That this is an ancient Divinely light of love. Based on that love, you are pulled. That which you gravitate towards and that you're magnetically inclined towards is in the hands of Allah 🕊. So, it means that this Earth stays where it is because of Allah's 🕊 command. Its love and its understanding of what it has to do and it's in its love and its *ishq* and its spin. The moon is in its orbit by its love and its *ishq*. The sun is in its orbit by its love and its *ishq*.

The immensity of the solar power that comes from the sun, its love and its *ishq* is a power that sends out and tells exactly the moon where it's supposed to spin, how close it can come, and how far it has to stay away. Everything is under that command of that sun. So, the sun is the source of *ishq* and love and it sends the gravitational command for the Earth, its distance and its proximity that it is to stay. It means that we described in *Laylatul Qadr* (Night of Power), '*Malaikatu war Roh beiznillah wa kullin amr. Salamun, hiya hatta matla'il Fajr.'*

تَنَزَّلُ الْمَلَائِكَةُ وَالرُّوحُ فِيهَا بِإِذْنِ رَبِّهِم مِّن كُلِّ أَمْرٍ ﴿٤﴾ سَلَامٌ هِيَ حَتَّىٰ مَطْلَعِ الْفَجْرِ ﴿٥﴾

97:4-5 – "Tanazzalul malaikatu war Roh, fiha beizne Rabbihim min kulle amr. (4) Salamun, hiya hatta matla'il Fajr. (5)" (Surat Al-Qadr)

"The angels and the Spirit descend therein by permission of their Lord for every Command/affair. (4) Peace it is until the emergence of dawn. (5)" (The Power 97:4-5)

By the permission of Allah ﷻ, these commands are coming. The central power of our galaxy, its understanding is the sun. That every command is coming from that ocean of light, meaning what? It tells the Earth exactly what its sustenance will be, what its power will be, what its lights will be, what its blessings will be, and where its orbit is to be, and the movement of its orbit. Because if the central command is the power, it's like the video game; it's the one telling the Earth what to do and where to go. Because that which is eternal is the power. That sun is telling the moon exactly where it's supposed to be. Not aliens! It's *'Izzatullah* (Allah's ﷻ Might and Magnificence).

The Sun Has an Eternal Authority Over Other Planets

That sun, when it want to send a punishment, it sends a flare from itself and you see a 'poofff' [solar flare sound effect] and they show this solar flare. They say its reaching all the way to the end of the galaxy and it can wipe

84

out all of the satellite communications. It can wipe out life on planets. It can take out all of the life of this Earth, if it begins to send its, I don't know how you describe, its power. They call 'solar flare.' They call it a 'solar storm,' magnitude 4, 5, 6. If the sun begins to send its power upon the Earth, it can burn all of the inhabitants of the Earth. That's why Sayyidina Yusuf ﷺ described that, 'Allah ﷻ put me in command of the sun and the moon and the eleven planets.'

إِذْ قَالَ يُوسُفُ لِأَبِيهِ يَا أَبَتِ إِنِّي رَأَيْتُ أَحَدَ عَشَرَ كَوْكَبًا وَالشَّمْسَ وَالْقَمَرَ رَأَيْتُهُمْ لِي سَاجِدِينَ ﴿٤﴾

12:4 – "Idh qala Yosufu li abeehi ya abati innee raaytu ahada Ashara kawkaban wash Shamsa wal Qamara raaytuhum le sajideen." (Surat Yusuf)

"[Of these stories mention] when Joseph said to his father, "O my father, indeed I have seen eleven stars and the sun and the moon; I saw them prostrating to me." (Joseph, 12:4)

That was from Surat Al-Yusuf, but its reality when we described in Surat Al-Qadr. That this station of power for our understanding, only for our galaxy is the importance of the sun. What commands comes from that. *"Ar Roh wa malaika"* (Holy Qur'an, 97:4), the Muhammadan representative and the angels that fulfill the command of the Muhammadan representative that commands that station.

Sayyidina Muhammad ﷺ is the Star Maker

They don't know yet, but they will know *inshaAllah* someday, that that sun was created by the annihilation and the black hole into the reality of Sayyidina Muhammad ﷺ. He is the Star Maker. *"Mahiz zunub wa Muhyil qulub"* (eraser of sins and reviver of hearts).

يَا مُحْيِي الْقُلُوْبِ، سَلَامٌ عَلَيك يَا مَاحِي الذُّنُوْبِ ،
سَلَامٌ عَلَيك

Ya Muhyil qulubi, Salaam 'Alayk
Ya Mahidh dhunubi, Salaam 'Alayk

O the reviver of the hearts, O the eraser of the sins, Peace be upon you

That which he annihilates all, all and bring it to its reality of light. So, when they find those Muhammadan *haqqaiqs*, those are the black holes within this universe. That anything that enter into that hole, it will come out into a reality of *baqa* (eternal existence). It will lose its mass and enter into the oceans of eternal light. As a result, it manifest as a star. This is all from *ishq* and love and *muhabbat*. Not the physical love people are confusing from the material world but the essence in which Allah ﷻ, *inshaAllah*, created this creation from this immense love.

What Led People to Become Idol Worshipers?

Then we get an understanding of the importance of the love for Sayyidina Muhammad ﷺ. It keeps the *aqidah* (belief) to be correct. For without that love everyone says, 'Why we don't just talk about the love of Allah ﷻ?' It is that love. If you don't mention the Muhammadan *haqqaiqs* (realities), then you become from those who think you became one with Allah ﷻ or that you will become one with Allah ﷻ.

How all these people became *bud parast* and idol worshippers and *mushrikeen* (polytheists)? How they called their saints to be gods? How they called something to be a god?

That was the danger. When you don't put creation in front of you and that your only way is to enter into the reality of the most purified station of creation called *"Muhammadun Rasulallah* ﷺ.*"* That Prophet ﷺ knows how to keep the barrier, the distance, and the *adab* from saying that he's one with Allah ﷻ, *astaghfirullah*. As a result of the firmness in that understanding, then you kept within the barrier of entering in. The most you can enter in is into the *haqqaiqs* of *Muhammadun Rasulallah* ﷺ; keeping us in the perfect *tawheed* (oneness) of *"La ilaha illAllah"* which means 'Nothing is there with it' and all that other than that is *"Muhammadun Rasulallah* ﷺ.*"*

When they didn't have that, they thought they were entering into oneness with the Divine. Then communities afterwards would describe them that, 'Who were they, what were they, how did they know?' I say, 'I don't know but they became one with the god,' and then they became called 'gods,' *astaghfirullah*. That's how their confusion and their belief and their *aqidah* had corrupted their truth. That's why the perfected truth is the Muhammadan truth. That nothing is one with Allah ﷻ. Allah ﷻ is with Allah ﷻ. For our ascension and our reality is into the ocean of *"Muhammadun Rasulallah* ﷺ.*"*

The Power of Praising Upon Sayyidina Muhammad ﷺ is Unimaginable

Then by this love, this *ishq*, imagine the power of each of these *Mawlids* (celebration of the birthday of Prophet ﷺ). The power of the actual birth [of Prophet Muhammad ﷺ], the power of celebrating the birth, the power of *salawats* (praises upon Prophet Muhammad ﷺ). That every difficulty you have, there is a *salawat* for that. So, imagine then when they're teaching all these essences, all these realities of lights, all of the universes and paradises, all of the *samayi wal ard* – from the heavens

to the earths, all are under that command. Then imagine the power of making *salawat* on Sayyidina Muhammad ﷺ!

We pray that Allah ﷻ dress us, bless us, and expand our heart for understanding. Anyone confused with their head, you probably have to watch couple more times so that you don't rush to judgment or think something else was said. The words are chosen to be very, very precise and delicate as to not move left and right in the wrong understanding, *inshaAllah.*

Subhana rabbika rabbal 'izzati 'amma yasifoon, wa salaamun 'alal mursaleen, walhamdulillahi rabbil 'aalameen. Bi hurmati Muhammad al-Mustafa wa bi siri Surat al-Fatiha.

Be Truthful to Love to Build Magnetism

Nurul Huda ﷺ is a Magnetic Reality

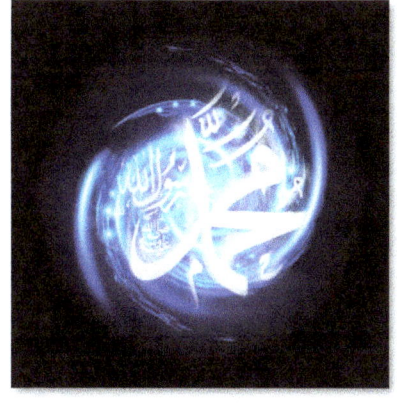

The *Nurul Huda*, that one of the names of Prophet ﷺ is '*Nurul Huda*' – the Light of Guidance or the Guiding Light. We talked the other night and always a reminder these subjects that are so immensely deep that we *tafakkur* and contemplate. That light is a magnetic reality, and that when people think only from physicality then these talks and this way doesn't make sense. If they can arise above their physicality and think from the World of Light. That Allah ﷻ give these titles, *"Nurul Huda"* – that this Guiding Light and this Light of Guidance and that, that light is magnetic, has an energy, has a *juzba* (magnetism), has a *faiz* and emanation.

Our Spiritual Practices are a Calling to the Muhammadan Light

That this love that we put into it, every love that we put in life, we have to be cautious. That that which we love, we will be with. Whom you love, you will be with and whom you love will be with you is the secret of

89

magnetism. That which we direct our light to it, it will magnetically pull us. This is a reality of guidance.

عَنْ أَنَسٍ رَضِيَ اللَّهُ عَنْهُ: ... فَقَالَ (رَسُولُ اللهِ ﷺ): " أَنْتَ مَعَ مَنْ أَحْبَبْتَ. "
[اَلْمَصْدَرْ: مُسْلِمْ: ٧٥٢٠]

'An Anasin (ra): ... Faqala (Rasulullahi) ﷺ: "Anta ma'a man ahbabta."

Narrated Anas ibn Malik (ra) that ...the Messenger of Allah (pbuh) said: "You will be with whom you love." [Source: Muslim 7520]

When we want to go deep into the understanding of guidance and why these practices and what's the reality of these associations? Because the *dunya* (material world) people, they say, 'Why they have to sit so much in praising? Why they have to continuously have *awrads* (daily practices) and recitations?' All of that is developing its understanding that every recitation that you make, it's a calling. You're calling to that light. You're calling to the reality of that soul. Then from these teachings, those lights have magnetic draw to them. Whether we're calling from the names of Allah ﷻ and we have to understand from *"Atiullah, atiur Rasul"* (Holy Qur'an, 4:59), that even when you call the name of Allah ﷻ, it has to pass through the permission of the light of Sayyidina Muhammad ﷺ.

...أَطِيعُوا اللَّه وَأَطِيعُوا الرَّسُولَ وَأُولِي الْأَمْرِ مِنْكُمْ... ﴿٥٩﴾

4:59 – "...Atiullaha wa atiur Rasula wa Ulil amre minkum... (Surat An-Nisa)

"... Obey Allah, Obey the Messenger, and those in authority among you..." (The Women, 4:59)

Sayyidina Musa ۩ Was Annihilated By the Light of Prophet ﷺ

We described that before that Allah ﷻ says, 'If I reveal My Speech to the mountain, it will be dust.' Even Allah ﷻ described to His prophet, Sayyidina Musa ۩, that, 'Not only I do not reveal My speech but you can't even look at Me. And look to that mountain and see if it's still standing when I reveal My glory upon it.'

لَوْ أَنزَلْنَا هَٰذَا الْقُرْآنَ عَلَىٰ جَبَلٍ لَّرَأَيْتَهُ خَاشِعًا مُّتَصَدِّعًا مِّنْ خَشْيَةِ اللَّهِ... ﴿٢١﴾

59:21 – "Law anzalna hadha alQurana 'ala jabalin laraaytahu, khashi'an mutasaddi'an min khashyatillahi..." (Surat Al-Hashr)

"Had We sent down this Qur'an on a mountain, verily, you would have seen it obliterated to dust (from its power)..." (The Exile, 59:21)

وَلَمَّا جَاءَ مُوسَىٰ لِمِيقَاتِنَا وَكَلَّمَهُ رَبُّهُ قَالَ رَبِّ أَرِنِي أَنظُرْ إِلَيْكَ ۚ قَالَ لَن تَرَانِي وَلَٰكِنِ
انظُرْ إِلَى الْجَبَلِ فَإِنِ اسْتَقَرَّ مَكَانَهُ فَسَوْفَ تَرَانِي ۚ فَلَمَّا تَجَلَّىٰ رَبُّهُ لِلْجَبَلِ جَعَلَهُ دَكًّا
وَخَرَّ مُوسَىٰ صَعِقًا ۚ فَلَمَّا أَفَاقَ قَالَ سُبْحَانَكَ تُبْتُ إِلَيْكَ وَأَنَا أَوَّلُ الْمُؤْمِنِينَ ﴿١٤٣﴾

*7:143 – "Wa lamma jaa Musa limeeqatina wa kallamahu Rabbuhu,
qala rabbi arinee anzhur ilayka, Qala lan taranee wa lakini onzhur ilal
jabali fa inistaqarra makanahu, fasawfa taranee, falamma tajalla
Rabbuhu lil jabali ja`alahu, dakkan wa kharra Musa sa`iqan, falamma
afaqa qala subhanaka tubtu ilayka wa ana awwalul Mumineen."
(Surat Al-A'raf)*

*"And when Moses arrived at Our appointed time and his Lord spoke to
him, he said, "My Lord, show me [Yourself] that I may look at You."
[Allah] said, "You will not see Me, but look at the mountain; if it
should remain in its place, then you will see Me." But when his Lord
manifested His glory on the mountain, He made it as dust, and Moses
fell unconscious. And when he awoke/recovered his senses, he said,
"Glory be to You! to You I turn in repentance, and I am the first of the
believers." (The Heights, 7:143)*

Sayyidina Musa ﷺ, when he saw even the light of that reality, which later
it is understood. In these *na'ats* (prophetic praisings) we asked that, 'Ask
Musa ﷺ: Ya Musa ﷺ, what did you see?' That even the light of
Prophet ﷺ made Nabi Musa ﷺ *khashiya*, to be dust and completely
annihilated.

کس کو دیکھا یہ موسیٰ سے پوچھے کوئی

آنکھوں والوں کی ہمت پہ لاکھوں سلام

Kis ko dekha, yeh Musa se pooche koyi
Aankho waalo ki himmat pe, Laakho salaam

Someone should ask Prophet Moses (as), Whom did he see?
Millions of salutations upon the Courageous Eyes that could witness that
glory.

All Ismullah Must Pass Through Ismur Rasul ﷺ

It means that for somebody to think that they can take from that *qudra* – the energy of Allah ﷻ is impossible. The *adab* (manner) for understanding is that every *Ismullah* (Name of Allah ﷻ) has to pass through *Ismur Rasul* ﷺ (Name of the Messenger ﷺ). That's why we have articles on 'Nurmuhammad' listing the 99 names of Allah ﷻ and which of the 99 names of Sayyidina Muhammad ﷺ these names will pass through.

These are the keys of our understanding. That when Allah ﷻ want to send His light and power, it must pass through the reality of Sayyidina Muhammad ﷺ and from Prophet ﷺ then down and moving, flowing towards creation. This becomes the reality of the understandings of guidance. That when this light wants to reach to us, Allah ﷻ sends the light to the soul of Prophet ﷺ.

Even when we're making our *zikr* (Divine remembrance) and when we say *Ismul Jalalah* (the Majestic Name of Allah ﷻ), "*Allah, Allah, Allah, Allah,*" it must be passing through Nabi Muhammad ﷺ. It means then these lights and these energies that coming through us, it passes through the reality of Prophet's ﷺ soul. Then the light of that energy then comes towards the servant to dress them and bless them. That's the importance of these understandings.

So, even when we're making the *zikr* of Allah ﷻ, there's a magnetism. They understand the *adab* of that magnetism, that it all must flow through the soul of Prophet ﷺ, right?

Allah ﷻ is in the Heart of Prophet ﷺ Which is Manzil ul Qur'an

Because we said that Allah ﷻ not on heaven and not on Earth but Allah's ﷻ power is in the heart of His servant.

عَنْ وَهَبِ بْنِ مُنَبِّهْ، قَالَ رَسُولَ اللهِ ﷺ، قَالَ اللهُ عَزَّ وَجَلَّ: " مَا وَسِعَنِيْ لَا سَمَائِيْ وَلَا أَرْضِيْ وَلَكِنْ وَسِعَنِيْ قَلْبِ عَبْدِيْ الْمُؤْمِنْ." [حَدِيثْ اَلْقُدْسِي – اَلْغَزَالِي فِي اَلْإِحْيَاء، وَ اِبنِ عَرَبِي فِي اَلْتَرَاجِمْ، صفحه ٢٢٤]

'An Wahab ibn Munabbeh, Qala Rasulallahi ﷺ, Qala Allah (AJ):
"Maa wasi'anee laa samayee, wa la ardee, laakin wasi'anee qalbi 'Abdi al Mu'min."
[Hadith al Qudsi, Al Ghazali fi al Ihyaa, wa Ibn 'Arabi fi al Tarajim, Safha 224]

Narrated by Wahab the son of Munabbeh that the Messenger of Allah (pbuh) said, that Allah (AJ) said: "Neither My Heavens nor My Earth can contain Me, but the heart of my Believing Servant."
[Holy Hadith, by Imam al-Ghazali in Al Ihya, and by Ibn 'Arabi in al Tarajib, Page 224]

That's what we were talking the other night, it is *Manzil ul Qur'an* (where the Holy Qur'an emanates). This is the month of Ramadan. That to reach to only Allah ﷻ is outside for us to understand. We are in an ocean of creation. The center and the

heart of that creation is Sayyidina Muhammad ﷺ. Allah ﷻ define that for us, 'I'm not in heaven, I'm not on Earth of what you want of your *ma'rifah* (gnosticism) but I'm in the heart of My servant.'

We think, 'Oh, this means for us,' but for its *haqqaiq* (realities) is Allah ﷻ is directing, 'My power is in the heart of My servant, known to you as Sayyidina Muhammad ﷺ.' That heart is *Manzil ul Qur'an*. It's the house of Holy Qur'an. That heart is emanating Qur'an. Allah ﷻ wants to speak, He speaks through the heart of Sayyidina Muhammad ﷺ. That is the power door, nothing beyond that.

Zikrullah and Salawats, Like a Magnet, Call Us to That Reality

When we fully understood that, when we say, '*Ar-Rahman*' (The Most Compassionate), that the pull that you're asking from *sifat ar-Rahman* (attribute of The Most Compassionate), it must be coming through the key of Sayyidina Muhammad ﷺ. It means it moves through the soul of Prophet ﷺ from that Divinely heart. So, it means Allah's ﷻ *qudra* (power) is moving, it dresses through a key from the name of Prophet ﷺ, and then begins to move to the servant and dress them and bless them.

As a result of even the *salawats* (praises upon Prophet Muhammad ﷺ) that we do, the *zikrs* that we do, all of the associations that we do, these are then magnetically charged. These lights and these energies that we are calling upon, they are like magnets. They begin to draw us into their reality. That Allah's ﷻ lights and attributes and essences – they begin to dress our soul, bless our soul, and they begin to call us into that reality.

Prophet ﷺ is the Key and the Light of Guidance

It means then the most powerful light of that guidance is when we're saying, *"Allah."* When we leave everything as a distraction on this Earth and we call ourselves to Allah ﷻ. Then the perfection of faith is that when you believe in Allah ﷻ but then Allah ﷻ directs us to *Muhammadun Rasulallah* ﷺ. Because in our life, we came to say, *"La ilaha illAllah,"* there is nothing. There is no one. There is nothing but the Creator known to us as *La ilaha illAllah,* so it negates everything.

لَا إِلَهَ إلاَّ اللهُ مُحَمَّدًا رَسُولُ الله ﷺ ﷺ

"La ilaha illallahu Muhammadun Rasulallah ﷺ*"*

"There is no deity but Allah, Prophet Muhammad (pbuh) is the messenger of Allah"

Allah ﷻ begins then to direct us to the secret of guidance that, 'You came to My Oneness. Now I want you to come to the secret of guidance, *Nurul Huda* (light of guidance), in which you begin to say *Muhammadun Rasulallah* ﷺ.' It means it's a *Miftah ur Rahmah* – it's the key of Allah's ﷻ *rahmah* and mercy. Because as soon as our life opens up with the reality of *Muhammadun Rasulallah* ﷺ, it means then now every name and attribute that we recite, it's coming from the light of Prophet ﷺ because the only one who obeys Allah ﷻ, *Atiullah* is Prophet ﷺ. So, every *zikr* (Divine remembrance) of Allah ﷻ is coming through the dress of the light of Prophet ﷺ and then dressing the servants, dressing creation, dressing every reality.

'You'll Be With Whom You Love' is the Secret of Magnetism

That's why then these associations are immensely powerful. When they sit in these *zikrs*, they sit in these *majlis e sali alan Nabi* ﷺ (association of praising upon Prophet Muhammad ﷺ), they're being dressed by these lights, blessed by these lights and magnetically charged is coming. That's

why that holy *Hadith* is a description of that, 'You'll be with whom you love.' That's magnetism, that's a *juzba*. So, all of these words in Arabic – *juzba* is a magnetism.

عَنْ أَنَسٍ رَضِيَ اللَّهُ عَنْهُ: ... فَقَالَ (رَسُولُ اللهِ ﷺ): " أَنْتَ مَعَ مَنْ أَحْبَبْتَ."
[اَلْمَصْدَرْ: مُسْلِمْ: ٧٥٢٠]

'An Anasin (ra): ... Faqala (Rasulullahi) ﷺ: "Anta ma'a man ahbabta."

Narrated Anas ibn Malik (ra) that ...the Messenger of Allah (pbuh) said: "You will be with whom you love." [Source: Muslim 7520]

Faiz is Directed Precisely to the Magnetic Charge of the Soul

Faiz is emanation. How does that emanation come towards a servant? It's through a magnetic charge. Why doesn't it just dress everyone? Why doesn't the *faiz* (emanation) just go and find its own location or erroneously land upon the chair as soon as you move? *Faiz* is not an undirected emanation, but it's precisely guided by its magnetic reality. That as soon as you open the magnetic charge within your soul and begin to praise upon Allah ﷻ. You begin to praise upon the reality and make *salawat* and *durood sharif* (praising) upon the soul of Sayyidina Muhammad ﷺ, opens for us this reality of magnetism that exists within the energy and the light.

So, people are wondering like, 'Is it a big magnet?' No, but later they'll find that actual magnetism is in light. As soon as you activate that magnetism, actually that light now is directed specifically to your soul, specifically to your light. That's why as soon as you begin to make your chants, you're opening up your magnetic charge. As a result, these names, these attributes and these *durood sharif* (praising on Prophet

Muhammad ﷺ) are now coming and directing themself towards the servant. As much as they make *zikr*, as much as their magnet is being drawn to these lights and to these blessings.

By Salawat, Activate Your Magnet Towards the Most Powerful Magnet ﷺ

As soon as you make *salawat* on Prophet ﷺ, you're activating the most powerful magnet. The most powerful magnet! That you have now the attention of that reality of

Prophet ﷺ; *Nurul Huda*. What we say, '*Nurul Huda, Shafi' al Wara* (the light of guidance, the intercessor of mankind).' It means all of these *salawats* (praises upon Prophet Muhammad ﷺ), all of these *nasheeds* (songs of praise) were all of these realities in a melodious way. That the shaykhs are teaching by these endless and blessed recitations, all these *haqqaiqs* (realities).

'*Nurul Huda, Shafi' al Wara,*' that as soon as we reciting these, we're activating our magnet towards the greatest magnet of Allah ﷻ. It means that light of Prophet ﷺ becomes active and now begins to draw the servant towards his reality and the gravitational pull is drawing us.

يَا شَفِيْعَ الْوَرَى، سَلَامٌ عَلِيك   يَا نَبّيَ الْهُدَى، سَلَامٌ عَلِيك

خَاتِمُ الأَنْبِيَاء، سَلَامٌ عَلِيك   سَيّدُ الْأَصْفِيَاء، سَلَامٌ عَلِيك

Ya Shafi' Al Wara, Salamun 'Alayk; Ya Nabiy al Huda, Salamun 'Alayk
Khatimul Anbiya, Salamun 'Alayk; Sayyidul AsfiYa, Salamun 'Alayk

O Intercessor of mankind, peace be upon you; O Prophet of guidance, peace be upon you; The Seal of the prophets, peace be upon you; Master of the purified ones, peace be upon you

The Gravitational Pull of the Sun Holds All Planets in Their Orbits

That's why when we understood, Allah ﷻ described, 'I teach you upon yourself and I'll teach you upon the horizon.' It means they'll learn. They'll see the reality within themselves and they'll see the reality upon the horizon.

$$\text{﴿٥٣﴾} \dots \hat{ق}ُّ الْحَقُّ أَنَّهُ لَهُمْ يَتَبَيَّنَ حَتَّىٰ أَنفُسِهِمْ وَفِي الْآفَاقِ فِي آيَاتِنَا سَنُرِيهِمْ$$

41:53 – "Sanureehim ayatina fil afaqi wa fee anfusihim hatta yatabayyana lahum annahu alhaqqu..." (Surat Al-Fussilat)

"We will show them Our signs in the horizons and within themselves until it becomes clear to them that it is the truth..."
(Explained in Detail, 41:53)

It means then actually the sun, its gravitational pull is the one commanding all our planets. The sun, its gravitational pull is commanding all the planets. The *isharah* (sign) and the command within the sun is holding these planets in their orbit. If the command comes stronger, the planets would have moved into the gravitational pull of that sun. It means the secret of their spin and their orbit, the secret of their proximity, their dress and their *tajalli* (manifestation) is all under the command of that sun. Because Allah ﷻ want us to understand the outside for us to understand the inside.

100

Allah ﷻ Wants Us to Contemplate on His Creation

People whom their mind is narrow in understanding, they say, 'What you're talking about? Everything is Allah ﷻ.' We said before don't, don't make everything too easy like that. It means you didn't contemplate. Allah ﷻ wants a *saalik* and a seeker that contemplates His creation, not just oversimplify and say, 'This is all Allah ﷻ.' But that's not the way of *ma'rifah* (gnosticism). The way of *ma'rifah*, Allah ﷻ want you to see the secret within its reality.

Allah's ﷻ Command to the Sun Enables Us to Breathe

Once you understand, 'Do you see the secret of that sun? You breathe from it.' Anybody has a question? Helpme@nurmuhammad.com. Say, 'No, no, you breathe from Allah ﷻ.' No, no. Allah ﷻ gave a command

to the sun to send a light to have photosynthesis on this Earth. As a result, it produces an oxygen for you to breathe. If Allah ﷻ didn't send that command to the sun and didn't have the green vegetation that would take the sunlight and give to you oxygen, (you couldn't breathe). They could have given out carbon monoxide and they would have been like polluted cars that kill you.

At night some plants in your home, you're not supposed to keep at night in your room because they actually put out carbon monoxide, not dioxide. So, it means all of these *haqqaiqs*, there are plants that they give oxygen. Other plants at night, they reverse their system and they actually take the oxygen and give you poison. If you keep them in your room, you become lightheaded.

Our life and death, everything is by Allah ﷻ but He made this creation of an immense intricacy. As a result of that sun, we breathe because of photosynthesis. So, that's why on certain times of the year, don't cut all the green trees.

That satan is influencing you to cut billions of green trees and cutting our oxygen, as if you're making a suicide upon this Earth.

If the Sun Comes Too Strong, It Will Turn Everything to Dust

Then this sunlight gives us vision. It comes with a specific spectrum of light. As soon as it hits the atmosphere of this Earth and give you vision. It gives you breath, gives us our sustenance. Had the sun come in too

strong, it would have burned all the crops. In the last days, the heat of the sun begins to torment the Earth because Allah ﷻ is not happy, right? The atmosphere begins to evaporate and the sunlight begins to burn all vegetation. Allah ﷻ describes that in the Qur'an that, 'When all their crops are turned to dust,' like burnt. Everything looks like it's burned. It means until now, Allah ﷻ sent a *rahmah* (mercy).

The Soul of Prophet Muhammad ﷺ is More Powerful Than the Sun

That *rahmah* of the sun and its understanding, we eat from it, breathe from it, see from it and receive the *tajallis* (manifestation) and the emanation and the warmth of it. All of that and the sun controls the orbit

of all the planets. They're not just randomly moving and choosing the way they want to move. Allah ﷻ give the *isharah* to the sun and the sun commands the outermost planet exactly how far it's going to stay away because the *juzba* is under control. If the sun turns on its gravitational pull which is its *juzba*, its attraction, that planet would move off of its orbit and been directed into the sun.

It means everything is under the control of that reality. Allah ﷻ wants us to know. Why? Because you say, 'Is the sun greater or the soul of Sayyidina Muhammad ﷺ?' The soul of Prophet ﷺ is beyond anything of understanding because all this *dunya* is made from *Nurul Muhammad* ﷺ (Light of Prophet Muhammad ﷺ). If the sun controls these planets and the sun gives this light, these vision, this breath, these realities – imagine then the reality of the light of Sayyidina Muhammad ﷺ. That, that light comes to us from Allah ﷻ through the soul and the heart of Prophet ﷺ and begin to dress you. It begins to bless you.

The Light of Prophet ﷺ Has Authority Over All Creation

It is the secret of the wi-fi for all the created universes. That *Nurul Muhammadi* ﷺ is moving the entire universes. Every command of Allah ﷻ is in those spectrums of light that touch every point of  this galaxy and the universes. To the point in which when Allah ﷻ creates new universes, that light has to give the authority of that reality, all its commands, and all of its *isharahs* (signs). Everything that coming into existence, that wi-fi light of Prophet ﷺ, just for us to understand, must be touching everything. It means its capacity is something that can't even be understood but we can only get a little sample of it just by looking on the exterior.

Why Allah ﷻ gave that authority to a sun? That sun is something created. That's why when you put all these teachings together, we begin to understand that's created and that's created from a Muhammadan light. If that has that authority, imagine what the soul which is the entirety and the *haqqaiq* of that Muhammadan light.

That's why then these are *Nurul Huda* – these are the lights of guidance. These are the realities of guidance. When we make our *zikr*, when we make our associations, when we make our *salawat*, we build this love. And love is the thing that develops the magnet. Love is the reality of the magnet.

Faith is a Light That Enters the Heart

We said before if you put your equation – what is faith? Faith is a light that enters into the heart and to the soul. It's an event. It's not something that you say you have or someone else says, 'You have faith.' Allah ﷻ has to grant faith. Faith is a light and that light has to enter the heart.

Prophet ﷺ described, 'Ya Umar, that you have to love me more than you love yourself.' He gave the secret of faith. 'You have to love me more than you love yourself.' That is the perfection of *iman* (faith).

وَعَنْ عُمَرَ عَلَيْهِ السَّلَامُ قَالَ: فَوَجَدْتُ نَفْسِي أَقُولُ: وَاللهِ يَا رَسُولَ اللهِ، إِنِّي أُحِبُّكَ! فَقَالَ لَهُ النَّبِيِّ ﷺ: " أَكْثَرَ مِنْ أَهْلِكَ يَا عُمَرُ؟" قُلْتُ: نَعَمْ. قَالَ ﷺ: " أَكْثَرَ مِنْ مَالِكَ يَا عُمَرُ؟" قُلْتُ: نَعَمْ. قَالَ ﷺ: " أَكْثَرَ مِنْ نَفْسِكَ يَا عُمَرُ؟" قَالَ: لَا.

فَقَالَ النَّبِيِّ ﷺ: "لَا يَا عُمَرُ، لَا يَكْمُلُ إِيمَانُكَ حَتَّى أَكُونَ أَحَبَّ إِلَيْكَ مِنْ نَفْسِكَ."

يَقُولُ عُمَرُ: فَخَرَجْتُ فَفَكَّرْتُ. ثُمَّ عُدْتُ أَهْتَفُ بِهَا: وَاللهِ يَا رَسُولَ اللهِ لَأَنْتَ أَحَبُّ إِلَيَّ مِنْ نَفْسِي. فَقَالَ النَّبِيِّ ﷺ: "اَلْآنُ يَا عُمَرُ اَلْآنَ."
[صَحِيحُ الْبُخَارِيِّ، الْمَجْلَدُ الرَّابِعُ، رَقْمُ الْحَدِيثِ ٥٩٤]

Wa 'an 'Umar (as) qala: "Fawajadtu nafsi aqoolo: Wallahi ya Rasulullahi, inni uhibbuka!

Faqala lahu anNabiyu ﷺ: "Akthara min ahlika ya 'Umar?"
Qultu: Na'am. Qala ﷺ: "Akthara min malika ya 'Umar?",
Qultu: Na'am. Qala ﷺ: "Akthara min nafsika ya 'Umar?", Qala: La.

Faqala anNabiyu ﷺ: "La ya 'Umar, la yakmulu imanoka hatta akuna ahabba ilayka min nafsika." Yaqoolo 'Umar (as): Fakhrajtu fafakkartu. Thumma 'udtu ahtafu biha: Wallahi ya Rasulullahi la anta ahabbu ilayya min nafsi. Faqala anNabiyu ﷺ: "Alan ya 'Umar, alan."
[Sahih al-Bukhari, al-Majladu al-Rabi'o, raqm al-hadith 594]

Narrated by Sayyidina 'Umar (pbuh) that he said: "I found myself saying, 'By Allah, O Messenger of Allah, I love you!' The Prophet (pbuh) said to him, 'Is it more than your love for your family, O 'Umar?' I said, 'Yes.' He (pbuh) said, 'Is it more than your love for your wealth, O 'Umar?' I said, 'Yes.' He said, 'Is it more than your love for yourself, O 'Umar?' He said, 'No.'

The Prophet (pbuh), said, 'No, O 'Umar, your faith will not be complete until I become more beloved to you than your own self.' 'Umar said: So I went out and thought. Then I returned and shouted, 'By Allah, O Messenger of Allah, you are more beloved to me than myself.' The Prophet (pbuh) said, 'Now, O 'Umar, now [you got it].'
[Sahih al-Bukhari, Volume 4, Hadith #594]

Love Equals Faith Which Equals Magnetism

As a result of that light and that love, its equation is magnetic charge. When the light begin to enter from these lights of reality, Allah ﷻ is granting love. When He grants, love equals faith. Faith equals magnetism. Faith equals magnetism – *juzba, rabita* (connection). We have all these words. *Rabitat chetora baa oon?* (how is your relationship/connection with him/her)? We have also *muraqabah* (spiritual connection). I heard it somebody was using in a sentence and it came into my ear. But all of these are traditional languages for us to understand that this love, this light, and this magnet has to be activated.

Be Sadiq (Truthful) in Your Love!

When they don't have love and their practices are not based on Divine love, because they have to have good *khulq*, good character. Love answers everything. When you study with the shaykh and you love and you think that you entered into an ocean of love, that love is your discipline. How could you ever harm that shaykh? How could you come against that shaykh? Even every horrible thing you could imagine you think the shaykh did to you in life. But because of you are a servant of love, *'Man ba ishq sadiq bodam'* (I was truthful to love). You've heard those in songs?

باور كن هميشه باور كن   كه من به عشق صادقم

Bawar kon hamisha bawar kon   *Ke man ba ishq sadiqam*

Believe, always believe me   *That I am truthful to love*

That I was truthful to love. My allegiance was to love. I abided and

upheld the laws of love, not the laws of people and not the laws of somebody. I didn't do things for other people. But if I was a *sadiq* (truthful) for *ishq* and love, Divine love. We're not talking about relations. We're talking about somebody whom used their soul with another soul for the love of

Allah 🕮 and the love of Sayyidina Muhammad 🕮. They were truthful in love. *'Man sadiq e ishq bodam'*, means that 'My truthfulness to love upheld my honour and my way.' Not what I claim as my character, not what I claim as my *aqidah* (belief). Not what I claim as I think I know and somebody else doesn't know, but we were servants of love.

Ask for Madad to Activate Your Magnetism

That's this secret of magnetism and they tried their best to uphold the law of love. That, *'Ya Rabbi*, you granted a love within my heart. They taught me *madad* (support) and then I fell in love', because my heart was activated, my magnet was activated. As a result, I was taught with this magnet and this love and this heart of mine; be a *sadiq* of *ishq* and love.'

شدم عاشق، تمنای مدد کردم   فقط در عاشقی یا رب، مدد گفتم

Faqat dar asheqi ya rab, madad goftam
Shodam asheq, tamannaye madad kardam

In this divinely love, I only asked for Your support and took the leap of faith and fell in love. And I begged for more support to endure this pain and trial of love.

Stay Truthful Even Through Testing and Hardship

Don't uphold yourself to what you think is a *shari'ah* (Divine Law), what you think is a law, what you think. Whatever you think of laws, they could be wrong in your mind. That's why there are a thousand books on every *usool* (fundamental principles of Islam) and everyone has a different opinion of what that *usool* means. Because those are scholars of *had e dunya* (worldy affairs).

But the scholars of *muhabbat* (love) and *ishq*, the ones of *ma'rifah*, then Allah ﷻ asked from them, 'Be *sadiq* to your *ishq*. Be truthful in your deeds and in your action to your love.' As a result of their love, Allah ﷻ tested them, gave  things that were not pleasing to them, gave situations in which they felt that they were betrayed. We know, we lived through it. And as a result, Prophet ﷺ asked, 'Just be truthful to your love.'

It means what would you do then? You stay quiet. You show the best of manners because this is love. You show the best of character. That no matter what, you kept the way of love, the best of character. That answers then everyone's question. With good character, you kept the way, you kept the relation. You kept everything because you were truthful in love and that's what's important.

Your Belief Has No Meaning If You're Not Truthful in Love

Don't ever argue on this *aqidah* (belief), that *aqidah*. It means nothing if they're not truthful in love. It means they fell in love with Allah ﷻ, they fell in love with Sayyidina Muhammad ﷺ and then everything from a lesser understanding. Everything from *dunya* (material world), whatever they were taught, at least they understood, '*Ya Rabbi*, that I became an '*ashiq* – a lover of Prophet ﷺ. Let me to uphold my truthfulness and my good character for love.' That was their *aqidah*, that was their whole *deen* (religion), that was their whole way. It answers every situation in their life. So then, it's not understood how somebody thinks they can be pious and they begin to attack and begin to get into hate. Then begin to go beyond hate and begin to attack.

Divine Love is a Light of Iman That Enters Into the Heart

It means this is then the reality of *ishq* and *muhabbat*. When Allah ﷻ opened for that, it means He opened for the servant now from that love, opened for them magnetism, opened for

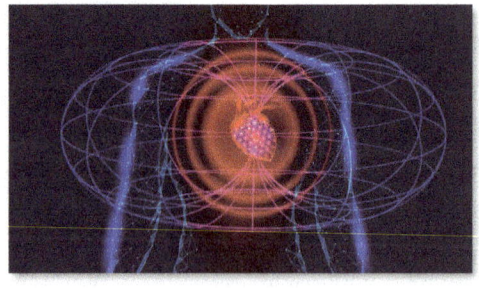

them *iman* and faith. If the servant has Divine love – is a gift, a light that entered into the heart. It means then that servant has been granted *iman* and faith. A real *iman*, not self-professed *iman*. Real *iman* in which they've been tested and tried and they always come back up with the truthfulness of love. That they will not harm because of their allegiance to Prophet ﷺ in *ishq* and *muhabbat*. As a result, Allah ﷻ made their hearts to be a magnet and magnetism.

Awliya Receive Faiz Because of Their Divine Magnetism

It means they have an immense magnetism. As a result of their

magnetism, they are receiving the *faiz* (downpouring emanation) of those whom are above; it means the *awliya* (saints) of the much higher realities and realms. Because that's a Divine magnetism, that's a Divine magnet of *ishq* and love; they receive immense amounts of *faiz* and lights and

energies and blessings and knowledges because those are also the servants of love. They're all magnetized. They have immense *juzba*. They're all emanating from that emotion and that ocean.

Imagine then as soon as the associations begin like the songs of the birds. That it describes that all the birds are sitting in a beautiful paradise, these are all the big *awliya*. And they see another *majnun* (madly in love) entered into their garden and they begin to

sing. Because they see us, that these are *'ashiqeen* (lovers), and these *'ashiqeen* are entering into their *zikr* and their association. Then that magnet begins to pull their *faiz* and bring that *faiz* into the association, those whom watching and those whom online.

111

Make Your Heart a Magnet With Honest Love

That's why they teach then make your heart a magnet, begin to open up your love, begin to be truthful in love. There's no arguing over this *aqidah* (belief), that *aqidah*, petty issues, and bad character. Just be truthful in love. Keep your symbol of love. Have the character of love. That, 'For the sake of love, I'm keeping the way, keeping the respect, keeping this *adab* (manners).' As a result, Allah ﷻ begins to send light into their heart.

That's why when they speak, other people don't have any understanding what they're talking about. 'Where you came with this? How you got from this?' Because they don't have that love; they don't have that light of faith like that. As a result, they don't have a magnet that's attracting these realities.

Activate Your Heart's Magnet to Pull the Faiz From Your Shaykh

Those whom have that reality, they teach their students – begin to open your love. Begin to open your light within your heart, begin to make your connection. If you don't practice these realities and begin to connect, how are you going to activate the magnet within your heart? As soon as

your heart has that magnet, it begins to attract these lights from the light of the shaykh. So, then there's millions of magnets or a thousand magnets out there beginning to activate. As soon as they activate, they're pulling the *faiz* from the shaykhs in this world of love.

So, they (shaykhs) pull from the power sources they have to bring. As a result everyone else is feeding off of their light, and with their *juzba*, they're pulling with that love. And that's the reality and the *haqqaiq* of Prophet ﷺ describing in his holy *Hadith* that, 'You'll be with whom you love.' So, it means this station of 'be' is what's important. How to 'be' in that love, how to nourish that love, how to bring about that love and that reality. It will become the magnet of your guidance in life.

عَنْ أَنَسٍ رَضِيَ اللهُ عَنْهُ: ... فَقَالَ (رَسُولُ اللهِ ﷺ): "أَنْتَ مَعَ مَنْ أَحْبَبْتَ."
[اَلْمَصْدَرْ: مُسْلِمْ: ٧٥٢٠]

'An Anasin (ra): ... Faqala (Rasulullahi) ﷺ*: "Anta ma'a man ahbabta."*

Narrated Anas ibn Malik (ra) that ...the Messenger of Allah (pbuh) said: "You will be with whom you love." [Source: Muslim 7520]

The Strong Magnet of Prophet ﷺ Pulls Us Out of Obstacles

As a result of this *ishq*, everything in life is like obstacles but when your magnet is strong and connected to their source, connected to the heart of Prophet ﷺ, what happens? That's what we described the night before like the child and childish games that we had when we were young. That, that magnet is now pulling and drawing. Its charge is so strong that it begins to pull. Imagine that it's pulling us over every difficult terrain, every mistake. Everything that we're doing, that magnet's charge is so strong that it's pulling us.

When we don't know what choice to make of left and right, the magnet pulls that, 'Come.' And all the choices become more and more correct, more and more correct, with such immense blessings, immense *faiz*. That if you were to look yourself coming in, you would say that, 'This is something closed, no way I can pass it.' But the magnet, it opens every closed issue. It begins just pulling your reality towards it and everything closed becomes open. Every obstacle becomes attainable.

Nothing Stops the Call and Faiz of Sayyidina Muhammad ﷺ

It means there's nothing that can stop. When the call is from Allah ﷻ and hits to the Muhammadan heart, when the *faiz* and emanation and the call of Sayyidina Muhammad ﷺ is coming, nothing can stop it. Nothing can change it and this is the *'Azimat* (Might) of Allah ﷻ, *'azimat* of Sayyidina Muhammad ﷺ and *"Ulil amre minkum"* whom Allah ﷻ gave this dress and gave these blessings (Holy Qur'an, 4:59).

We pray that from the lights of *Nurul Huda* that Allah ﷻ guide us, bless us to the immensity of the love and the *ishq* of Sayyidina Muhammad ﷺ, and those whom are holding and custodians of that love upon this Earth. That they activate the magnet within our hearts and call us into that presence over every obstacle and every difficulty. Everything blocking us and the fear that our eyes may see that, 'This is something blocking. This is something impossible. This is something you know I can't attain at my age.'

Allah ﷻ is reminding that, *"HasbunAllahu wa ni'mal Wakil"* (Sufficient for us is Allah, and [He is] the best Disposer of affairs).

حَسْبُنَا اللَّـهُ وَنِعْمَ الْوَكِيلُ ﴿١٧٤﴾

3:173 – "HasbunAllahu wa ni'mal Wakil." (Surat Ali 'Imran)

"Sufficient for us is Allah, and [He is] the best Disposer of affairs."
(The Family of 'Imran 3:173)

It means your faith and trust is in Allah ﷻ. If Allah ﷻ give the command to the Muhammadan heart, there is nothing that will stop it, nothing that cannot be done by Allah ﷻ, and every grace and blessings and emanation to dress upon the servant.

Subhana rabbika rabbal 'izzati 'amma yasifoon, wa salaamun 'alal mursaleen, walhamdulillahi rabbil 'aalameen. Bi hurmati Muhammad al-Mustafa wa bi siri Surat al-Fatiha.

Activate the Heart's Magnet Through Muraqabah (Spiritual Connection)

Sunlight is Our Eternal and Infinite Source of Power

We are on the lowest scale of understanding because we're using

combustible power. We are exploding things to make power. But all of the higher realm of knowledges, they understood that Allah 🕮 is giving us an eternal, infinite source of power which is the sunlight. But because mankind is at a point in which they want to make money from energy, they're using fossil fuels and things that are combusting and exploding.

But the real energy and the higher levels of beings' understandings of energy, it's all free from sun. They're taking the plasma, the rays and the energy of the sun as an eternal battery pack. They use it as a wi-fi charger or wherever their devices are moving, it's taking from the power of the sun.

Calibrate and Focus Your Magnet Through Meditation

It means the immensity of that Muhammadan light and its *haqqaiq* (realities) and its ability to dress and bless. That is why, why this is being taught? It's because this is an ocean of guidance. 'Why you have to meditate? Why do I have to contemplate? Why do I have to make the connection?' But then on the same email, 'Please guide me and please keep me guided. Please help me to reach Allah's ﷻ satisfaction.' That's the reality that how are we going to guide ourselves to a co-ordinance when every other magnet is pulling us in different directions. Everything has a magnetic charge. It pulls us in that direction. It takes our desire in our heart and directs us.

The Shaykh is a Magnet That Keeps Us from Distractions

So, the most important organ that we have is the heart. The heart is like a magnet that what you direct it to, it will be attracted. This material world and everything within it is also magnets and each magnet is pulling people towards its direction. Then the reality and the understanding, the breaking down of guidance is this understanding. That, 'Why I have to take a shaykh? Why I have to learn *muraqabah* (meditation)? Why I have to do all these things? I'm just worshipping Allah ﷻ.'

Say, no! But Allah ﷻ is giving to us an understanding that your imitated worshipness, unless it's connected to that magnet, connected to that source, you're going to be distracted by everything in this material world. Even now more because the immensities of the material world on how much they're putting a charge upon people.

Activate Your Heart With Zikr (Divine Remembrance) to Increase Your Magnetism

So it means that I make my *muraqabah*, I make my connection. I found the way towards the shaykhs and they described the Muhammadan love. Why? Because my heart is a magnet. I have to activate that magnet. As soon as I activate it with *zikr* and polishing and cleaning the surface of my magnet, then its charge and its *juzba* (magnetism) is this immense love for the Divinely Presence and the love of Prophet ﷺ.

So, then by learning how to meditate, how to breathe and how to connect, how to love Prophet ﷺ more than I love myself, my magnet becomes activated. That's the reality of guidance. Their job is to activate the hearts of people, help them to polish their heart, direct their heart towards the most powerful and eternal magnet of Allah ﷻ.

عَنْ أَنَسِ بْنِ مَالِكٍ رَضِيَ اللهُ عَنْهُ قَالَ، قَالَ رَسُولُ اللهِ ﷺ: "لاَ يُؤْمِنُ أَحَدُكُمْ حَتَّى أَكُونَ أَحَبَّ إِلَيْهِ مِنْ وَالِدِهِ وَوَلَدِهِ وَالنَّاسِ أَجْمَعِينَ ."

[صَحِيحُ مُسْلِمٍ، حديث ٤٤، وَالْبُخَارِي، كِتَابُ الْإِيْمَانْ، حديث ١٥]

"'An Anas ibn Malik (ra) qala, qala Rasulullahi ﷺ: *La yuminu ahadukum hatta akona ahabba ilayhi min walidihi wa waladihi wan nasi ajma'yeen."*
[Sahih Muslim, Hadith 44, wa Al Bukhari, Kitabul Iman, Hadith 15]

"Narrated by Anas son of Malik (ra) that Prophet Muhammad (pbuh) said: None of you will have faith till he loves me more than his father, his children, and all mankind."
[Authentic by Muslim, Hadith 44 & by Al Bukhari, Book of Faith, Hadith 15]

We Reach 'La Ilaha IllAllah' Through the Door of 'Muhammadun RasulAllah ﷺ'

That's all under *tawheed* (oneness), all under the worshipness of Allah ﷻ because it's *La ilaha illAllah* and the only way to reach *La ilaha illAllah* is through the door of *Muhammadun Rasulallah* ﷺ. It means anything other than that is like an idol that blocks us from Allah's ﷻ Presence because their name is not associated with Allah's ﷻ name. When Allah ﷻ is describing for us, *'La ilaha illAllah Muhammadun Rasulallah* ﷺ – only way to Me is through the door of *Muhammadan Rasulallah* ﷺ and that reality and the immensity of that guidance.'

لَا إِلَهَ إِلاَّ اللهُ مُحَمَّدًا رَسُولْ الله ﷺ

"La ilaha illallahu Muhammadun Rasulallah ﷺ."

"There is no deity but Allah, Prophet Muhammad (pbuh) is the messenger of Allah."

Cleanse and Charge Your Magnet to Approach Prophet ﷺ

So with this love, with this *ishq* that when we do the *zikr*, we do the contemplating, then we're realizing our heart is a magnet and that which I direct it to that love, direct it to the *ishq* (love) of Prophet ﷺ. Every time I make *salawat* (praises upon Prophet Muhammad ﷺ), I'm making a *zikr*. I make *istighfar* (seeking forgiveness) to clean my magnet, I make *salawat* to charge my magnet. That's why Prophet ﷺ described, 'If you make one *salawat*, what happens? Your magnet will have called my magnet and I will come to [make] ten praisings upon you.'

عَنْ أَنَسِ بْنِ مَالِكَ رَضِيَ اللهُ عَنْهُ، قَالَ: قَالَ رَسُولُ اللهِ ﷺ:
"مَنْ صَلَّى عَلَيَّ صَلاةً وَاحِدَةً، صَلَّى اللهُ عَلَيْهِ عَشْرَ صَلَوَاتٍ، وَحُطَّتْ عَنْهُ عَشْرُ
خَطِيئَاتٍ، وَرُفِعَتْ لَهُ عَشْرُ دَرَجَاتٍ."

"'An Anasin ibn Malik (ra) qala: Qala Rasulullah ﷺ: Man Salla 'alaiya Salatan wahidatan, Sallallahu 'alayhi 'ashra Salawatin, wa Huttat 'anhu 'ashru khaTeatin, wa ruf'at lahu 'ashru darajatin."

"Prophet Muhammad (pbuh) said: Whoever sends blessings [Praises] upon me, God will shower His blessings upon him ten times, and will erase ten of his sins, and elevate [raise] his [spiritual] station ten times." [Hadith recorded by Nasa'i]

Prophet ﷺ Conveys Lights of Qur'an Upon Our Soul

It gives the humility of saying that, 'Allah ﷻ will release my soul to come and make ten praisings upon you,' but the *adab* (manners) for us to always understand is that I will go begging into the presence of Sayyidina Muhammad ﷺ. With every *salawat* Allah ﷻ  will open the soul, 'Go into the presence to receive your ten gifts, your ten *salawats*. Whatever gifts that are imaginable upon your soul with that association.' That becomes the infinite power of *durood sharif* (praising on Prophet Muhammad ﷺ) and *salawat an Nabi* ﷺ.

It powers the magnet. It builds the love and keeps your heart in the presence of that *Nurul Huda* (guiding light). So imagine that presence, that light, that dress. Anybody wants to read Qur'an, make *salawat* on Sayyidina Muhammad ﷺ – that is the light of Qur'an. What Prophet ﷺ want to give to you ten times? He's going to convey the lights of Qur'an upon the souls of people.

There are Salawats and Duroods for Every Difficulty

This is our magnet. This is our guidance. This is what keeps us on our path. Through every difficulty – imagine when the world is directing you in a different direction and you're from the *muhibbin* (lovers of the way) and *'ashiqeen* (lovers), that your magnet is facing Prophet ﷺ and a strong *dunya* (material world) connection begins to distract you.

What happens? Make your *durood sharif* so that your magnet goes back

and calibrates. That's why they keep giving the *durood sharif*. They say, 'Oh, you're sick – make this *salawat*. You're anxious – make this *salawat*. You have doors closed – make this *salawat*.' Why? So that your soul's magnet calibrates to the one who can give everything. If you're short on anything, any door that's closed, any difficulty, sickness, anything that's happening, with *durood sharif* the magnet directs itself. And what we said, from *La ilaha illAllah* will flow through *Muhammadun Rasulallah* ﷺ and reach to the servant.

That becomes the proper *adab* so that they are not asking Allah ﷻ alone but they're asking through their *durood* and through their *salawat*. That

by this love and this *ishq* when I'm praising upon Prophet ﷺ, they have *duroods*, all the different *duroods*. There's *durood* for opening, *durood* for *rizq* (sustenance), *durood* for sickness. All of these, why? Because if Prophet ﷺ begins to praise back, all of it is a *shifa* and a healing. All of it is with permission of Allah ﷻ energized and dressed by the realities of Allah ﷻ upon that *durood*.

Praise Upon Prophet ﷺ for Your Du'a to Be Accepted

That was the *shari'ah* (Divine Law) of *du'a* (supplication) for *Ahlus Sunnah* (People of Prophetic Tradition). That, if you want your *du'a* to be accepted, praise Prophet ﷺ before, make your *du'a* and close the *du'a* with *salawat*. So, between the two *salawats* that are infinitely going to the heaven and they're never checked, that *du'a* will be inserted within that reality.

Every other *du'a* has to be checked; if there's negative energy, what's the intention? What's the servant trying to achieve? But between the *salawat* upon Sayyidina Muhammad ﷺ the *du'a* that's packed in the middle and the *salawat*, it encases the prayer and goes without any type of security check. Because the *durood* itself has cleansed everything, took every negativity, every bad intention out. The *Durood e Pak* make everything to be purified and perfected and reach towards the Divinely Presence.

We pray that Allah ﷻ give us more and more understanding and open for us the immense lights, immense blessings, and the immense understanding of lights of guidance. With *ishq* and love is the only way towards that guidance, *inshaAllah*.

Subhana rabbika rabbal 'izzati 'amma yasifoon, wa salaamun 'alal mursaleen, walhamdulillahi rabbil 'aalameen. Bi hurmati Muhammad al-Mustafa wa bi siri Surat al-Fatiha.

The Binary Code for
Attraction and Repulsion

Ramadan – the 9th Lunar Month Takes Us Towards Nothingness

Alhamdulillah, Ramadan is an immense *barakah* (blessing) from

Allah ﷻ as a great reset in which the munificence of the power of 9. That its reality is a *nuqt* (dot). And that 9 fused, multiplied by anything renders itself back to a 9 and in essence, becomes a *nuqt* and annihilates everything.

From its angelic reality to the *dunya* (material world) reality, Allah ﷻ put within the 9th lunar month, the holy month of Ramadan in which to annihilate the servant. To take them down back towards nothingness and is a great *rahmah* (mercy) and reset for *insan* (mankind). That's immense mercy from Allah ﷻ.

The Binary Code Teaches How to Move Towards Allah ﷻ

When we try to understand magnetism, binary code, all these sciences that should be in the last days, make more sense for people than telling them, 'Be good.' Good is different in the minds of different people based on preconceptions and life's conditions. What is good for you may not be good for me and maybe something else for  someone else. Its *haqqaiq* and its science is free from all of these interpretations and renders us the cleanest understanding. That in this life of ours, we are trying to reach towards Allah ﷻ. That has to do with this binary code and the reality of magnetism. That if Allah ﷻ is ONE, the ONE, the only ONE, then Allah ﷻ is asking for us then, 'You have to be nothing.' Because the only way anything is attracted with its magnetism is that you have to be nothing.

Satan Inflates Our Ego So We Repel Away From Allah ﷻ

That 1 in binary code is positive. It's a positive charge. If you act as if you're the ONE, then your positive charge will repel you from Allah ﷻ. So, this is a very simplified understanding in this reality. That Allah ﷻ asks for us, 'I am the ONE! And any illusion you have of being a ONE and something in comparison to Allah ﷻ' – what they call *'ananiya* (I-ness), so *Fir'aun* (Pharoah) and arrogance. And all that the devil wants for people is to push them away from Allah ﷻ.

How to push people away from Allah ﷻ is make them the ONE. Tell them in their magnetism that, 'You're the ONE. You're the positive ONE. You're the great ONE.' So, you watch on social media, they talk very bad to people, 'You're this, you're that, you got to be that, you got…' It's the devil actually talking in the carnate of people. It's not even hidden anymore that the way in which they talk, the aggression in which they talk. The character in which they talk – it's to teach people to be one, to be the ONE. To be the ONE with the positive charge. As a result, just from their energy understanding, it will repel.

Admitting We Are a Negative Charge Magnetically Pulls Us Towards Allah ﷻ

They taught magnetism in school. If Allah ﷻ is a positive charge, then you have to admit that you're a negative charge. Only by admitting you're a negative charge, you will be magnetically pulled towards Allah ﷻ. So, we said the doorway to these *haqqaiq* (realities), *"La ilaha illa anta Subhanaka, innee kuntu minazh zhalimeen."* That's your negative charge. 'There is nothing but Allah ﷻ, glory be to Allah ﷻ and I am an oppressor to myself.' It means I'm deflating.

...لَّا إِلَهَ إِلَّا أَنتَ سُبْحَانَكَ إِنِّي كُنتُ مِنَ الظَّالِمِينَ ﴿٨٧﴾

*21:87 – "... La ilaha illa anta Subhanaka, innee kuntu minazh
zhalimeen." (Surat Al-Anbiya)*

*"...There is no god/deity except You; Glory to you: Indeed I have been of
the wrongdoers/Oppressor to Myself!" (The Prophets, 21:87)*

To Believe You Are a ONE is Disbelief

Everything that the *dunya* (material
world) is trying to do and *shaitan*
(satan) is trying to do to me, by
making me think I'm the positive
charge, I'm the great one, I'm the
one to be listened to – it's my ego
that's been offended. This is the
source of every anger. When you
write down on your paper, 'What is
anger?' Anger is when you think that you're something and you didn't
achieve and people didn't listen to you the way that you thought you
deserve to be listened to and you were not recognized. It means your
oneness was insulted. So, it means the devil makes everyone to think that
they're something. Its sicknesses are anger and that's why anger is
disbelief. Why? Because the one is disbelief. To think that your *'ananiya*
that, 'I am! I am, my I is strong' – it's a disbelief.

Sins Make Us Believe We Are of a Positive Charge

The whole path, very simplified, is to be nothing. Nothingness is not
achieved by sins because people say, 'Oh, the sins are a negative charge.'
Say, 'No, the sins actually make you more positive.' The sins make you
to think you're a more positive charge, you're more of a oneness, you're
more independent of anything. You think that you are escaping
Allah's ﷻ judgment, Allah's ﷻ punishment. That nothing can reach to
you, therefore, you sin.

That the real concept of negativity and to reduce ourself to the negative sign, Allah ﷻ is the positive sign. This is the essence of binary code. This is the essence of magnetism because the binary code is magnetism. Then our life is to be a negative charge. Negative charge means humility, not sins. My negativity in this understanding is my humility.

How much can I reduce my positive charge? *"Wa la ilaha illa anta Subhanaka, innee kuntu minazh zhalimeen."* (Holy Qur'an, 21:87) *"Subhanaka"* is that Allah ﷻ is my positive, is my ONE and I am verily an oppressor to myself and I acknowledge, *ya Rabbi*, I am negative and nothing.

Our Life's Struggle is to Be Nothing and Become a Negative Charge

In my negativity, if it becomes sincere and through the *tariqahs* (spiritual paths) and practices. Because once you took the step of *tariqah* – you want, you don't want, you think you can check out willingly, unwillingly – doesn't matter for Allah ﷻ. He guided the servant. You're on a path to now establish the reality of, *"La ilaha illa anta Subhanaka, innee kuntu minazh zhalimeen."* That Allah ﷻ will teach the servant through *ruhani* (spiritual) or *nafsani* (egocentric) that, 'You are nothing.' What does that mean? Allah ﷻ brings you down willingly or unwillingly. Allah ﷻ doesn't care.

...لَّا إِلَٰهَ إِلَّا أَنتَ سُبْحَانَكَ إِنِّي كُنتُ مِنَ الظَّالِمِينَ ﴿٨٧﴾

21:87 – "... La ilaha illa anta Subhanaka, innee kuntu minazh zhalimeen." (Surat Al-Anbiya)

"...There is no god/diety except You; Glory to you: Indeed I have been of the wrongdoers/Oppressor to Myself!" (The Prophets, 21:87)

Allah ﷻ said, 'I enrolled you. The first thing they taught you *'La ilaha illa anta Subhanaka, innee kuntu minazh zhalimeen'* (Holy Qur'an, 21:87). That you're in a school and your life is about how to be the negative charge. Not how to sin but how to deflate oneself. That, *'Ya Rabbi*, I'm nothing.'

Those Who Fight Back When Tested Repel Away From Allah ﷻ

Then every test will come that don't open your mouth. 'I'm nothing.'

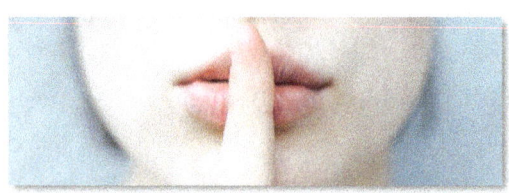

Every, every difficulty comes – don't justify your *nafs* (ego). 'I'm nothing.' Don't, don't try to validate yourself, so that I can become nothing. If the servant is sincere, Allah ﷻ grant them more of their negative charge in which He establishes, 'You really are trying to be a negative charge.' Then as a result of that negative charge, its nature will draw close to the positive. So, it's in our hands. That's why when we come to the *tariqahs* (spiritual paths), they give us the understanding of, you're being tested. When you're tested, remain silent.

When you are tested do not answer back, do not fight back, do not show aggression. That is your inclination from the *shaitan* inside to reiterate to you, 'Be the ONE. Don't let Allah ﷻ to

deflate you. Remain as you're a positive charge.' And the more the person is a positive charge then the two positives deflect. Before you know it, you're actually drifting from Allah ﷻ. Then they become more sinful, more negative character, more angry, more aggression. These are all of the characteristics that Allah ﷻ is showing to the servant.

Through Humility, We Can Move From a State of Negativity to Annihilation

Then *awliya* (saints) have these understandings and realities – that life was about being nothing. Nothing is through the test of humility in which whatever test come in my life, it's to remain nothing, silent. As a result, Allah ﷻ draws the servant into His Divinely Presence. So, then this state of negativity enters into what they call – this is the *fana* (annihilation). These are these Arabic terminologies understood with science and math.

The *fana* is when Allah ﷻ takes you from your thinking you're someone and begin to deflate you with all of life's testings. Testings, testings, testings – family, children, relatives, shaykhs, teachings, everything until you're nothing. When you feel that nothingness, Allah ﷻ is drawing you. 'This is the ocean of *fana* in which you are being annihilated.'

In that ocean of annihilation, it's years of *tariqah* that you're entering into oceans of annihilation. One bombardment, from another bombardment, from another bombardment, from shaykh talking bad to you, everyone saying something. And never once opening your mouth and staying quiet, stay quiet, stay quiet because this ocean of *fana* is not something easy. It's not something somebody does one time and then think they accomplished all the rewards of the heavens. It's a lifetime.

Allah ﷻ Exposes Our Dirty Character Through Testing

It's a lifetime of *Ashab ul Kahf* (Companions of the Cave) – the dog was thrown rocks at. Allah ﷻ showing your *najes* (dirty) character. Allah ﷻ will make the world to throw rocks. These are the *mushkilat* (difficulties) and tests and difficulties of life that they make the character of the person and they teach them to be a nothing. *"La ilaha illa anta Subhanaka, innee kuntu minazh zhalimeen."*

$$...لَّا إِلَٰهَ إِلَّا أَنتَ سُبْحَانَكَ إِنِّي كُنتُ مِنَ الظَّالِمِينَ ﴿٨٧﴾$$

21:87 – "... La ilaha illa anta Subhanaka, innee kuntu minazh zhalimeen." (Surat Al-Anbiya)

"...There is no god/ diety except You; Glory to you: Indeed I have been of the wrongdoers/ Oppressor to Myself!" (The Prophets, 21:87)

Sitna Maryam ﷻ Took a Path of Annihilation

What Sitna Maryam (Mary) ﷻ described in surah (chapter) 19, *"Nasyam mansiyya* – Oh I wish that I was nothing"* – a *nuqt*, a line, nothing, not appearing.

...قَالَتْ يَا لَيْتَنِي مِتُّ قَبْلَ هَذَا وَكُنتُ نَسْيًا مَّنسِيًّا ﴿٢٣﴾

19:23 – "...Qalat ya laytanee mittu qabla hadha wa kuntu nasyam mansiyya." (Surat Maryam)

"...She cried (in her anguish): Oh, I wish I had died before this! And I was a thing forgotten and out of sight!" (Mary, 19:23)

Allah ﷻ showed the *fitna* (confusion) that would be attributed to her birth and to herself and what the people would call her of a Divine nature. When these were the servants in which they wanted to not even appear and be annihilated. That was a great learning for ourselves that take a path in which *"Nasyam mansiyya"* that, 'Ya Rabbi, I wish that I'm nothing.'

When Awliya Reach the Ocean of Fana, Allah ﷻ Revives Them as ONE

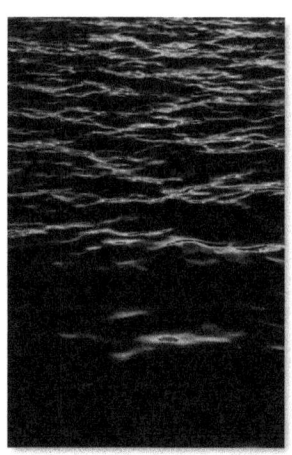

As a result of drawing in their ocean of *fana* (annihilation) – so, you write the negative charge is in a journey – continuously bombarding and continuously being taught to be humble. In that journey of negativity, Allah ﷻ begins to revive the servant. We talked last night about *Jabal Qaaf* (Mount Qaaf), this mountain of *Qaaf* they described as oceans of darkness. The shaykhs have been taken through this in seclusion where it's an like eternal ocean of black. It's just black. It means it's an ocean of non-manifest and in this ocean of non-manifest, means nothing. You're in a continuous state and dress of *fana*.

Then this ocean of *fana* eventually opens in which Allah ﷻ is redressing the servant. That, 'You came to Us as nothing. And as a result of that nothingness, now We revive you within our ocean of something-ness.' As a result, they were turned back ON. In that ocean that is a *nuqt* which nothing is there, Allah ﷻ turned that servant back ON. As a result, they were dressed with the oneness.

The Shaykh is a Reflection of ONE, Sent Back to Guide Humanity

As a result of that reality, Allah ﷻ gives them in their seclusions that, 'You have reached your death. You have reached these oceans of nothingness. You may remain here to be nothing in these oceans of *fana*, or you go back to guide humanity.' As a result of their guidance and when Allah ﷻ want to open for the servant guidance, they are sent back onto the Earth, back amongst people. Then they become a reflection of that ONE and they're out to train people now.

They train people. That the shaykh has been trained. When he's making his connection with his Lord, he's nothing. In that nothingness, he receives the dress of the ONE. And when he's amongst his people to teach and to guide, he teaches them to be nothing and he is the ONE. Because the minds of people that are corrupt, they listen to the teaching. They say, 'Okay, oh [Shaykh says I am nothing] nothing, nothing, then why we have to listen to you.' This is because the sickness of the character of people.

When the Shaykh is ON, We Must Be OFF!

That from Allah ﷻ, this is the dress of guidance. This is magnetism and *juzba* (attraction). This is the reality of what we described in *faiz* (downpouring blessings). This is the whole of *tariqah*. That when you come to the understanding of this ONE and nothing. Then realize that the shaykhs – not all shaykhs – everyone calls themself a shaykh but they have to have been dressed, guided, and in seclusions, and all of their realities and each teach about the reality. How can somebody be from a reality they don't even know how to describe?

When they've been dressed by that reality, their only purpose is guidance because Allah ﷻ trained them. They're not ON all the time so that everybody will walk on eggshells. They've been taught there's ON and OFF for them. When the time for their teaching, their *majlis* – their associations, they are ON. When they are ON, everybody else has to be trained to be OFF.

As a result of keeping the company with these shaykhs of binary code and magnetism, they teach you. It's the same analogy. If you accept somebody is your shaykh, and you accept that they are the positive charge, they are the charge that Allah's ﷻ sending from, *"Atiullah atiur Rasul wa Ulul amre minkum"* is to obey this *Ulul Amr* (saints). It means he's a positive charge. He represents the Divinely Presence, the presence of Sayyidina Muhammad ﷺ, the presence of *awliyaullah* (saints). As a result, your life is that he is the positive and I am the negative.

$$...أَطِيعُوا اللَّهَ وَأَطِيعُوا الرَّسُولَ وَأُوْلِي الْأَمْرِ مِنْكُمْ... ﴿٥٩﴾$$

4:59 – "...Atiullaha wa atiur Rasula wa Ulil amre minkum..."
(Surat An-Nisa)

"... Obey Allah, Obey the Messenger, and those in authority among you..." (The Women, 4:59)

Technology Depicts the Binary Relationship Between Master and Student

That's what we described last night in all technology. Right? They say, 'Okay, Shaykh is not making this up. Look at the technology.' There is a master server and there is a slave server. When you say 'slave' it's bad  choice of words but technology people made this up. There is a master unit and then there is the empty unit. There is a master server and then the empty servers which just obey and follow the master unit. Same with the remote. You can get the universal remote – it's a master remote. The servant remote – the student remote is supposed to be completely empty. Not thinking of all of its ego and all its buttons and all its choices.

Humble Yourself in the Presence of the Guide to Receive His Light

When they empty themself and take a path in which I'm nothing, *"La ilaha illa anta Subhanaka, innee kuntu minazh zhalimeen."* (Holy Qur'an, 21:87), *'Ya Rabbi,* I'm nothing, I'm nothing, I'm nothing.' As soon as I accompany that guidance, I can then move into their presence and receive

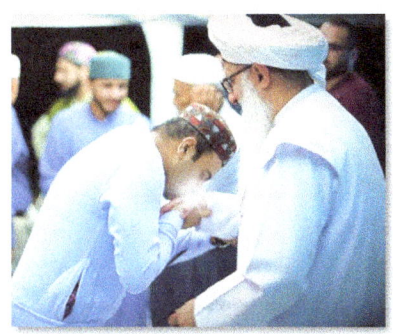

their *tajallis* (manifestations) and their lights. The more I humble myself, that even I know Arabic better than him, I humble myself, 'Don't say a word.' I know math better than him, I humble myself, 'Don't say a word.' I know everything better than him, 'Don't say a word.' You took a path of humility.

Allah ﷻ Gave Salvation to Those Who Admit They Have Oppressed Themselves

Every time we struggle with that, that can be through email, through online, through listening on your couch that, 'I don't agree with anything

you're saying.' Any time you take that path, remember that's what Allah ﷻ wants, that you to deflate yourself. Take a path of humility. The more you say, 'I'm nothing,' *"La ilaha illa anta Subhanaka, innee kuntu minazh zhalimeen"* (Holy

Qur'an, 21:87). It means in *Salat un Najat* (Prayer of Salvation) continuously recite that 7 times for your 7 names in 7 paradises. *"La ilaha illa anta Subhanaka, innee kuntu minazh zhalimeen."*

Then what is Allah's 🕊 reply? *"Fastajabna lahu wa najjayna hu minal gham."* That Allah 🕊 provides a *najat* (salvation) for those whom have offended and those whom have oppressed themself.

وَذَا النُّونِ إِذ ذَّهَبَ مُغَاضِبًا فَظَنَّ أَن لَّن نَّقْدِرَ عَلَيْهِ فَنَادَىٰ فِي الظُّلُمَاتِ أَن لَّا إِلَٰهَ إِلَّا أَنتَ سُبْحَانَكَ إِنِّي كُنتُ مِنَ الظَّالِمِينَ ﴿٨٧﴾ فَاسْتَجَبْنَا لَهُ وَنَجَّيْنَاهُ مِنَ الْغَمِّ ۚ وَكَذَٰلِكَ نُنجِي الْمُؤْمِنِينَ ﴿٨٨﴾

21:87-88 – "Wa Zan Nooni idh dhahaba mughadiban fazhanna al lan naqdira 'alayhi fanada fizh zhulumati an la ilaha illa anta Subhanaka, innee kuntu minazh zhalimeen. (87) Fastajabna lahu wa najjayna hu minal ghammi, wa kadhalika nunjee almumineen. (88)"
(Surat Al-Anbiya)

"And [mention] Zulnun [Yunus (Jonah) (as)], when he went off in anger and thought that We had no power/decree over him! But he cried out through the depths of darkness, "There is no god/diety except You; Glory to you: Indeed I have been of the wrongdoers/Oppressor to Myself!" (87) So We responded to him and saved him from the distress. And thus do We save the believers. (88)" (The Prophets, 21:87-88)

"Fastajabna najjayna minal gham." It means that Allah 🕊 will give a reply to the servant who acknowledges and accepts that as their reality. 'We give a *najat* for those whom have offended and harmed themselves.' But first you have to admit to that; you take a life to that.

Allah 🕊 Determines Whose Heart is Sincere Through Testing

Then you understood then Allah 🕊 said, 'You want to come to My Presence? You practice with them.' If you can't achieve a binary state with the shaykh, imagine then trying to reach that with Allah 🕊 without the shaykh – that's infinitely more difficult. But to

138

receive and to achieve a binary state with the shaykh in which you take the teachings, you take the understandings, you take all the guidance. And you tell yourself continuously every night that, 'I'm an oppressor to myself, *ya Rabbi*, let me to be nothing.'

That when they teach, in my nothingness, as soon as I'm sincere   and it's not for yourself   to   determine. Allah 󠁓 has a, like a counter that monitors the heart and goes 'Zzzz, zzz, zzzz' [counter moving noise]. It's not you thinking, 'I'm

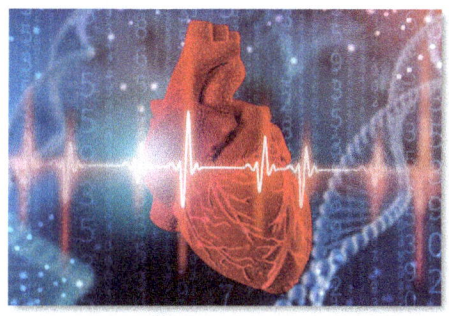

sincere.' Allah 󠁓 will test the person and then Allah 󠁓 will see when the heart is sincere. As they are sincere, they are drawing near into the heart of the shaykh.

Then the *faiz*, the lights and the energies of the shaykh are being conveyed. They are not being conveyed by the will of the shaykh. That, 'Oh, I like you more. I like you less. I, therefore, give to you.' Well, that would be *nafsani* (egocentric). It has nothing to do with the will of the shaykh. It has to do with the character of the students. When their character is sincere and they humbled themselves to Allah 󠁓, humbled themselves to the presence of Sayyidina Muhammad 󠁷, and humbled themself to the path in which, '*Ya Rabbi*, I'm here to serve and I'm nothing. Whatever I know, whatever You bestowed of me of knowledges, I'm nothing.'

The Binary System Was Hard Even for Sayyidina Musa ﷺ With Sayyidina Khidr ﷺ

This was the difficulty with Sayyidina Musa ﷺ and Sayyidina Khidr ﷺ

because Allah ﷻ gives from the highest standard. Look how high Sayyidina Musa ﷺ is and how difficult it was just to be nothing, just to be humble. Every step of the way, you have to say something. Until Sayyidina Khidr ﷺ said, 'Look, the

binary system is not going to work anymore. (Holy Qur'an, 18:78) There is no way for me to convey what you wanted from Allah ﷻ. You wanted to know of a higher knowledge. A knowledge, *"ilmu ka rushd."* The words in Qur'an was to be *rushd* – to be cooked, to be brought to a whole new level of reality.

قَالَ لَهُ مُوسَىٰ هَلْ أَتَّبِعُكَ عَلَىٰ أَن تُعَلِّمَنِ مِمَّا عُلِّمْتَ رُشْدًا ﴿٦٦﴾

18:66 – *"Qala lahu Musa hal attabi'uka 'alaa an tu'allimani mimma 'ullimta rushda."* (Surat Al-Kahf)

"Moses said to him: May I follow you, so that you teach me from that (knowledge) which you have been taught that make you grow?"
(The Cave, 18:66)

How is a binary system of magnetism because the essence of its science is more real than the *kalaam*, of words and fancy Arabic that confuse everybody. The science of it is understood that he's saying, 'How my energy going to dress onto you when you're being a ONE and I'm a ONE? We're actually now repelling each other. There is no magnetism. There's no flow of energy from me to you. For every time I want to convey a knowledge to you through my heart, you're identifying yourself. You're speaking, showing your title. As a result, you are now repelling.'

قَالَ هَذَا فِرَاقُ بَيْنِي وَبَيْنِكَ ۚ سَأُنَبِّئُكَ بِتَأْوِيلِ مَا لَمْ تَسْتَطِع عَّلَيْهِ صَبْرًا ﴿٧٨﴾

18:78 – "Qaala haazaa firaaqu bainee wa bainik; sa unabi 'uka bitaaweeli maa lam tastati' 'alaihi sabraa" (Surat Al-Kahf)

"He answered: 'This is the parting between me and thee: now will I tell thee the interpretation/significance of (those things) with which you could not have patience.'" (The Cave, 18:78)

The Magnetic Charge and Faiz of the Heavens Dress the Shaykh

Magnetism and the reality of magnetism is that, 'I'm nothing.' When I was nothing with Allah ﷻ, He drew near. When Allah ﷻ taught us to be nothing in the presence of Sayyidina Muhammad ﷺ, our *wujud* (existence) draws near. Not my mind and *'aqel* (intellect), my soul, our souls go. As a result of drawing near, then they said, 'These are your guides. They represent the Muhammadan reality.'

As a result, I became nothing. My soul draw near to them. We described that in magnetism before. As a result of that nothing, then you're in a continuous magnetic charge to these immense souls. And as a result of being nothing but charged to their love, their *faiz* and magnetic energy from paradises are continuously dressing the soul, not the *'aqel*. They don't dress the brain of the shaykh.

They taught him that whatever comes to you is a test in life, be nothing. As a result of that nothing, you have an immense love. With that love, your soul is a magnet connected to us, yearning for us. As a result of whatever Allah ﷻ charges us with of lights and *faiz* and emanations, it's flowing to you. Not from brain and ego; it's flowing to you, free onto your soul. The shaykh is not picking and choosing in the heavens, picking, choosing, 'Oh not this shaykh, this shaykh.' But whomever is approaching with sincerity and love and the magnetism of their *wujud* is locked onto these realities. The *faiz* of the heavens dresses upon them.

Arrogance and Wanting to Be the ONE Repels Us From the Shaykh

Then that system is taught on Earth that, 'Teach your students to love you, respect you, honour you.' You can't go to five magnets and do that. That's why then the student loses. They're just dissipating

everywhere, deluded. The system of magnetism is you give your love, you come, you took the path, you heard the teachings. 'I'm nothing, nothing, nothing.' When he talks, you listen. There is even people talking on the other side; the ladies are talking while the shaykh is talking. What kind of student is that? Show a complete disrespect for the words of Allah ﷻ, the words of Sayyidina Muhammad ﷺ, and the words of *awliya*. It means your magnet is very far from that reality and drawing farther away from that reality.

Everything is an immense science. If we took a path of humility – that's why the shaykh can see, it's like a doctor's office. When you're not serving, when you're not cleaning, and you're coming to be served, it means you're coming and saying, 'I am a ONE and I'm related to a ONE and I am the ONE.' The danger – why the shaykh has to identify that – the danger is you're not receiving any *faiz*. You're not receiving any magnetism. You're not drawing near to the reality. You're actually repelling yourself from the reality.

Without Love and Respect, There is No Magnetic Charge or Connection

If you are repelling from the shaykh, then imagine everything else that you're repelling away from. How could you be drawing near to Allah ﷻ but you're repelling from such an easy practice which is a shaykh? Allah ﷻ Almighty is the Creator of all universes. How many 800 forbiddens He's written and how many of them are you achieving on a daily basis? Probably 799.

It means Allah ﷻ, *"Atiullah"* (Obey Allah) is impossible. That's why Allah ﷻ gave, *"atiur Rasul"* (Obey the Messenger) because only Prophet ﷺ can adhere to what Allah ﷻ wants. Then even Prophet ﷺ is impossible, so Allah ﷻ, *"wa Ulil amre minkum"* and 'Follow these Ulul Amr (saints).' They teach with a mercy, they teach with a compassion but they're teaching the same system.

... أَطِيعُوا اللهَ وَأَطِيعُوا الرَّسُولَ وَأُوْلِي الْأَمْرِ مِنْكُمْ ... ﴿٥٩﴾

4:59 – "...Atiullaha wa atiur Rasula wa Ulil amre minkum..." (Surat An-Nisa)

"... Obey Allah, Obey the Messenger, and those in authority among you..." (The Women, 4:59)

If you are rude to them, you don't listen to them. You are arrogant with the teachings and in their presence. You could be at home and being rude and you think, 'The shaykh doesn't see me.' It's not important for the shaykh to see you. He's not coming with a stick like the Indian solider come and hit you for no reason. But you're showing your *wujud* and your being. There's no *ihtiram* (respect), there is no adherence, there is no love. As a result, you're not making a magnetic charge and connection.

Love Creates a Bond Between the Souls in the Ocean of Light

Then there are people who want so much to achieve that reality. They sit with all sincerity and they participate, that you understand now. Then they click here, they do this, they do that, they do all of these things that have been given as a guidance. As a result, they have an immense love. And Allah ﷻ is the one whom then releases their soul to be bonded in the ocean and in the light of the shaykh.

As a result, that shaykh's light is already in the presence of his shaykhs bonded. And his shaykhs are bonded all the way to the presence of Sayyidina Muhammad ﷺ. It's not a ship you have to board and figure out what your destination will be. It's an elevator that already is associated with the heart of Prophet ﷺ. That's why, "...*atasimo bihab lillah.*" Allah 🌙 is giving the example, 'Hold tight to their rope' and, 'Don't *tafarraq* – don't separate from them.'

$$\text{وَاعْتَصِمُوا بِحَبْلِ اللَّهِ جَمِيعًا وَلَا تَفَرَّقُوا ۚ ﴿١٠٣﴾}$$

3:103 – "Wa'tasimo bihab lillahi jamee'an wa la tafarraqo..."
(Surat Ali 'Imran)

"And hold firmly to the rope of Allah all together and do not separate..." (Family of Imran, 3:103)

Your Love Boards You to the Shaykh's Ship Regardless of Distance

This love and this respect, it builds the magnetism. Through your soul, not through the brain and through your physical. You use your physical body to take you to that state of love and respect in which you want the knowledges, you want the teachings. The shaykh is talking and people are beginning to look bored. Then what did they come for? They came for a dinner?

So, people then are sitting at home never seen that but yearning for the

reality. They want the knowledge, they want the *faiz*, they want the energies. As a result, their soul is drawing near into it and they start emailing that, 'I'm in the presence of Prophet 🕌. I'm feeling this, I'm feeling that, I'm feeling all this.' Well, because of sincerity.

With sincerity, the soul, like a magnet, immediately attaches. That becomes the *"Fulkil mashhoon."* These are loaded ships. The soul of the shaykh is like a ship and as soon as people attach themself, they're being drawn near into that reality.

وَآيَةٌ لَّهُمْ أَنَّا حَمَلْنَا ذُرِّيَّتَهُمْ فِي الْفُلْكِ الْمَشْحُونِ ﴿٤١﴾

36:41 – "Wa ayatul lahum anna hamalna dhurriyyatahum fil fulkil mashhooni." (Surat YaSeen)

"And a sign for them is that we have carried their atoms/forefathers in the loaded ship." (YaSeen, 36:41)

That becomes the reality of magnetism. To keep their negative charge, they took a path of humility. As a result of that humility, they were able to draw close to the positive charge. As a result of drawing close to the positive charge, they receive the lights, the emanation and the *faiz*. That is what's important to make the connection, feel the connection, to be dressed by that connection. We pray that Allah ﷻ give us its reality and more and more deeper realities of these lights and these emanations.

Subhana rabbika rabbal 'izzati 'amma yasifoon, wa salaamun 'alal mursaleen, walhamdulillahi rabbil 'aalameen. Bi hurmati Muhammad al-Mustafa wa bi siri Surat al-Fatiha.

Losing Magnetism by Reverse Polarity

The Connection of Love is Like a Magnet

If people didn't achieve it with a level of purity and they felt a little bit of magnetism, then they can lose their magnetism. If they reverse the magnet, then things can change. We described before in the understanding of love and the connection of love – it is a magnet. When you study magnets, it's an iron, [another] iron, and they're magnetized.

Allah ﷻ creates the polarity. That when somebody's attracted to somebody, Allah ﷻ is allowing that polarity to come. So, when Allah ﷻ wants us to be attracted to the Divine, He changes the polarity of the person, 'You're now attracted to  Allah ﷻ.' Then, 'Now you're attracted to the heart of Sayyidina Muhammad ﷺ.' So the good deeds, good actions – all these characteristics then, it's drawing ourself closer into that polarity.

Shaitan (Satan) Reverses the Polarity of the Magnet

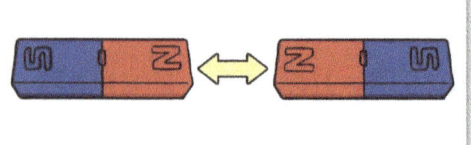

Shaitan's role in life is to come and flip people's polarity; make them to do something bad to flip the magnet away. So, as soon as they make *istighfar* (seeking forgiveness), Allah ﷻ brings the magnet back, right?

When we studied the magnets, if you hit the magnet – let's say, the two are attracted, these two magnets. If you hit one magnet, you can actually reverse the polarity of the magnet in which it no longer attracts. It repels each other. So, if you see one magnet, you reverse it this way [the side that repels]. It goes 'Woo' and pushes out. Your charge is actually pushing you away. That's the role of *shaitan*. Why he makes people fight? Because he's hitting their magnet with a rod. As a result of hitting it, he changed the polarity and the people are repelled from each other.

Arguments Flip Polarity and Make People Repel Each Other

So, before the Divine, imagine individual people who have a love for each other. *Shaitan* makes them to fight. As a result of their fight, the magnet flipped and they're no longer attracted. If you ask for forgiveness and make *istighfar*, Allah ﷻ will reverse the polarity and bring you back into a magnetic field, reverse the polarity.

But if we keep doing, keep doing, keep doing or people don't ask for a forgiveness, they start to abuse the relationship of each other. As a result of *shaitan* hitting, then the polarity flips and they actually begin to repel each other. There's no way to bring them back into each

other's presence. They have nothing to do with each other because the magnets of their reality have been pushed away.

If We Don't Seek Forgiveness, We Could Lose Our Faith

So, our whole life is based on understanding magnetism. That's what

istighfar is. As soon as we ask, '*Ya Rabbi, astaghfirullah al-'Azim* (I seek forgiveness of Allah the Magnificent),' that, '*Shaitan* has now hit my polarity, hit my magnet. I'm begging Your forgiveness.' Then Allah ﷻ flips it back.

But a day may come if we keep doing bad, keep doing bad, keep doing bad, that Allah ﷻ doesn't flip the polarity. Then we see or we hear from people, no matter how high [their station] they left. They left Islam, they

left their belief, they left everything. Their magnet was flipped away from Allah ﷻ and towards the *dajjal* (man/system of deceit) because they start to do crazy, crazy things that you can't imagine anybody

with a mind thinks like that. That's the polarity!

Good Deeds Make the Magnet Pull Stronger

The magnetism itself becomes weakened. It's like faith. So, the shaykh's

practices have to continuously be strong. The love for Prophet ﷺ has to be nourished and the nourishment are the good deeds. That's why they go out and encourage people to give, give, support, do. Do the recitation, do these projects, put out these videos. Because they want the *nazar* (gaze) of Prophet ﷺ upon themselves so that their magnet is continuously getting stronger and stronger because Prophet ﷺ is happy with those whom are doing these acts of love and *ishq*. As a result, all those whom are doing it, their magnets are becoming stronger. So, it's the good deeds that make the magnetic pull to each other stronger and stronger and stronger.

Spiritual Gravitational Pull is Through Unseen Ropes of Love

That's what they don't understand about gravity. Whatever formula they have for gravity, they still don't understand it because they're into their mind. But *ishq* and love has an immense reality with gravity. That has to do with magnetism, understanding the true nature of magnetism. Because you study the physical to understand the reality of the physical which is concealed within our spiritual reality. Because our spiritual light, how is it attracted to something? It's the magnetism of it; its gravitational

pull that it orbits around the love of Sayyidina Muhammad ﷺ and begin to be pulled to it.

If it should lose its gravity and lose that connection, it would be like an astronaut in space just 'shh,' float away. There will be nothing holding you. So, it means the reality of gravity are unseen ropes where Allah ﷻ has unseen ropes. These ropes are of *ishq* and good character and magnetism. That's what makes the reality of somebody to be drawn to somebody.

Love Prophet ﷺ at the Atomic Level to Enter Into His Orbit

We said before – that's again in your electrons, that Allah ﷻ puts this love within my being to love Sayyidina Muhammad ﷺ. I became now an electron in his orbit. He is the nucleus of my existence. That's when he meant that, 'You have to love me more than you love yourself.' He's talking at our atomic reality. So, Prophet ﷺ is describing in that holy *Hadith* of faith, 'Ya Umar! You've to love me more than you love yourself for your *iman* (faith) to be *kamil* (perfected).'

وَعَنْ عُمَرَ عَلَيْهِ السَّلَامُ قَالَ: فَوَجَدْتُ نَفْسِي أَقُولُ: وَاللهِ يَا رَسُولَ اللهِ، إِنِّي أُحِبُّكَ! فَقَالَ لَهُ النَّبِيِّ ﷺ: " أَكْثَرَ مِنْ أَهْلِكَ يَا عُمَرُ؟" قُلْتُ: نَعَمْ. قَالَ ﷺ: " أَكْثَرَ مِنْ مَالِكَ يَا عُمَرُ؟" قُلْتُ: نَعَمْ. قَالَ ﷺ: " أَكْثَرَ مِنْ نَفْسِكَ يَا عُمَرُ؟" قَالَ: لَا.

فَقَالَ النَّبِيِّ ﷺ: "لَا يَا عُمَرُ، لَا يَكْمُلُ إِيمَانُكَ حَتَّى أَكُونَ أَحَبَّ إِلَيْكَ مِنْ نَفْسِكَ."

يَقُولُ عُمَرُّ: فَخَرَجْتُ فَفَكَّرْتُ. ثُمَّ عُدْتُ أَهْتِفُ بِهَا: وَاللهِ يَا رَسُولَ اللهِ لَأَنْتَ أَحَبُّ إِلَيَّ مِنْ نَفْسِي. فَقَالَ النَّبِيِّ ﷺ: "الْآنُ يَا عُمَرُ الْآنَ."

[صَحِيحُ الْبُخَارِيِّ، الْمَجْلَدُ الرَّابِعُ، رَقْمُ الْحَدِيثِ ٥٩٤]

Wa 'an 'Umar (as) qala: "Fawajadtu nafsi aqoolo: Wallahi ya Rasulullahi, inni uhibbuka!

Faqala lahu anNabiyu ﷺ: "Akthara min ahlika ya 'Umar?"
Qultu: Na'am. Qala ﷺ: "Akthara min malika ya 'Umar?",
Qultu: Na'am. Qala ﷺ: "Akthara min nafsika ya 'Umar?", Qala: La.

Faqala anNabiyu ﷺ: "La ya 'Umar, la yakmulu imanoka hatta akuna ahabba ilayka min nafsika." Yaqoolo 'Umar (as): Fakhrajtu fafakkartu. Thumma 'udtu ahtafu biha: Wallahi ya Rasulullahi la anta ahabbu ilayya min nafsi. Faqala anNabiyu ﷺ: "Alan ya 'Umar, alan."
[Sahih al-Bukhari, al-Majladu al-Rabi'o, raqm al-hadith 594]

Narrated by Sayyidina 'Umar (pbuh) that he said: "I found myself saying, 'By Allah, O Messenger of Allah, I love you!' The Prophet (pbuh) said to him, 'Is it more than your love for your family, O 'Umar?' I said, 'Yes.' He (pbuh) said, 'Is it more than your love for your wealth, O 'Umar?' I said, 'Yes.' He said, 'Is it more than your love for yourself, O 'Umar?' He said, 'No.'

The Prophet (pbuh), said, 'No, O 'Umar, your faith will not be complete until I become more beloved to you than your own self.' 'Umar said: So I went out and thought. Then I returned and shouted, 'By Allah, O Messenger of Allah, you are more beloved to me than myself.' The Prophet (pbuh) said, 'Now, O 'Umar, now [you got it].'
[Sahih al-Bukhari, Volume 4, Hadith #594]

This is a direct direction from Prophet ﷺ to the atomic reality of Hazrat Umar ؓ, that your *ishq* and love has to overcome everything for me so that you can enter into my orbit. So, only now the scientists understand this atom and electron.

Sayyidina Muhammad ﷺ is the Nucleus for Creation

So, when we bring ourself into that immense love of Prophet ﷺ because we need the human love, the Divine love will flow. *"Qul in kuntum tuhibbon Allah"* – 'Tell them if they love Me, follow you.' So, this is not a love that you can have for Allah ﷻ because you're a creation. Allah ﷻ is the Creator.

قُلْ إِنْ كُنْتُمْ تُحِبُّونَ اللَّهَ فَاتَّبِعُونِيْ يُحْبِبْكُمُ اللَّـهُ ... ﴿٣١﴾

3:31 – "Qul in kuntum tuhibbon Allaha fattabi'uni, yuhbibkumullahu..." (Surat Ali 'Imran)

"Say, [O Muhammad], "If you should love Allah, then follow me, [so] Allah will love you..." (Family of Imran, 3:31)

So, Allah ﷻ is giving us this hint that, 'The best of My creation, the most beloved of My creation, move yourself into his holy orbit.' Then think of yourself like an electron and he is the nucleus of my existence.

The Two Forces of Love That Hold the Electron Into the Orbit

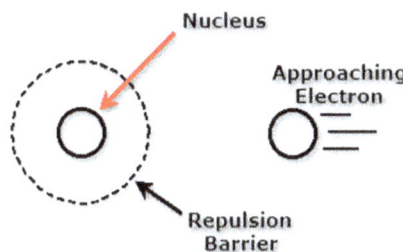

So, then what happens with your electron? It's a strong nuclear force and a weak nuclear force. These are the two forces that hold an electron in the orbit of an atom, of a nucleus, right? There are two forces that hold the electron in the orbit of the nucleus.

- One – the force of Prophet ﷺ loving me more ancient than my love for him.
- Two – me, my love immense directed.

As a result of these two forces, our love is drawing my electron to collide. I want nothing more than to die and be in his presence. But as a result of not being and not being given that permission, what happens with the electron? As it's trying to draw closer, it

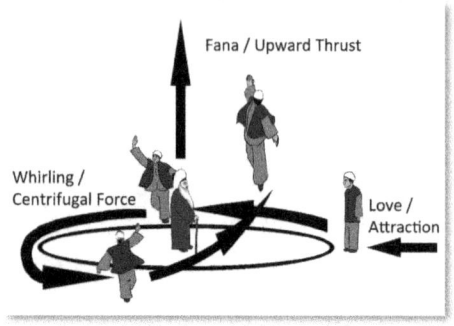

doesn't reach. But it doesn't mean it stops. What we described in the reality of the *sama'* (whirling), the electron begins to spin because it's looking for an opening to come. So, if you knew Prophet ﷺ was in that room and they shut all the doors to that room – you're going home or you're going to go all around the building looking for a way to get in? If he says, 'Tomorrow, I'm going to be appearing here,' all of us going to break through every window trying to get in. You don't go home, say, 'It's finished.'

The Electrons Don't Give Up Until They Reach the Nucleus

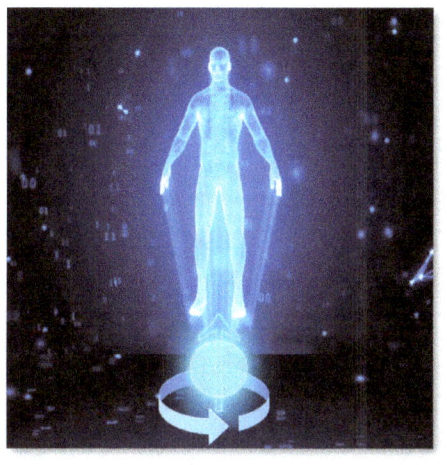

So, the electron as it's moving, it's now beginning what they call 'centrifugal spin.' It's beginning to spin to get into the nucleus. It begins to spin so much trying to find a way into the nucleus that as a result of spinning fast, fast, fast, fast, what happens? It begins to rise. So, the attraction is pulling it in. It's spinning and then rising. So, that's how we are created. You're a hologram. You're just a bunch of atoms that are appearing. *InshaAllah*, we leave that for another conversation.

Subhana rabbika rabbal 'izzati 'amma yasifoon, wa salaamun 'alal mursaleen, walhamdulillahi rabbil 'aalameen. Bi hurmati Muhammad al-Mustafa wa bi siri Surat al-Fatiha.

Second Power

Haqiqatul Faiz

Reality of Downpouring

Emanation

How to Attract and Retain Divinely Emanation

Heavenly Realities Can Only Be Achieved Through a Spiritual Path

We talked about this path when they break down its realities. That the 'Levels of The Heart' [book] is dedicated to the entire understanding of the house of Allah ﷻ. Anybody who wants to occupy and move within that reality, then should have been reading that understanding and educating themselves in the *Lataif ul Qalb* (subtle energy points of the heart). That is the pathway into the reality of the heart. When Allah ﷻ wants to dress His servants, He gives them and dresses them from the six powers of the heart. Those are the powers that complete their *wilayah* and dress that sainthood and dress its lights and its blessings.

Those are achievable by those whom Allah ﷻ guides to the *turuqs* (spiritual paths). By virtue of teaching these realities, we can see that without the *turuqs*, it's not possible to achieve. If it's exception that Allah ﷻ dress

whomever He wants, however He wants. But the rule is that when we understand how these *maqams* (stations) are achieved, we understand the importance of the *turuqs* and the *tariqahs*, the spiritual path. It's not self-help. It's not you read or you read on Sufism and that you achieve these realities. They're very difficult realities to achieve, the basis of which is love and *muhabbat*.

To Love Allah ﷻ, You Must Love Sayyidina Muhammad ﷺ

They have to have an immense love for Allah ﷻ. Their path is based on this immense *ishq*, immense *muhabbat* and love. That Allah ﷻ begin to reflect in their heart that, 'If you love Me, love Sayyidina Muhammad ﷺ.'

قُلْ إِنْ كُنْتُمْ تُحِبُّونَ اللَّـهَ فَاتَّبِعُونِيْ يُحْبِبْكُمُ اللَّـهُ ... ﴿٣١﴾

3:31 – "Qul in kuntum tuhibbon Allaha fattabi'uni, yuhbibkumullahu..." (Surat Ali 'Imran)

"Say, [O Muhammad], "If you should love Allah, then follow me, [so] Allah will love you ..." (Family of Imran, 3:31)

So they can't achieve this if they're not immensely immersed within the love of Sayyidina Muhammad ﷺ. With that immense love and *ishq*, Prophet ﷺ begins to put into their heart because 'Whom you love you'll be with.'

عَنْ أَنَسٍ رَضِيَ اللهُ عَنْهُ: ... فَقَالَ (رَسُولُ اللهِ ﷺ): " أَنْتَ مَعَ مَنْ أَحْبَبْتَ."
[أَلْمَصْدَرْ: مُسْلِمْ: ٧٥٢٠]

'An Anasin (ra): ... Faqala (Rasulullahi) ﷺ*: "Anta ma'a man ahbabta."*

Narrated Anas ibn Malik (ra) that ...the Messenger of Allah (pbuh) said: "You will be with whom you love." [Source: Muslim 7520]

When Prophet ﷺ loves that one who loves him ﷺ, he puts what's dear within his heart. So, dear into the heart of Sayyidina Muhammad ﷺ is love of Allah ﷻ and Holy Qur'an, love of his holy family, love of his holy companions. As a result, begins to guide them to the love of *awliyaullah* who are the Muhammadan representatives of that reality on Earth. So, if they're not from this *ishq* (love), these are realities again that cannot be achieved.

1. Haqiqatul Juzba (Reality of Attraction)

We Can't Understand Inner Purification Without Tafakkur

As a result, when Allah ﷻ dresses them with this light and this love, what happens then? The *Haqiqatul Juzba* (Reality of Attraction). That they'll sit and train with these *ulul amr* (saints) on how to enter into their heart. How to fight the inner fight of devils, bad character, bad desires. How to open up the energy of their being, understanding the energy. So, imagine now somebody who doesn't make *tafakkur* (contemplation), how he's going to achieve all these realities?

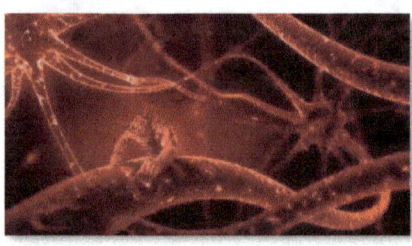

How is he going to achieve now the understanding of inner purification, inner cleansing, inner realities? How is he going to understand that his iron and his blood – or he or she, doesn't matter – their blood and iron has to be perfected and cleaned so that *shaitan* (satan) is not moving within them to an immense degree.

عَنْ أَنَسٍ قَالَ، قَالَ رَسُولُ اللَّهِ ﷺ: "إِنَّ الشَّيْطَانَ يَجْرِي مِنَ الْإِنْسَانِ مَجْرَى الدَّمِ."
[الْمَصْدَرْ: صَحِيحٌ مُسْلِمٌ ٢١٧٤]

'An Anasin Qala Rasulallahi ﷺ: *"Innash Shaitana yajri minal Insani majra addami." [Sahih Muslim 2174]*

Narrated by 'An Anas (ra) that the Messenger of Allah (pbuh) said, "Satan circulates/flows through the human being as blood circulates/flow in the body." [Authentic by Muslim 2174]

Purified Iron, Like a Satellite Dish, Attracts and Stores Emanations

As a result of the inner purity and inner realities, the *faiz* (downpouring blessings) that Allah ﷻ dressing, the *faiz* that Sayyidina Muhammad ﷺ dressing, and the *faiz* that *awliyaullah* dressing upon them is adhering and sticking on them. It's not a blessing that comes and passes and goes. It's a blessing that they are able to bring upon themselves and contain upon themselves.

The iron within them is being purified. That iron, each cell of that iron like a satellite dish making the hairs to stick up when energy comes. Each cell of iron beneath the hair that sticks up is 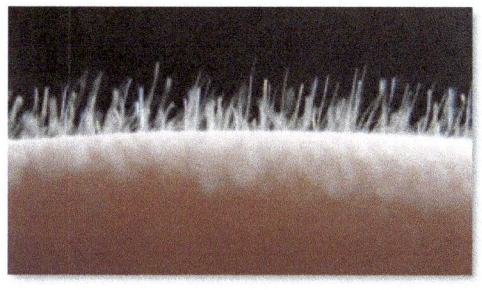 like a satellite dish that collecting and activating all these *faiz* and energies. '*Faiz*' is emanations, lights, blessings, Divine grace – whatever people want to call it. These lights that are coming upon the soul of somebody is coming by virtue of their iron and their body purification. Their iron is bringing it, the blood is bringing it, the reality is dressing them, blessing them, bringing that energy upon themselves. As a result, the energy is moving upon their *badan*, upon their physicality.

Haqiqatul Juzba is Needed to Move Towards Haqiqatul Irshad & Guidance

 So if not doing those practices, not doing those understandings then how they going to receive that *juzba* (attraction). The *juzba* is magnetism. As a result of their magnetic force, they are literally like a magnet. That they put out a charge and as a result, people are attracted to them. So, the energy that emanate in *Haqiqatul Juzba* is what is needed. It means that these six powers, if Allah ﷻ doesn't dress the servant with these six realities, they cannot be given this type of guidance and *irshad*.

For *Haqiqatul Irshad* (Reality of Guidance) – and the *haqiqah*, the reality – because we have a lot of people watching these videos that don't understand Islamic terminology. We met with some and they said they spend like an hour just trying to understand these words that we use. Like you have to have a dictionary on the side to go through each word. So, *haqiqah* means the reality of magnetism. To open this reality of magnetism and to be a magnetic character in which your heart and soul's power is emanating an immense power, immense reality.

Allah ﷻ Turns On the Magnetic Charge in Our Hearts to Guide Us

As a result of that and it moves at and away from space and time. It means space and time is not a barrier for their *juzba* (magnetism). Not only they attract seen but they attract unseen. They not only attract living and they attract those whom passed. The *juzba* of their soul through their magnetism attracts many realities towards them.

One – the students that are in need of guidance. So as a result, that magnetic charge is released upon them. The students hearts, we've described before in other understandings, that when Allah ﷻ want to guide somebody, He turns on the magnetic charge within their heart. So, it's not that our brain is guiding us, that we saw some videos and we became interested in it. It's actually Divine opening up the heart. Immediately, He turns the charge that, 'Love Me.'

This is what Abu Yazid al Bistami ق described that, 'In all his journeying toward the Divinely oceans of power, when he finally reached into what he wanted to reach, he found that Allah's ﷻ love for him was more ancient than his love for Allah ﷻ.'

The Magnetic Charge Directs Us to the Love of Prophet ﷺ and Holy Souls

It means we only have this love because Allah ﷻ turned the magnet on. If for a moment Allah ﷻ, God forbid, should become angered by us, God forbid, that magnet if it turns off, everything drops. Everything the servant does is not in the way of Allah ﷻ, not with the love of Allah ﷻ. They may do many things they think Allah ﷻ loves but actually it's what *shaitan* loves. They begin to do very corrupt and bad actions.

The true magnetic energy is when Allah ﷻ turns the *qalb* (heart) and as a result, they are and their entire *wujud* – their entire being is directed towards their Lord Almighty. Then Allah ﷻ turns that magnet and then they become directed towards the love of Sayyidina Muhammad ﷺ. Then again, again all of those descriptions, Prophet ﷺ begin to turn the charge and they have then the love for *Ahlul Bayt* (Holy family of Prophet ﷺ), the love of holy companions and the love for *Ulul Amr*, the *awliyaullah* who will be guiding them. Only by means of that magnetic reality within them, they're finding their co-ordinance.

The Iron Within All of Creation is Guided by Allah's ﷻ Co-ordinance

It means how does a bird find where it has to go? How does an ant know? You've seen an ant, he's so tiny in just the space of your floor of your house. Who's guiding that ant to get its piece of rice all the way in another part of the house? Your house to the ant is like a traveling throughout the continent. By the size of it and where it has to go to get its sustenance – who's guiding that ant? With what magnetism Allah ﷻ puts within that creature that, 'Your sustenance is here,' and immediately, it sets out. Who guides the bird to fly? Where they're supposed to be in winter, where they're supposed to be summer? Where they're supposed to fly to get their *rizq*, and their sustenance, their food?

It means that everything around us is on that Divine GPS. The iron within it is guiding by Allah's ﷻ co-ordinance. So, Allah ﷻ puts the co-ordinance, the angels send the co-ordinance. The GPS and Global Positioning Satellites from the Divinely Presence are activated and creatures are moving the way Allah ﷻ wants them to move. He says that, 'Everything moves within an orbit like a track.' It's nothing random. Everything is exactly programmed the way Allah ﷻ wants it programmed.

لَا الشَّمْسُ يَنبَغِي لَهَا أَن تُدْرِكَ الْقَمَرَ وَلَا اللَّيْلُ سَابِقُ النَّهَارِ ۚ وَكُلٌّ فِي
فَلَكٍ يَسْبَحُونَ ﴿٤٠﴾

36:40 – "Lash shamsu yambaghee laha an tudrikal qamara wa la allaylu sabiqun nahari, wa kullun fee falakin yasbahoon."
(Surat YaSeen)

"It is not permitted to the Sun to catch up the Moon, nor can the Night outstrip the Day: Each (just) swims/floats along in (its own) orbit."
(YaSeen, 36:40)

That's why then when these people, they fire off weapons into the oceans that destroy the magnetic charge of these creatures. Or they explode weapons into the air that has an effect upon the electromagnetic pulse and  energy of these creatures. You see the birds drop out of the sky. You see the whales and the dolphins coming up on shore because their entire positioning and guidance system has been destroyed.

To Activate the Magnetic Charge, the Heart Must Be Activated First

So, it means that everything around us is based on this *juzba*. So Allah ﷻ says, 'There is no guidance unless I guide.'

...وَقَالُوا الْحَمْدُ لِلَّهِ الَّذِي هَدَانَا لِهَٰذَا وَمَا كُنَّا لِنَهْتَدِيَ لَوْلَا أَنْ هَدَانَا اللَّـهُ ۖ﴿٤٣﴾...

7:43 – "...Wa qalo Alhamdulillahi al ladhee hadana lihadha wa ma kunna linahtadiya lawla an hadana Allahu,..." (Surat Al-A'raf)

"... And they will say, Praise be to Allah, who has guided us to this [joy and happiness]; and we would never have been guided if Allah had not guided us." (The Heights, 7:43)

It means this is from the *Haqiqatul Irshad* – the reality of guidance. That Allah ﷻ has to activate that inner heart so that the charge is activated. That is for the one whom is being pulled in, that their call is being directed from their magnet to seek what

Allah ﷻ wants them to seek. Then the ones whom are establishing themself in that ocean so that Allah ﷻ make them to inherit that magnetism.

That's the *juzba* and magnetism that they begin to dress from the magnet, dress from the magnet, dress from these oceans of power and the charge within their heart. The magnet is in the cleanliness in which God wants it of His Divinely Presence, love of His beloved Prophet ﷺ, love of His holy books, love of the best of character, the companions, the family of Prophet ﷺ. When it's all dressed the way Allah ﷻ wants it, their magnet is activated. As a result, Allah ﷻ begin to dress their magnet with magnetism and people are attracted to their reality. People are called to that reality and that is the reality of magnetism.

2. Haqiqatul Faiz
(Reality of Downpouring Emanation)

Real Magnetism is the Ability to Collect Divinely Emanation

The next reality that flows and all of them [6 powers of the heart] are continuously opening. So it's not just only one opens but Allah ﷻ is dressing upon all of them as they're all interconnected. That *Haqiqatul Juzba* and *Haqiqatul Faiz* (Reality of Downpouring Emanation)

means the reality of Divinely emanation. So, how can somebody receive a *faiz* if they don't open the reality of their magnetism?

So, it means that there can be ten people sitting and people come new, they dress from the blessings. The blessing comes to them and within no time, they've lost it by a day or two days. The blessing came, it went and dissipated from their lives. The reality of *Haqiqatul Faiz* is that they understood on which to hold that charge. That all their meditation practices, all of their connection practices, all of the cleanliness because it's all being built upon this reality. That all of their *Haqiqatul Juzba*, their magnetism, was to collect this emanation.

When Magnetic Character is Developed It Attracts Divine Grace

So, their magnetic character that is being developed. At the same time, Allah ﷻ begins to open, Prophet ﷺ begins to open and *awliyaullah* begin to open a magnetic character which is now magnetized and pulling *faiz* and blessings and emanations. So, it means whatever *faiz* is in the air, their soul is pulling it and the magnetism of their body is drawing it and holding it. Whatever they recite, they begin to bring that emanation and blessings, Divine grace. So, it's not just passing through but because of their cleanliness, their meditation, their practices, these are very powerful magnets being developed. As a result, it attracts all of this Divine grace and blessings.

Whatever they recite, it pulls. Wherever they attend, they pull. Whatever emanation is coming for that night or whatever Divine grace is Allah ﷻ dressing on a night, a holy night, throughout the night, *zikr* (Divine remembrance) nights, their soul and their magnetism is calling upon it and collecting it. As a result, they become a source of immense blessings. They have an immense amount of *tabarak* and blessings upon themselves because the soul is becoming energized.

The Body Attracts the Faiz and the Soul Stores It Like a Battery

A soul without that magnetism will lose the charge. So, it means that's why Allah ﷻ put us within this physical body. To understand the body, the soul, and the mind is essential for the path. You can't say, 'It doesn't matter what my body does. My soul is good, I'll catch these blessings.' No, if the body is not disciplined in the way that Allah ﷻ wants it, the body has to be able to attract the charge and the soul is like a battery that begins to take it and store it, and store it, and store it.

You know, just to put the solar panel on your roof, you say, 'Okay, it's sunny outside. I'm going to put solar panels on my roof.' But if you don't have a battery to store the power, it's not going anywhere. The sun is actually charging the panel and the panel is depleted because nothing has been stored. What was most important in their understanding of solar power was the  development of the battery. So, not only you need something that collects the energy which is the magnetism, but to have the battery and the soul that is being prepared to take this *faiz* and begin to store it.

Shaykh's Juzba Attracts Immense Blessings From Other Awliya

Take the blessings and begin to store it. Until Allah ﷻ describes like them, 'They are *fulkil mashhoon*,' in Surah YaSeen ﷺ. That these big *awliya*, they are like 'loaded ships.'

وَآيَةٌ لَّهُمْ أَنَّا حَمَلْنَا ذُرِّيَّتَهُمْ فِي الْفُلْكِ الْمَشْحُونِ ﴿٤١﴾

36:41 – "Wa ayatul lahum anna hamalna dhurriyyatahum fil fulkil mashhooni." (Surat YaSeen)

"And a sign for them is that we have carried their atoms/forefathers in the loaded ship." (YaSeen, 36:41)

171

One – they have an immense amount of *juzba*. So as a result, they put out a charge and many things are attracted to them. They say the students are attracted to them, the

jinn (unseen beings) are attracted to them, *awliya* are attracted to them. That's why Mawlana Shaykh ق would describe that, 'When these *awliyaullah* speak, all of them are listening.' One – because they have an attraction, they have a *juzba* and a connection to them. Two – they are recipients of immense *faiz*. As soon as they speak, the big, big *awliyaullah*, they're sending their *faiz* and their support. That's what enables them to speak in such a difficult condition and difficult world. So, the two are now working together. Because of their magnetism, they have the ability to attract onto those immense magnets.

The Jinn World Listens and Benefits From Awliya's Teachings

As a result of their connection, they can pull the *faiz* from these *awliyaullah* and begin to distribute it to those whom are listening and benefiting. Most are from the *jinn* (unseen being) world. They immensely benefit from these energies and these realities. These are all from the *mu'min* (believer) and *tariqah* realities and *tariqah* spiritual beings. They take from these energies. They take the blessings of these energies because they know that these shaykhs are magnets to these immense shaykhs. That their network is pulling energy and making connections.

So, I don't know if it makes sense by the tongue. That the magnetic charge of the shaykh, he connects and begins to make a magnetic connection to his shaykh and to the association of shaykhs. As a result of the strong magnetic force, it releases the *faiz* and the blessings and the emanations from their souls. That's why they speak what other people can't speak because the association above them is continuously dressing them with immense amounts of Divinely light and blessings.

To Represent Tariqah, One Must Be Trained and Have a Connection

So, what's necessary in our life is that understanding of *tafakkur* (contemplation). They make the connection, they make the cleansing, they connect with their *juzba*. The reality of their *juzba* is their lifeline. If they don't establish their *juzba*, if they don't establish their magnetism with their shaykhs, how can they guide? Right?

So, you can't go into town and say, 'Okay you, you, you. You're going to represent the *tariqah*.' You can, but it's of absolutely no value. That doesn't make any sense because that person has not been trained in meditation. That person not been trained in their connection. They definitely have no magnetic connection to the shaykh that talking to them or the shaykh before them that didn't even train them. So, when we understand the inner works, we can understand the fallacy and what doesn't make sense. Right?

Your Loyalty is What Makes Your Magnet to Be Locked

Then the shaykh can only give that reality to someone whom been trained by them, who connected and the connection is a perfected connection. As a result of that perfected connection, that shaykh knows that that one has a strong magnetic connection to them. So, their magnets are locked. That's why the loyalty of the *tariqah*; it's not an authoritative thing. Because they don't care – you listen, you don't listen – that's up to you. But to achieve this reality and these realities then you adhere to that, you connect to it. You make sure that, 'I have to connect to this magnet and this is my life and death.' When I connect, you know when your heart is connected. You know when your magnetic connection is strong. You feel the pull, you feel the *faiz*.

Awliya Have Learned When to Turn OFF and Be Approachable

We described in other talks, they feel the energy. Last night, they asked good questions on zero point energy. That they trained, they trained, they trained and they begin to put less effort and immediately, they ignite because you know, these magnets are like a switch. They hit the switch and they immediately feel the charge coming. As a result, the shaykh also will train them is turn your switch 'OFF' when you're not in need of it. Don't walk around with that

switch 'ON' because it's going to be heavy for people and agitating for people to continuously be connected and then be hard upon people. So, a part of their perfection and that's why Prophet ﷺ described to his holy companions, 'Lower your wings for people.'

عَنْ أَبِي الطُّفَيْلِ: قَالَ أَمِيرُ الْمُؤْمِنِينَ إِمَامُ عَلِيُّ ابْنِ أَبِي طَالِبْ عَلَيْهِ السَّلَامُ: "حَدِّثُوا النَّاسَ بِمَا يَعْرِفُونَ." [صحيح البخاري ١٢٧]

'An Abi al Tufayl: Qala Amirul Muminin Imam 'Ali ibni Abi Talib (as): "Haddisu an naasa bima ya'rifuna." [Sahih al Bukhari 127]

Abu al Tufayl reported that the Leader of the Believers, Imam 'Ali the son of Abi Talib (pbuh) said: "Convey/speak to the people according to the level of their knowledge and what they can understand. [Authentic by al Bukhari 127]

Because he knows that your *ummah* (nation), you're all angels. The *Sahabi kiram* (Honored Companions of Prophet ﷺ), they're like angels, higher than angels. So, he's teaching that the believer has to lower their wings. It means turn 'OFF' your charge so people can draw near to you. So that you have a time in which to be of an approachable reality.

When Shaykh Turns ON the Magnet, He Pulls the Heavenly Emanation

Then when they're 'ON,' their teaching is 'ON.' It's merely a flick of a switch within their heart and the charge comes to the higher magnets and begins to pull the reality of *faiz* towards them. Because there's no ego in their association. They're not up there saying, 'No. No, no, we don't like him. No, he's from this country. We don't support him.' They have no ego. They're in the oceans of the fountains of abundance. As a result of that abundant energy and abundant reality, all that they require is that, 'You should be sending your magnet to us. That your *juzba* should be connected to us and that we open the reality of this.' Allah 🕮 sends *faiz*, Prophet 🕮 sends *faiz* and then the *ulul amr*, they begin to send their emanation and their *faiz*.

The Blessed Voice and Image of Awliya Eternally Dresses People

As a result, that's a *Shaykh ul Tabarak*. That's a person of immense *tabarak* (blessing). Right? So, he's now like a power plant for *faiz*. As soon as their association – and again space and time is of no relevance for them. Say, 'I have to be sitting on the carpet.' You don't have to be sitting on the carpet [in the association of the shaykh]. You can listen to this ten years from now and Allah's 🕮 power is always eternal. Allah's 🕮 reality is *daayim* (eternal).

You watch Shaykh Nazim ق now and he passed away how many years ago. He's more powerful now. Because you're able to hear, said from his holy lips and his speech is live and real and is alive in a frequency from Allah's 🕮 oceans of *daayim*. So, it means these words of *awliyaullah* that been captured for video and audio – this is a *barakah* (blessing) and a *ni'mat* of the last days. Because imagine if you had tapes to listen to Shaykh Abdul Qadir Jilani ق. What type of energy would be coming from that sound? So, this is something that can't be understood but it's in the oceans of eternity.

As a result of these energies, they're dressing, they're blessing. Then that is an immense source of *faiz* and emanation. That everything that we listen to them, every sound that comes from them, every association  that we're attending from them, they're dressing upon us. So, the one whom is meditating and connecting and polishing, he's in a continuous state of able to attract that *faiz*. So, it means they're able to build themself to an immense state of realities depending upon how much they want to put into it. So, they want to listen everyday. They put the subscription, they listen everyday. They meditate earlier and then when the association starts, they're in a meditative connection, and they're catching the *faiz* upon their reality. They're dressing themself from that reality. That Allah ﷻ dress them and bless them.

Subhana rabbika rabbal 'izzati 'amma yasifoon, wa salaamun 'alal mursaleen, walhamdulillahi rabbil 'aalameen. Bi hurmati Muhammad al-Mustafa wa bi siri Surat al-Fatiha.

Duality of Light – Leave Particle Existence to Reach Wave Reality

Quantum is the Study of Light and Eternity

Alhamdulillah, that Allah ﷻ guides humanity and sometimes humanity may catch up with its understanding of guidance through their sciences and through their understandings. It means that in science – we were talking the night before with the gentlemen here – in science, they discovered when they studied light and what they call 'quantum.' So, quantum sciences was their study of light, what we would call the *malakut*, the world of eternity, that which is eternal.

Double-Slit Experiment

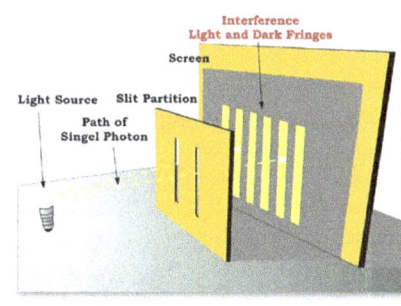

When they studied the light, they understood that the reality of the duality of light. That when they darkened a room and they put a piece of paper and they put two holes on that paper at the end of a distance, they darkened the room and they put out a spectrum of light. When they watched the light in their experiment, it always went through one hole because there's two at the end of the paper.

They did that and did that until one time they decided, 'Well, maybe let's not watch it. We'll turn the other way and we won't observe it and let's do the experiment.' To their surprise, the light went through two holes. So they understood now, their sciences started to open on the reality of the duality of light. Once to their amazement, that light was reacting to them. It was reacting to its observation. When it deemed itself being observed, it stayed within the confine of its particle existence. When that light was not observed, it went into its wave format and was able to go through two holes when it wasn't being watched.

Every Light has a Duality: Particle Form and Wave Form

This is an ancient reality. It means Allah's ﷻ realities are ancient and taught amongst the prophets ﷺ and the saints towards humanity. Every so often, Allah ﷻ releases a permission in their sciences to understand as a guidance, to bring people towards a reality. So, when they're studying that every light has a duality, has a particle and has a wave and the *tariqah* (spiritual path) comes to teach from what Prophet ﷺ had brought and perfected this science of light – this science of reality – that you have a particle existence and you have a wave existence.

The particle existence is that which people observe. But the science is telling people, 'No, we also have a wave existence.' It means you have a form of light that is moving. They barely understand where it's moving and that's just the light of you. Imagine then the atomic reality of you, the electrons of you. How are those exactly within a very defined orbit and what happens if you try to move one of those forcefully?

Enter Your Wave Reality By Not Being Observed By Others

Everything is so defined and so perfect but for us on this subject of the duality of light, this is the teaching of *tariqah*. That if you want a particle existence, this is your *mulk*, your form, for us to understand and make it simplified. Or do you want to train in your light reality which we call the *malakut* and the 'heavenly reality.' Everybody has these two realities but it's based on observation. So, what they understood from their sciences, this is the teachings of *tariqah* (spiritual path). As much as people observe you, you remain locked within your particle existence.

When people don't observe you, you can enter into your wave reality. So, that's why then the *tariqahs* come and teach people that, 'Be nothing.' So, this concept of 'be nothing' was so that they could reach their reality. It means that you have these two realities but if you're not opening them, your understanding is only of a very physical nature and you lose the whole concept of your spirituality. You lose the whole possibility of your spirituality.

The Wave Reality in the All-Encompassing Light of Sayyidina Muhammad ﷺ

Wave, how could wave even be understood? That your wave reality –

how fast can it travel? Where can it be? What would be limiting its reality? Your wave reality, would it only be moving within this plane, within this *dunya* (material world),

181

within this galaxy, within this universe? It means the potential of our understanding within the wave reality, the light reality of *insan* and people, is limitless because we still don't know what Allah ﷻ has created. How many infinite creations and galaxies and universes and how much of that light of yours exists within that galaxies and those universes.

If all of those are under *Muhammadan Rasulallah* ﷺ, 'The one who knows himself will know his reality, know his lord' and will enter into the Muhammadan light that encompasses every aspect of this universe.

قَال رَسُولَ اللَّهِ ﷺ : " مَنْ عَرَفَ نَفْسَهْ فَقَدْ عَرَفَ رَبَّهُ."

Qala Rasulullahi ﷺ: *"Man 'arafa nafsahu faqad 'arafa Rabbahu."*

The Messenger of Allah (pbuh) said: "Who knows himself, knows his Lord."

Not only the *dunya* (material world), not only the universe but everything within the heavens. Every angel is in a Muhammadan light. If Prophet ﷺ give to you access within the light, that within the reality of not only finding yourself, but entering into the Muhammadan light that you can enter your light into the reality of the different *malaika* (angels) to understand their reality.

Diffuse Your Light Within the Muhammadan Light to Be of a Timeless Reality

So, if everything has a light and they're teaching that this is all a *Muhammadun Rasulallah* ﷺ, by knowing yourself, you will know your lord and it means you'll know what governs you. You have the potential of entering into every aspect of light from all its planets and all its universes. And all of that all the way into the *sama* and into the heavens. From into the heavens, *Baitul Mamur*, into the '*Arsh* (The Divinely Throne), into the angels, into everything that is created by that light.

So, it means you take a light, you shine another light and you see how that light diffuses within the light and it enters into it. If Prophet ﷺ gives you the code to go, that, 'I'll allow your light to move within my light to understand everything.' That it's all created from his reality ﷺ. It means then the potential and the limit is limitless and that's why it's a 'timeless reality.' If we stick within the confines of time and particle and form – very limited *dunya*, very limited existence; life that doesn't even touch a drop of its reality. So, then Allah ﷻ was sending guidance from the heavens to teach them your duality but didn't use these scientific words; taught them 'be nothing.' Why? Escape the observation of people. So, the *tariqah* (spiritual path) comes and teaches you have these two realities. Everyone has these two realities.

You Will Never Reach Your True Reality By Wanting to Be Observed

But if you're raised in a way that you want to show yourself, identify yourself, propagate yourself, Facebook yourself, Instagram yourself, what's *shaitan* (satan) doing? He's making sure you're completely under observation, right? Because he knows these two theories. He knows that this person will never reach their reality if they're under observation.

So, now 99% of all creation is making themself more observed. Even some guy in the middle of – I don't want to insult anybody – a village of anywhere, he has a mobile phone for some reason and he's posting himself. He'd be on a rickshaw with nothing, just has a mobile phone posting himself where nobody would have observed him. *Shaitan* plays with him that, 'Observe. Let people to observe you. You will never reach your destiny.'

The Role of the Nafs (Ego) Restricts Us to the Particle Form

Somebody has asked that what is the role of the *nafs* (ego) in this understanding? It's to keep the servant from becoming a wave. So, it means that everything that the *nafs* inflicts upon a person and their humanity is to keep and restrict them  from achieving their wave reality, to achieve the light reality that's within them. That's the role that the *nafs* is playing is to keep the person to be in their physical and in their physical desires. That's the difficulty of achieving any spirituality or any significant improvement in our spirituality if we can't reach to the wave reality.

So, that was an interesting email that somebody had asked that, 'What's the role of the *nafs* (ego) in the particle and the wave?' Allah ﷻ put the *nafs* there as a source in which to keep us as a particle and that's our testing in life. If we're going to follow the *nafs*, then the *nafs* whole duty is to make us a particle in which we are not capable of observing ourself and that we don't reach to any spiritual maturity so that we constantly are required to remain under supervision. As a result of that supervision, we cannot reach to our wave reality.

What is Modern-Day Idolatry?

Those that follow their *nafs* (ego) too much and their desires, then you can see that its completely making them particle; so much particle almost like a statue. That they're not just semi-*dunya* (material world), they're like full *dunya* and they become what they call what? What's a popular terms for these people? Idols. So, there's nothing hidden. *Shaitan* (satan) makes everything to be out. It's that people just don't have ears and eyes to see it. That when they become so much in their *dunya*, they actually become *mujassamiyoon*. They become a statue, they become an idol. They have no longer any relationship to their soul and to their wave reality. They have calcified and actually have become a statue.

As a result of their 'statue-ness,' they call out to people to worship them, what they call their 'fans' and those whom are idols and idol worshippers. So, you can see how much difficulty *shaitan* (satan) has put upon this Earth. If you think at idol worshipping before was for what? That they took a symbol of something and thought by putting their attention on it which is worshipness, putting all their thought and their mind and following. Everything

about their being is put upon that idol thinking it had some sort of benefit for it. Allah ﷻ would describe that neither it can benefit you nor harm you. It actually has absolutely nothing to do or for you.

قَالَ أَفَتَعْبُدُونَ مِن دُونِ اللَّهِ مَا لَا يَنفَعُكُمْ شَيْئًا وَلَا يَضُرُّكُمْ ﴿٦٦﴾

21:66 – "Qala afata'budoona min doonillahi maa la yanfa'uukum shay-an wa laa yadurrukum." (Surat Al Anbiya)

He said, "Then do you worship instead of Allah that which does not benefit you at all or harm you? (The Prophets, 21:66)

Look at modern day idolism. It's from their own words, not words we've made up. They call themself 'idols.' They have shows to make an idol.

Everybody who follows these idols, they're like worshipping them; every moment what they're doing, how they're eating, what clothes they wear. Allah's ﷻ reminding that the old school idol worshipping which is backwards compared to today's idol worshipping because today's idol worshipping, they have brought an immense amount of technology into their idol worshipping. Old school idol worshipers would look at us and say, 'Whoa, where you guys took this. You've taken it such an advance level.' They had one little statue and look how much Allah ﷻ was angry with them.

We're Distracted By Idols Instead of Focusing Upon Our Own Realities

Now everything in our existence on this Earth is an idol. Which idol you think you're going to follow that will lead you to somewhere, have some sort of benefit for you? Watch what they drive, watch what they eat, watch what they dress; none of which you can do, none of which has any benefit for you and has a tremendous amount of harm.

That it wasted human life, it wasted their focus. Instead of focusing upon the reality and on the heavens and closing our eyes from this world and trying to reach within our spiritual reality then Allah ﷻ is reminding for us, 'Look at how *shaitan* has brought idol worshipping into your realm,' and how significant it is that 90% to 99% of the population are all following it.

Prophet ﷺ Warned Us About Following Other Nations

We said before there are people with a certain style of recitation that come from South Central Los Angeles but now they're being the same recitation in Japan, in Hong Kong, in Indonesia, all of the world. They have never seen these people but they sound like them, they dress like them, they act like them. All of that is from the *Hadith* of Prophet ﷺ that, 'You'll follow people, you'll follow them. You'll follow them all the way until they take you within the hole.'

عَنْ أَبِي سَعِيدٍ الْخُدْرِيِّ، عَنِ النَّبِيِّ ﷺ قَالَ :" لَتَتْبَعُنَّ سُنَنَ مَنْ كَانَ قَبْلَكُمْ شِبْرًا شِبْرًا وَذِرَاعًا بِذِرَاعٍ، حَتَّى لَوْ دَخَلُوا جُحْرَ ضَبٍّ تَبِعْتُمُوهُمْ ." [صَحِيحُ الْبُخَارِيّ ٧٣٢٠]

'An Abi Sa'yeed Al Khudri (ra), anin Nabiyi ﷺ qala: "Latat taba'unna sunana man kana qablakum shibran shibran wa ziraan bi ziraa'in, hatta law dakhalu juhra dhabbin tabi'tumu hum."

Narrated Abu Sa'yeed Al Khudri (ra): The Prophet (pbuh) said: "You will follow the ways/customs/traditions of those nations who came before you, span by span and cubit by cubit (step by step and inch by inch). So much so that even if they were to enter a hole of a lizard, you would follow them." [Sahih al-Bukhari 7320]

187

So, they left their Islamic identity and they began to associate with these idols and begin to worship them. They give their money to them. They give their heart to them. They give their eyes, their ears, and their breath to them. We pray that Allah ﷻ destroy idol worshipping within our hearts, within our lives, within our families and our children and our communities. That He open from His blessings, this love and this *ishq* for Divinely Presence, that only Allah's ﷻ light can save us.

Be Nothing and Hide Yourself From the Eyes of Others

So, then *turuqs* (spiritual paths) come and teach, if we know that this law and this reality, that if you're under observation, you're held by that observation. Right? If ten eyes are looking at you, you're held by it. You didn't reach your reality. You're just held by their observation. Their observation is like frozen you from achieving anything.

So, *tariqahs* would come and Prophet ﷺ was teaching, 'Be nothing. Be nothing. Hide yourself and move yourself from the eye of people.' Blessed are those whom understood to hide their reality because *tariqah* training is not that you become a particle and then propagate your particle. You'll never reach your reality.

Only as a Wave Reality Can We Move Towards Muhammadun Rasulallah ﷺ

The particle's power is very limited to its material understanding. Only through your wave, if you're trained through your wave reality, where you broke it, you broke the observation; that you isolated and secluded yourself from the eyes of people and the eyes of observation. Then they began to teach you and seclude and seclude and that to open

your wave reality. Only at the wave reality, your light is moving into their realms, into their hearts, and into their souls, and into the oceans of realities and knowledges which are called *Muhammadun Rasulallah* ﷺ.

Each shaykh is a custodian of a Muhammadan secret. Each secret separate from the other. No two secrets are the same. This is *'Azhamatullah* (Allah's ﷻ Might and Magnificence). Allah ﷻ doesn't recycle. He doesn't say, 'I have to have two secrets. One for you, one for you because I'm short on secrets.' Each reality, Allah ﷻ uniquely different than the other and all of them, its key is Sayyidina Muhammad ﷺ.

Our Light Diffuses into Everything and Keeps the Knowledge of Its Experiences

Only through the wave reality, it means that only through casting your light into that ocean and into that reality, you can begin to move through

it because that light is an energy. Energy is not destroyable and energy picks up its residue everywhere it goes, right? So, the light bulb here, we're talking, the energy here says, 'I went into a light bulb. I experienced that. I went into a nuclear power plant. I experienced that. I went into a mobile phone. I went into a TV.' It's the same electricity. It's just moving and experiencing everything that Allah ﷻ wants it to experience, but it picks up the residue of what it experienced. It keeps the knowledge of what it experienced.

Now the light, which is far superior than electricity, is that when you enter into your wave reality and your light reality, your light goes everywhere. It's diffused into everything. Based on that, you are like a Google, that whatever you're asking from

DOWNLOADING

that light, it's moving into what's in Taufeeq's [audience members' name] heart and immediately retrieving all his information, right? You're not encrypted. Now they understood in their computers, they want to do that. They want to make your computer into a node, into a hub. They want to take everything off of your information and your database and your hard drives. They want to use a billion computers for computing, not one computer!

Real Guides Can Read Everything Written on Your Light

Allah ﷻ said, 'We already had this long time ago.' It means that if you  move through your soul, you're moving through the light of everything. Wherever it moves, they go. They move into your heart and into your soul. You're not encrypted, you're not locked. Through your heart and soul, they know what you're wanting and what you're asking. You're happy, you're sad, you're mad, you're glad – it's all written on your lights. You're not hiding it.

Wonder that's why they say, 'Oh, when we log on, we asked a question. We already got the answer.' Well, the one who gave you the question and the one answering you is the same. It's all from the heavens. It's all been already established on a world of light and those whom operating from that light, they're just sort of moving within that dimension. What knowledge has to be brought, the light moves into it, picks it and immediately by the speed of thought and light, that light is retrieving that knowledge back.

You Can Access Immense Knowledge With Your Wave Reality

So, it means everything is happening in the wave reality. If the student achieves their wave reality, they achieve everything; what they would call *'uloom ul awaleen wal akhireen* (knowledges of the beginning and the end), right? Because once you achieve your wave reality, there's no limit to where Allah ﷻ will send that light. That's only based on Allah ﷻ.

If He allows the *darajat* (station) of the light that, 'That light now is getting more powerful. We're allowing it to go into this realm.' They can talk above the *maqam* (station) of Sayyidina Jibreel 🖼 because their light is penetrating even deeper and deeper and deeper. As a result of penetrating, they're retrieving. They're retrieving all the informations through their light and that's how this system operates.

Your Light Sends a Signal to the Shaykh When You Attend Associations

So, when people come and sit – no matter if through TV, video – this doesn't mean anything. We're talking about the seven heavens and

above. What does a video and somebody sitting in Alabama have anything to do with it? That's so much more easier than what they're describing. As soon as people are sitting, their light is sending a signal. Their data of the light of the shaykh is moving

through all of them and picking up every signal and every necessity. Where their light is coming short, he's putting in. Where their light is in excess, what they need to know, what they need to be protected from, that system is flowing.

The one who reached the wave, it's not him. He's nothing. In his training to be nothing, he represented something. In their nothingness, they can achieve immense, immense realities because the one whom is sending the signal is reaching to everyone. So, it means that *madad* (support) that they teach, the *madad* that dressing them, the *madad*, the *madad*, the *madad*. The *madad* of all of these huge souls, their lights are flowing through them and reaching to everyone's code, reaching what they're in need of, not what they're asking from, what they're in need of.

Shaykhs Listen to Your Soul, Not Your Ego

Because with the asking, we said before is what we would call a 'terrorist' but the computer is going to pick up a NSA (National Security Agency). Your bad character inflicts terror upon your soul. The one who's talking all the time is the ego. They're not listening to

egos and seeing what the ego has a question. The ego has this, the ego has a concern, the ego has a complaint. My goodness, that's not the way anyone would operate from the heavens. They're operating from the soul, right?

They just need you to be humble enough to come forward to participate. Your soul is communicating with their light and saying that, 'This *zalim* (oppressor) is doing this. This like this, this like this,' and the co-ordinance are coming and the *najat* (salvation) is moving, the lights are flowing, whatever realities have to be bestowed are happening.

Focus On Secluding Yourself to Achieve Your Wave Reality

So, then that's why the teaching was, be nothing. Leave your particle existence; it achieves nothing, it benefits no one. A lot of particle talking but they can't reach anything or do anything. So, the *tariqahs* (spiritual paths) come and teach that you have to be a wave.

All of the *adab* (manners) of *tariqah* is don't look to other people, what you think they are or what they think they're not. But just understand the teaching from the shaykh is that you have to be nothing. You have to have achieved your wave reality. That did you isolate yourself? Did you negate yourself? Did you hide yourself? Did you find yourself?

If you negated yourself, isolated yourself, draw no attention to yourself and then you went in to find yourself. That you sat and meditated, meditated, meditated, found all your characteristics, begin to battle them, ask for *madad* and support and energy to be dressing, dressing, and blessing. As a result, they were nothing. They're not visible in pictures. They're not known to anyone and they were not known to anyone. As a result, they achieved a wave status. They were sent into seclusion and then seclusion and seclusion so that their lights would be reinforced, reinforced, reinforced.

Be Like the Seed and Stay Quiet in Difficulty Until You Become Non-Existent

Allah 🕮 shows that in nature – and we talk about it all the time – is that are you going to live your life as a seed or are you going to plant it in the soil? You know, the seeds can talk all they want but in the end it's just a seed, doesn't mean anything. But if that seed is trained in which it entered the soil and the soil began to rip it apart. So, it means they stay quiet when it's very difficult. Everybody to say this to them, that to them, it doesn't matter. That's all soil sort of crushing them.

Everyone knows stories of our own existence. There were obnoxious people always around, always casting horrible comments and that was our training. It was like a boxing match every week. Sit into a room and then  Mawlana ق would say, 'Okay, say something.' Then they would start attacking, attacking, attacking everything. You just stay quiet, stay quiet, go home and cry. That these are a bunch of clowns and what am I going to do with them? But you gave so much money, you have nowhere to run. So, I'll go back again tomorrow, and you go, you go, you go, you go until you're ripped to pieces. You have nowhere to run until the thought of running stopped, until you felt like you were already dying.

It means it's been buried, it's been buried, it's been buried. They're not visible anywhere. We're not visible on any photo. They had an existence in which was non-existent. They didn't sign up to be existent. They wanted to reach to the presence of Prophet ﷺ and the *tariqahs* (spiritual paths) come and teach that if you reach to that wave in which you isolate yourself and reach and find your character, make your *muraqabah*, make your connection.

Focus on the Shaykh During His Training and Testing, Not Where He is Now

Don't look left and right and say, 'I want to be like that, I want to be like this.' Say, 'I want to be like nothing.' They would go and I told the  gentlemen when they go to see a shaykh, they see him at his end state. [They] said, 'Look, Shaykh is talking everywhere. I want to be like that. I talk everywhere, give everybody answers that mean nothing.'

195

No, no, look to the shaykh when he was training, not when he's in the position of his guidance. How was he trained? He was in no pictures. He paid for everything but he was not seen on anything. You can't find him in anything. He didn't want to be identified as anything.

Go look to Shaykh Nazim ق and say, 'No, he has baklava and a tea' and they would all sit like that with baklavas and teas and Shaykh would say that Shaykh Nazim ق was eating from the scraps of people in London. He was so upset with people throwing away things that he was taking them out and making people, 'Eat these, eat these.' How much he suffered, how much he went into seclusion.

He went to seclusion, five-year-old daughter died and he didn't come out of seclusion. He didn't quickly go and apologize to somebody and run for this and run for that out of fear and scared. They stayed in seclusion. They were men. They're lions of Allah ﷻ. Nothing interferes with Allah's ﷻ command for them. It means look to their character of what they were, how they got to where they got to go.

You Can Only Acquire Ijazah in Your Wave Form

It means that when they trained to be a wave, everything was broken down. They achieved a wave status and each wave may be even stronger than the other but they have to be a wave and only through their wave reality, they will be recruited by Prophet ﷺ.

It doesn't matter what anyone says, 'You're this. You're that. You're *khalifa* (representative) this, you're *khalifa* that.' That's all their own stuff. None of those titles matter until they're recruited by Prophet ﷺ. That your wave status is achieved and as a result, you talk. Because of the strength that you have in your wave reality with the *ijazah* (authorization), we give you to talk. Their particle form won't be confined by the eyes of people because they achieved the light. They achieved the wave.

You Will Not Experience Growth When You're Locked by People's Eyes

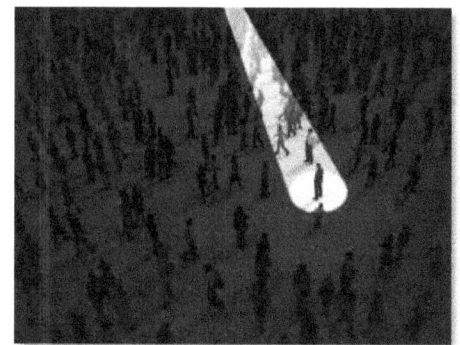

If you don't achieve the wave and you put yourself as particle, their eyes will lock you. Big shaykh in Pakistan was asked by his shaykh, 'You want particle or you want wave? You want to be *zahiri 'ulama*, external *'ulama* (scholar) or internal *'ulama*?' He said, 'External.'

It means you'll be locked by the eyes of people, you'll have no growth. I think now I think he realized he wants to be internal *'ulama*. He went back to Rumi ﷺ poetry. So, as much as people grab you, nothing will happen. You can memorize books and an orator and you'll speak out what you memorized, but the reality of wave and *malakut* (heavenly realm) is that you achieved the light and it reached to them and your light, like an energy, is connected to us and transmitting.

When Your Wave Reality is Established, You Cannot Be Bound By Others

As a result of your light committed and transmitting to us, we're sending you *faiz* (downpouring blessings) and you're receiving. As a result of this connection, we're going to let you now to talk, represent us because you're connected to us. You are a connected individual. Your *ijazah* (authorization) says you are connected.

As a result of that connection, they have that ability that the particle form – it means that when they're presenting themself, people's eyes are not holding them to anything because they have their wave energy already is established. They can reach anywhere to anyone at any time.

Connect With Your Heart to Transform Your Particle Into Wave Reality

So, their wave movement is always moving but their particle is being grasped by people and the people say, 'I only see him in the particle form.' They teach, 'Well, connect with your heart.' If you grab him in his particle form and connect your heart, immediately that light of his wave will hit into your heart and you begin to see his wave reality. That's what's important.

That they'll hold you and begin to send you lights within your heart and into your being and in your soul and begin to energize you and build you.

If you take from their example that what they begin to send to you of lights and emanations, you stay quiet. Don't show yourself so that they can dress you and annihilate you. As a result of that, there are students around the world who are achieving their wave reality and that's all that's important, not the particle. The particle is of no value to them. If they achieved the wave reality, then from amongst those, they'll be recruited and brought into the presence of Prophet ﷺ. At that time, they have a purpose and a reality. It means then from these, they all have to be from the wave reality.

Categories of Saints Who Aren't in Need of Speaking

From amongst these *rijal* (people of maturity) whom entered into their wave reality, some may be given service from Prophet ﷺ that requires no talking, right? So, you have categories of *Abdal* that are known and unknown; the *Budala*, whom they are the representatives that can be and hidden. So then in this category of understanding, because they're all of their wave reality, the one that Prophet ﷺ only from a few say, 'Now you talk to represent us.' But there are others whom Prophet ﷺ says, 'No need for you to talk. Absolutely no one should know you.'

As a result of no one knowing you, their wave reality is not confined to anything and they're everywhere at all times. They can manifest 24,000 places at the same time, enter into any association, and you don't even know who they are. As a result of not being observed, they serve the nation in that capacity. You understanding? [Shaykh asks audience]. So, if people know you, you can't be like that. Say, 'I just saw him in Indonesia. Look, I take a photo, I just saw him in Alabama. I just saw him in Texas.' It won't happen because that one's responsibility talk and not from that reality.

Then there are those of the *Abdal, Nuqaba*, you don't see them at all. You don't even know who they are and the reason you don't know is so that they're free to move in their wave format in any place, at any time, at anywhere. They appear, you don't know how they appeared and they vanished. You don't know how they vanished because you don't know them. So there is no eye watching them. As a result of no eye watching them, they serve the nation in that specific understanding.

The Rijal (Men of God) are Present in Your Prayer, Spiritually Working on You

They enter into your *salah* (daily prayer) and begin to move into your heart to fix what's necessary and you don't even know their presence is there. They don't even have to manifest. That's why when you call upon *rijalullah* (men of God), Allah ﷻ has many tools at His disposal. Whatever you can think of *dunya* (material world) having, Allah ﷻ has infinite more of its realities.

So, those *rijal* (people of maturity) whom are of a very powerful wave reality, when you're making *du'a* (supplication) and asking at *Fajr* (dawn prayer) time, making your *madad* (support), they're coming. You don't see their spirituality. You don't even see their wave form and they can be right in your face moving right into your heart, correcting your *lataifs* (subtle energy points), correcting everything that's wrong within your being. A sickness, they can come immediately to take that sickness away. By its healing, they can come in a physical format.

Shaykh Abdullah Daghestani's ق Powerful Reality

Shaykh Daghestani ق was one of the powerful ones of that reality. He

said many times when he was younger, his shaykh was sending him places to do things. There was somebody who was sick with tuberculosis at that time. [Shaykh Dahgestani ق] Said, 'I was sent by my shaykh to an individual. I appeared, went to the individual, say I've been sent for your *shifa* and your healing. You've been told to eat horse meat.' He began to eat the horse meat. They located where to get

horse meat. He ate the horse meat to take away his tuberculosis. Then he [Shaykh Dahgestani ق] said, 'Immediately with that power, I went back to my shaykh and I was being continuously dispatched.'

Tariqah is a Path in Which to Be Nothing

So, it means these *Tazkiratul Awliya* (Biographies of the Saints) and the story of *awliya* (saints), there are many. They have a job. They have a purpose, but the main point of tonight is that they all accomplished the wave

reality and that's why the *tariqahs* (spiritual paths) come, not just to bother people. 'Be nothing, be nothing, be nothing.' It's just you feel a pity if somebody is going to keep being a particle and they're not going to ever reach to their wave reality.

So, the *tariqah* comes to teach, you're losing the concept. The concept of this path is to be nothing. If you achieve that nothingness, Allah 'ﷻ opens for you the science of it because the wave only moves as a wave when it's not observed. You don't have the power of the observation until you're mature.

Angels Observe You Until You Become Spiritually Mature

So when you isolate, you've gone into another first rule. You're not under observation but the angels are observing you and so they're keeping you to be locked because it takes a key. So, as they're being blocked from observation that, '*Ya Rabbi*, I'm not letting anyone to look to me and I'm taking a life in which to continuously be nothing, be nothing, be nothing.'

But the angels are watching you and that's when Allah 'ﷻ wants clarification, 'What's their character?' They have to reach to a level of purity in which their character has sincerity and Allah 'ﷻ begin then to unlock in which Allah 'ﷻ tell the angels that, 'This one, this *rijal* (people of maturity) is sincere and no longer you have to observe that individual. He will be responsible to observe himself. As a result, he can enter his wave format at any time.' The angels don't lock him to be under observation.

Imam Ali ؏ is the Master of Wave Reality

We pray that Allah 'ﷻ dress us and bless us from the immensity of what Allah 'ﷻ has given, *"Wa laqad karramna bani adam."*

$$\{ ٧٠ \} ... \text{وَلَقَدْ كَرَّمْنَا بَنِي آدَمَ}$$

17:70 – "Wa laqad karramna bani adama..." (Surat Al-Isra)

"And We have certainly honored the children of Adam..."
(The Night Journey, 17:70)

That the immensity of what Allah ﷻ has given, "*Subhana man huwal Khaliq anNur.*" This is the month (Rajab) in which Allah ﷻ opens the realities of lights and opens the realities of seclusions and the *baab* and the gate of that reality, Imam Ali ﷺ.

$$\text{سُبْحَانَ مَنْ هُوَ الْخَالِقَ النُّورْ}$$

"Subhana man huwal Khaliq anNur"

"Glory to Him who is the Creator, the Light"

That *muhabbat*, that love, that *ihtiram* and respect is an immensity for the sword of nothingness. It means *Ulul Ahbab*, the People of the Door, their *imam* (religious leader) is Imam Ali ﷺ, teaching them that, 'With my *Zulfiqar* (sword of Imam Ali ﷺ), take off their head, take off their bad character, take off their thinking, take off all that their *nafs* (ego) is saying and enter into this ocean of nothingness.'

Sainthood Cannot Be Granted Without Imam Ali's ﷺ Approval

He is the master of the wave reality, the one whom signs upon *wilayat* and sainthood for anyone to achieve it. The order must come from *"Atiullah wa atiur Rasul wa ulil amre..."*

...أَطِيعُوا اللهَ وَأَطِيعُوا الرَّسُولَ وَأُولِي الأَمْرِ مِنكُمْ... ﴿٥٩﴾

4:59 – "...Atiullaha wa atiur Rasula wa Ulil amre minkum..."
(Surat An-Nisa)

"... Obey Allah, Obey the Messenger, and those in authority among you..." (The Women, 4:59)

He is the king of the *Ulul Amr* (saints) to sign for that reality when an order comes from Prophet ﷺ that, 'This one is going to be in the training  of nothingness.' When they achieve that nothingness, then Imam Ali ؑ has to sign its certificate of sainthood. This is from *Imam ar-Rabbani* ؓ in the Naqshbandi *tariqah* (spiritual path) confirming. We pray that Allah ﷻ dress us, bless us with the immensities of the *tariqah*, the immensity of the holy companions, the immensity of all the *Ahlul Bayt* (Holy Family of Prophet ﷺ), all *awliyaullah* (saints) *fis samayi wa fil ard* (in the heavens and on earth) and what Allah ﷻ has given to this Muhammadan kingdom, *inshaAllah*.

Subhana rabbika rabbal 'izzati 'amma yasifoon, wa salaamun 'alal mursaleen, walhamdulillahi rabbil 'aalameen. Bi hurmati Muhammad al-Mustafa wa bi siri Surat al-Fatiha.

Third Power

Haqiqatut Tawajjuh

Reality of Directing to the Divinely Face

Meditation is the Foundation for Receiving the Nazar and Tawajjuh

Meditation is the Foundation of Knowing Yourself

It's like building a house. If we want to talk about the roof and the windows but yet we didn't lay the foundation. So, this system that's taught is a systematic way of teaching that worry about the energy, worry about how to practice the energy.

90% of the replies to everyone who emails helpme@nurmuhammad.com is meditate because your question shows

you didn't meditate. The other person emails a question – they didn't meditate. You keep saying, why did I keep getting all these replies saying meditation?' It's because this is the foundation. If you're not doing the practice, you're not understanding energy. You're not spending the time to make your *tafakkur* (contemplation). You're not spending the time to make the connection with the shaykhs to ask for *faiz* (downpouring emanation) and ask for an accounting. 'What is my character? What is my *hisaab* (account)?' You don't want to know these things?

The Energy of the Shaykh is Like a Truth Serum

Many people are not comfortable to sit and meditate because they don't  want to know about themselves. If you're bold enough to find out about yourself, then the next phase is, 'I want to reach towards this energy. I want the energy of the shaykhs to be present with me.'

Because they're like a truth serum. If their light comes, it's going to force you to understand what you've done wrong. Because the light of truth comes and it doesn't keep a lie with you and agree with you in your lies. You with yourself are sufficient to lie to yourself, 'Oh, I'm the best. Everything is great. Everything I'm doing is perfect, perfect, thank you, *mashaAllah*. I'm great.'

The Truthful Guide Will Show Your Character Defects

But when you meditate and ask for Allah's ﷻ servants, *"Wa kono ma'as sadiqeen, ittaqollah."* Allah ﷻ says in Holy Qur'an, 'Have a consciousness and keep the company.'

يَا أَيُّهَا الَّذِينَ آمَنُوا اتَّقُوا اللهَ وَكُونُوا مَعَ الصَّادِقِينَ ﴿١١٩﴾

9:119 – "Ya ayyuhal ladheena amanoo ittaqollaha wa kono ma'as sadiqeen." (Surat At-Tawbah)

"O you who have believed, have consciousness of Allah and be with those who are truthful/ Pious/ sincere (in words and deed)."
(The Repentance, 9:119)

It means we keep the company all the time. It wasn't a physical. Allah ﷻ doesn't care about physicality. 'Keep their company.' So as soon as you meditate, this was Allah's ﷻ command, *"Wa kono ma'as sadiqeen."* So, you're meditating

and asking for *sadiq* (truthful), *'Ya Rabbi*, send Your *rijalullah* (men of God).'

As soon as you're sitting, their energy comes and begin a truth. What you did was wrong, what your character did is wrong. Why you're angry is wrong. All these things will come because they don't come to lie with you. They come to inspire that, 'What you're thinking was wrong. The character you had was wrong. The arrogance you have is wrong.' All of these characteristics. It comes with a truthful light into our life so that we can begin to work on ourselves.

Take the Path of Purification to Receive the Shaykh's Faiz

Nobody is saying they're perfect but at least they took a path in which to try. Perfection is only for Allah ﷻ. This is not a path of perfection. This is a path in trying. If you don't try, it's like going into the grave with cancer. You came into the grave without trying anything? Well, that's 70,000 times more difficult.

This life is about trying to clean ourselves, trying to recognize what I'm doing bad, trying to be inspired towards goodness. As a result, that's the foundation. When we did that and we meditated, we made the foundation. We made the connection with the shaykhs, the *faiz* of the shaykhs is coming – the rest of all those questions will become clear. That you work through all the bad characteristics. Then the *faiz* (downpouring emanation) of the shaykhs are coming, the energy is coming.

Allah ﷻ Increases the Voltage of Energy in Doses

We said before that as soon as you do the *madad* (support) and begin to do the practices, you feel energies coming onto you and they grab your heart. You feel like you're having a heart attack and you don't have to go to the hospital. You don't have to run anywhere. This is the *jalali tajalli* (majestic manifestation) that Allah ﷻ reflect onto the servant. We said it's like an earthquake. The immense positive light

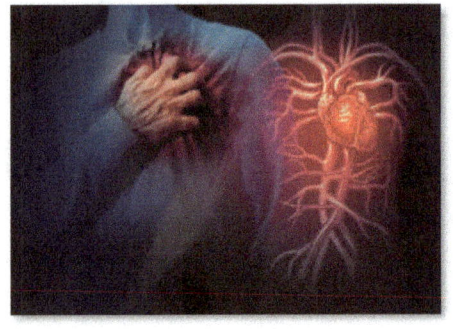

that reflecting, it conflicts with the negative standard light of people, right? So the low voltage, you're bringing on a high voltage. So, that high voltage, when it hits you, of course it creates a shock.

It keeps going up. So you're 50 watts today, you got hit and you do this again and Allah ﷻ says, 'Increase his voltage.' More light comes, again hit the person, and they go into a shock. They go into shaking because Allah ﷻ keeps increasing in doses. It never reaches a point where it just keeps flowing to you. This energy – Allah ﷻ is of an infinite capacity of power. Every time it comes with a *jalali tajalli*, of course, it's going to shake, it's going to crush. It's going to shake everything.

We Need Energy Training to Avoid Physical Health Issues

When it comes too much, then there are different difficulties upon the body. Because this energy is running on the spine and running throughout their system. They can overheat, their veins have difficulty. So, everything has to be through their training, through understanding, through moderation. If they send

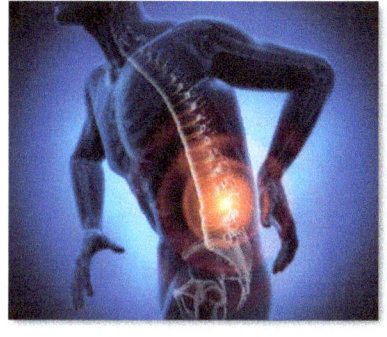

too much energy to somebody, they can have problems in their spine, their vertebrae and many heated issues throughout their body.

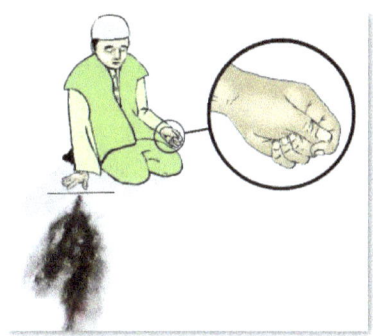

That's why they train them on how to bring the energy in, how to keep their *wudu* (ablution). How to ground their energy so that the positive is flowing, pushing the negative and grounding it out. Not to catch it and just keep it going around until it pop out of a vein and you get like something happening onto your body because the energy has to leave at a particular way. If you don't, then many different types of difficulty. That's why everything is going to go by step – step by step, step by step, and a gradual increase of energy and *faiz* (downpouring emanation). That's what is meant by the *faiz* of the shaykh.

Faiz of the Shaykh is From His Haqiqatut Tawajjuh (Reality of Directing to Divinely Face)

When we talk like this, other shaykhs who listen, they say, 'Oh, we never heard this stuff before.' That's okay because you shouldn't be discussing these teachings with any other shaykh. Each shaykh has a different understanding and maybe at a very different level. It's not handed out for everybody at the same.

The understanding of when people say, 'Get the *faiz* of the shaykh. Keep your *nazar* (gaze) upon us,' what does the *nazar* and the *faiz* mean? From their *Haqiqatut Tawajjuh* (Reality of Directing to Divinely Face) when they achieved *Haqiqatut Tawajjuh* and *Haqiqatut Tawassul* (Reality of Conveyance).

Haqiqatut Tawajjuh is that they were trained, and they were trained that when you reach to the *Hawla wa la quwwah* (there is no support, nor power) through the *wajh* (face). From their face to the face of Sayyidina Muhammad's ﷺ *ruhaniyat* (spirituality) is a *tawajjuh*. It means they're receiving  from the face onto their soul. They achieve those realities and that power is dressing continuously on them.

وَلَا حَوْلَ وَلَا قُوَّةَ إِلَّا بِاللهِ الْعَلِيِّ الْعَظِيمِ

"Wa laa hawla wa la quwwata illa billahil 'Aliyyil 'Azheem."

"And there is no Support/strength, nor power except by Allah, The Sublimely Exalted, The Magnificent."

Haqiqatut Tawassul (Reality of Conveyance) to the Holy Face

The *tawassul* is that through that same connection, they can pray back that, 'Please resolve this. Pray for this. Do to this.' They're not using physical. They're using from the connection of their soul which is an ocean of power.

So, normal people say, 'Oh, *nazar* – we've heard that.' Other people who know *tariqah* (spiritual path), they say, '*Faiz* – the *faiz* of the shaykh,' But can they explain it? Because you have to be from it.

Many Holy Faces Can Dress the Face of the Shaykh

The *Haqiqatut Tawajjuh* (Reality of Directing to Divinely Face) and *Haqiqatut Tawassul* (Reality of Conveyance), that they reached to a place in which their face reached the face of power. That face can keep alternating from the face of Sayyidina Muhammad ﷺ to the face of their shaykhs and *Ahlul Bayt* (Holy family of Prophet ﷺ) and *Ashab an Nabi* ﷺ (Holy companions of Prophet ﷺ).

One whom has an open heart in the associations, many faces are changing on the shaykh throughout the association. Throughout the whole *shajarah* (spiritual lineage), throughout all *Ahlul Bayt* can be dressing the face of the shaykh at any moment during the *khatms*, the *zikrs* (Divine remembrance) and the *mawlids* (celebration of the birthday of Prophet ﷺ) because that's the reality of that *tawajjuh*.

Tawassul is the way in which they convey their concerns and the needs of what's being needed upon this Earth from the servants of Allah ﷻ back and towards the oceans of power, *inshaAllah*.

Subhana rabbika rabbal 'izzati 'amma yasifoon, wa salaamun 'alal mursaleen, walhamdulillahi rabbil 'aalameen. Bi hurmati Muhammad al-Mustafa wa bi siri Surat al-Fatiha.

First Become Liquid and Establish Tawajjuh With Your Shaykh

Heavenly Knowledges are Needed Nowadays for Survival

Alhamdulillah, in this blessed month and the immensity of the Divine mirror and all that is being inspired within the hearts and the guidance and love and *ishq* of Sayyidina Muhammad ﷺ. As days become more difficult, the realities become more essential. What was once maybe for a benefit of seeking knowledge and feeling that, that knowledge was of some excitement, the knowledge now becomes more of a survival.

That, the direct remedy and the key for every difficulty has to be understood as things are becoming more and more negative and things become more and more confused. Then Allah ﷻ wants for those whom believe and *'ashiqeen* (lovers), those whom have a path of love. That you don't have to look left and right but you have to connect and to build the love and *ishq* for Sayyidina Muhammad ﷺ and that to love Prophet ﷺ more than we love ourselves. When every other love and every other thing in this *dunya* (material world) is of a disappointing and the love that is eternal, and the relationship that is eternal, is the most important.

عَنْ أَنَسِ بْنِ مَالِكٍ رَضِيَ اللهُ عَنْهُ قَالَ، قَالَ رَسُولُ اللهِ ﷺ: " لاَ يُؤْمِنُ أَحَدُكُمْ حَتَّى أَكُونَ أَحَبَّ إِلَيْهِ مِنْ وَالِدِهِ وَوَلَدِهِ وَالنَّاسِ أَجْمَعِينَ. "

[صَحِيحُ مُسْلِمٍ، حديث ٤٤، وَالْبُخَاري، كِتَابُ الْإِيْمَانْ، حديث ١٥]

"'An Anas ibn Malik (ra) qala, qala Rasulullahi ﷺ: La yuminu ahadukum hatta akona ahabba ilayhi min walidihi wa waladihi wan nasi ajma'yeen."
[Sahih Muslim, Hadith 44, wa Al Bukhari, Kitabul Iman, Hadith 15]

"Narrated by Anas son of Malik (ra) that Prophet Muhammad (pbuh) said: None of you will have faith till he loves me more than his father, his children, and all mankind."
[Authentic by Muslim, Hadith 44 & by Al Bukhari, Book of Faith, Hadith 15]

Our Love of Sayyidina Muhammad ﷺ is the Security of Our Faith

It means that love and that *ishq* of Allah ﷻ that He wants us to connect and make the connection with the love and the reality of Sayyidina Muhammad ﷺ. That becomes then the clarity of our faith, the security of our faith.

Then we begin to understand how different the knowledge is and the reality of *awliyaullah* (saints) from common people. That what was talked about last week; that the reality of our *salah* (daily prayer) and that the presence of the holy face of Sayyidina Muhammad ﷺ and it's in the dialogue. It's in the words, it's in all of the teachings. *Alhamdulillah*, it's *Maqamul Ihsan* (Station of Moral Excellence). It is the state of perfection.

Real Guides Achieve Their Status Through Spiritual Connection

These are also from the realities of the powers of the heart; the *Haqiqatut Tawajjuh* (Reality of Directing to Divinely Face) and *Haqiqatut Tawassul* (Reality of Conveyance). It means these realities are the essence of spirituality and the mastering of spiritual realities. What makes the student a student and qualified as a teacher is their  connection. It means it's not the concept of memorizing books and being a professor at a university teaching spirituality. But it's the understanding from the shaykh's knowledges that we achieved that and we took a path in which to receive and achieve.

Suit Up, Show Up, and Stay Quiet to Lose Your Form

In the teachings of the levels of the heart, in the teachings of the six powers of the heart, in the teachings of a star and the formation of a star, in which Prophet ﷺ describe, 'Follow my companions, any one of them is a star on a dark night.'

أَصْحَابِيْ كَالنُّجُـومْ بِأَيِّهِمْ اَقْتَدَيْتِمْ اَهْتَدَيْتِمْ

"Ashabi kan Nujoom, bi ayyihim aqta daytum ahta daytum."

"My companions are like stars. Whoever among them you follow, you will be rightly guided." Prophet Muhammad (pbuh)

217

These are all the beads that when we put our string and make this *tasbih* (prayer beads), make this *zikr* (Divine remembrance), and this praise of ours towards the Divine reality, they all connect. That we're trying to be a star and lose our form. We want to enter that which is eternal and the material world has to be brought down and the *malakut* (heavenly realm) and the spiritual realm has to be superior.

The gentlemen released the video on Saturday, and again, the miraculous nature of those talks; [they] could be a year ago. Somehow, they're inspired in which to formulate the talk, choose the talk. I don't choose the talks that are going to be aired and then from their choice they put things together and then it airs and it coincides with what's been talking about and the whole spirituality of what's been on the subject matter of 'Losing Our Mass.' So, it gives always an *isharah* (sign) that there's a Divine curriculum.

We suit up, show up and stay quiet so that the inspiration comes to us, both teacher and student. Because we're all students and see what Allah ﷻ, through the holy tongue of Sayyidina Muhammad ﷺ and inspiration of *awliyaullah* reach to us and what they want for us. So, you see then the talks then it coordinates with the videos that are being aired so that the curriculum is already been formed. We just show up and we try to take what they want for us to understand that this path of spirituality and losing our matter. So, those whom are science-heavy and say, 'Where is all of this?' It's in everything that we do.

Crushing Our Solid State is the Foundation of Our Spirituality

So, if we lose the matter and the solidness, what happens? That becomes the foundation of our spirituality and the solid only burns through heat. That heat can be *nafsani* (egocentric) or *ruhani* (spiritual). It means either Allah ﷻ can crush you physically with immense amounts of tests or we subject ourself and say, 'I don't need to be crushed. I don't need for You to to bang me left and right and smash and then have every type of difficulty come to me, *ya Rabbi*. I want to come through my *ishq* and love and I want to be hard on myself and meditate and contemplate. I bring the fire of spirituality on myself and upon myself to understand and how to stay quiet, how to be patient, how to look to my faults and my wrongdoings and correct them and assume that all my faults are seen by everyone.'

Assume Your Faults are Seen By Everyone

If you don't have that assumption, then you're not really in their school. If, for any reason, you feel that you can do something and that they don't see it, that's not a student of the way. That's not the *adab* and the manners of that student.

That we talked about before when Shaykh Abdul Qadir ق was telling his students, 'Go slaughter this chicken where Allah ﷻ won't see you.' But what he really wanted to find is that whatever you think of Allah ﷻ of seeing, Prophet ﷺ sees because Allah ﷻ in *Hadith al Qudsi* (Holy Hadith) says, 'I'll be the seeing in which you see.'

عَنْ أَبِي هُرَيْرَةِ رَضِيّ اللهُ عَنْهُ قَالَ، قَالَ
رَسُولُ اللهِ ﷺ : إِنَّ اللهَ تَعَالَىٰ قَالَ:"... وَلَا
يَزَالُ عَبْدِي يَتَقَرَّبُ إِلَيَّ بِالنَّوَافِلِ حَتَّى أُحِبَّهُ،
فَإِذَا أَحْبَبْتُهُ كُنت سَمْعَهُ الَّذِي يَسْمَعُ بِهِ، وَبَصَرَهُ الَّذِي يُبْصِرُ بِهِ، ..."
[حَدِيثٌ اَلْقُدْسِي – اَلْمَصْدَرْ: صَحِيحُ الْبُخَارِي – رقم:٦٥٠٢]

"'An Abi Hurairah (ra) qala, Qala Rasulullahi ﷺ: InnAllaha ta'ala qala: ..., wa la yazaalu 'Abdi yataqarrabu ilayya bin nawafile hatta ahebahu, fa idha ahbabtuhu kunta Sam'ahul ladhi yasma'u behi, wa Basarahul ladhi yubsiru behi, ..."
[Hadith Qudsi, Sahih al Bukhari, Raqam: 6502)

"Narrated by Abu Hurairah (ra) that: the Messenger of Allah (pbuh) said that: Allah the Almighty said: ...My servant continues to draw near to Me with voluntary acts of worship so that I shall love him. When I love him, I am his hearing with which he hears, his seeing with which he sees, ..." [Holy Hadith, Authentic by al-Bukhari, # 6502]

What Prophet ﷺ Receives From Allah ﷻ, He Gives to Ulul Amr (Saints) and Angels

So, it means then Allah ﷻ gave this quality of *nazar* (gaze) on Sayyidina Muhammad ﷺ. He sees his nation and Prophet ﷺ gives that seeing to his *Ulul Amr* and to his angels. *Malaika* (angels), they take from the power of Sayyidina  Muhammad ﷺ because it's *"Atiullah, atiur Rasul."*

...أَطِيعُواللَّهَ وَأَطِيعُواللرَّسُولَ وَأُوْلِي الأَمْرِ مِنْكُمْ... ﴿٥٩﴾

4:59 – "...Atiullaha wa atiur Rasula wa Ulil amre minkum..."
(Surat An-Nisa)

"... Obey Allah, Obey the Messenger, and those in authority among you..." (The Women, 4:59)

Not *"Atiullah, atiul malaikah and atiur Rasul."* The angels only take from the authority of what Prophet ﷺ gives to them. They're considered *Ulul Amr.* So it means that *"Atiur Rasul"* is the highest. So, whatever Prophet ﷺ is receiving, then he's giving that out. So, it means then the student is aware that the shaykhs are watching me, the angels are watching me, Prophet ﷺ is watching me and then my life is about testing, losing my solid state.

The Liquid State and Meditation are Essential to Become Patient

As soon as I lose my solid state and I feel the burn, I feel the difficulty, I'm trying with all my life to be patient and I see the sadness everywhere that this difficulty encompasses. As a result of their sacrifices and their choices in life, things become heavy and difficult. As a result, they  keep melting and melting and melting but as a benefit of that melt, they become very liquid.

The liquid state gives them a sense of patience. With that patience, they're able to accomplish what Allah ﷻ wants. That, *Haqiqatut Tawajjuh* is then from their liquid state; that in their liquid state they're continuously meditating. Otherwise, how could you be patient if you don't meditate? Every difficulty comes, you want to yell and scream or do something with your mouth or hands to resolve. You can't! So, the meditation becomes the essential part of life in which they go into their *muraqabah*, they go into their connection. They cry unto their lord, they ask Prophet ﷺ, they ask *awliyaullah* and that whole relationship is the key for their success and that becomes their *tawajjuh*.

Allah ﷻ Granted Us an Audience With Sayyidina Muhammad ﷺ Five Times a Day!

That's what was being taught last week. So, it means these are all the same subject. These are all coming in different ways for students to understand. That if we want our *salah* to be real, Allah ﷻ is showing us that if you're doubting the importance of *Milad* (celebration of the birthday of Prophet ﷺ), you  doubt the importance of the love of Sayyidina Muhammad ﷺ, Allah ﷻ, five times a day is granting us an audience, an audience with Sayyidina Muhammad ﷺ. That, 'His holy face will be looking at you,' and, 'I would not have sent him' – because that makes sense now – 'I would not have sent him except that he's a mercy for all of creation.'

وَمَا أَرْسَلْنَاكَ إِلَّا رَحْمَةً لِّلْعَالَمِينَ ﴿١٠٧﴾

21:107 – "Wa maa arsalnaka illa Rahmatal lil'alameen."
(Surat Al-Anbiya)

"And We have not sent you, [O Muhammad (pbuh)], except as a mercy to the worlds/creation." (The Prophets, 21:107)

223

Salah is the Most Blessed Gift Creation Can Receive

It means, 'I'm sending his holy *nazar* to be upon you in every *salah*.' The

reason for your *salah* is so that the *nazar* of Prophet ﷺ will be on his nation. The greatest nation, the most blessed nation in which Allah ﷻ granted them the greatest gift is the *nazar* and the face of Sayyidina Muhammad ﷺ looking at his

nation, praying for his nation. That, when I see their *'amal* (actions) because every time you go into *salah*, that *'amal* is shown to that Divinely face. If it's good he says, '*Alhamdulillah*,' and praises Allah ﷻ that, 'Oh, these servants their *'amal* and actions were good.' If the *'amals* are bad – and the overwhelming tide now is the *'amal* is bad – and, 'I ask Allah ﷻ for forgiveness.' This is the most immense and most blessed gift that creation can receive.

قَالَ رَسُولُ اللهِ ﷺ: "... تُعْرَضُ عَلَيَّ أَعْمَالُكُمْ، فَإِنْ رَأَيْتُ خَيْرًا حَمِدْتُ اللهَ، وَإِنْ رَأَيْتُ غَيْرَ ذَلِكَ اسْتَغْفَرْتُ اللهَ لَكُمْ."

Qala Rasulullahi ﷺ*, "... Tu'radu 'alayya 'amalukum, fa in ra'itu khayran hamidtu Allah, wa in ra'aytu ghayra dhalik astaghfartullaha lakum."*

The Messenger of Allah, Prophet Muhammad (pbuh) said: "... I observe the deeds of my ummah/Nation. If I find good [in it] I thank/praise Allah, and if I see bad, I ask forgiveness for them/on their behalf."

Shaykhs Inherit the Love and Softness From Prophet ﷺ

That's why the gift of Prophet ﷺ amongst all the gifts of all the messengers of Allah ﷻ was intercession. He's the grand intercessor in which his soul intercedes for all of creation. That *tawajjuh*  means the connection to the holy face; that becomes our lifeline. When we meditate and connect and before we can reach to that reality, then we're connecting with the shaykh.

As we have that love for the shaykh because the love for Prophet ﷺ is still unknown to those who come in fresh. They say, 'I don't know what Prophet ﷺ is like but I like the way that you teach. I like the way that you're loving. I like the way that everything is soft and everything is fragrant.' We found Prophet ﷺ through the love and the accompanying of Mawlana Shaykh ق. Because the *kamil* and the perfected example of love and compassion and such a mercy in which you said if this man represents mercy, my God, imagine what Prophet ﷺ was like.

Holy Companions Had an Immense Love for Sayyidina Muhammad ﷺ

 How his companions had such an immense love they would have died instantly if that was asked of them. It means they loved so much beyond the love of themselves, they would have done anything and they did anything for the love of Sayyidina Muhammad ﷺ. That becomes the reality of the *tariqah* (spiritual path). So that when

we're connecting, we're connecting with the shaykhs. We're asking to build that love, that connection. Ask that, 'I want to be in the presence of your face that your face to dress me, to bless me and I see myself as nothing.' Silencing my mind that, 'I don't have questions. I don't have my active mind.' Shutting that mind down and asking that, 'You fill my heart with light and reflect that light into my heart.'

All of those were the daily practices to build the *tawajjuh*, to build that connection because that *tawajjuh* becomes essential. Building the connection with the holy face, from the face of the shaykh and his spiritual face to the face of Sayyidina Muhammad ﷺ, to the face of Allah ﷻ Almighty, whatever that may be understood from people who understand. The building of that is the whole of this reality and power that coming and the dress that comes upon humanity.

Tawassul (Conveyance): Face to Face Through Established Connection

As a result of that face and those whom connect with the face, what then is the next step? If you can connect with a face, you can convey. *Tawassul* – I can convey my concerns if I'm connected. If somebody give you a phone and you need to call  India but you don't have a phone, what do you do? You go to your friend who has a phone and say, 'Can you call India for me please?' That's a *tawassul*. By means of that phone, you're going to contact where you have to contact. Well, that's why people go to the shaykhs who are connected. They trust in them. They know that their hearts are connected. Their love and *ishq* is the example of their fruit.

How do you have a tree that claims to love Prophet ﷺ but bears no fruit of that love, never speaks of that love, never gives an example of that love? It's a fruitless tree; something must be wrong. But the tree that continuously gives the fruits of that *ishq* and that love, well then, you know they're like a mobile phone. You go to them and say, 'Please, I need to make a call. Call them. Tell into the heavens my concern. Tell the issue into the heavens of this is my difficulty,' and that becomes the understanding and the concept that they use their *tawajjuh*. They use their connection with that face and all the faces that they've been trained with. That those faces are the faces that dress them and bless them and as a result of connecting, they're now capable of asking. And that's the *tawassul*.

Without a Connection, You're Screaming From a Closet Instead of Using a Smartphone

They convey because they have now a connection. They have a mobile phone that has video and audio. That's why other people, their prayers are like somebody who goes into a closet and screams to India, right? They don't see anything. They don't really even know what they're conveying to, who they're conveying. If they deny the love of Prophet ﷺ, can you imagine who they're conveying their concerns to? If they think it's to Allah ﷻ, Allah's ﷻ, 'Why you're not asking and loving Prophet ﷺ?' Maybe the *imam* (religious leader) whom is guiding you of *shaitan* (satan) and *shaitanic* thinking is distracting and diverting you. So, you can see how the blind and how difficult the interaction of the blind would be.

Tariqah Shaykhs are Connected Through Face, Heart, and Soul

The blessings of *tariqah* that Allah ﷻ gave to the *tariqahs* is that they're connected. As a result of being connected, they connected their heart, their face and their soul. As a result of that connection, they begin to convey. It doesn't mean it will be accepted and they don't convey every *du'a* (supplication). They know when to convey and when not to convey. It means they know when Allah's ﷻ hearing and seeing and that's enough. But if

they have to intervene to make the conveyance to Prophet ﷺ and then they have that ability, but is rarely used. But these are the realities that save us from the immense difficulties that are coming and that this love and this *ishq*, it has a purpose. It has a direction and a goal.

Become Liquid By Loving Sayyidina Muhammad ﷺ

If we can reduce our 'material' and 'matter' and 'the reality for trying to

keep our form' and enter more into the liquid state, that liquid state is more applicable to connect, more able to connect. That's what becomes essential in all of these teachings and this is all to perfect the station of faith in which we love Sayyidina Muhammad ﷺ more than we love ourselves.

عَنْ أَنَسِ بْنِ مَالِكٍ رَضِيَ اللهُ عَنْهُ قَالَ، قَالَ رَسُولُ اللهِ ﷺ: " لاَ يُؤْمِنُ أَحَدُكُمْ حَتَّى أَكُونَ أَحَبَّ إِلَيْهِ مِنْ وَالِدِهِ وَوَلَدِهِ وَالنَّاسِ أَجْمَعِينَ."

[صَحِيحُ مُسْلِمٍ، حديث ٤٤، وَالْبُخَارِي، كِتَابُ الْإِيْمَانِ، حديث ١٥]

'"An Anas ibn Malik (ra) qala, qala Rasulullahi ﷺ: La yuminu ahadukum hatta akona ahabba ilayhi min walidihi wa waladihi wan nasi ajma'yeen."
[Sahih Muslim, Hadith 44, wa Al Bukhari, Kitabul Iman, Hadith 15]

"Narrated by Anas son of Malik (ra) that Prophet Muhammad (pbuh) said: None of you will have faith till he loves me more than his father, his children, and all mankind."
[Authentic by Muslim, Hadith 44 & by Al Bukhari, Book of Faith, Hadith 15]

As a result, the servant be granted the light of *iman* (faith). With that light of *iman*, that can reach to *Maqamul Ihsan* where every prayer is they see their Lord and they know that their Lord is continuously seeing them. That's where we started – is if you want to reach to that, you have to know that your Lord sees you.

عَنْ أَبِي هُرَيْرَةَ رَضِيَ اللهُ عَنْهُ: (جِبْرِيلُ عَلَيْهِ السَّلَامُ) قَالَ: فَأَخْبِرْنِي عَنِ الْإِحْسَانِ. قَالَ ﷺ: "أَنْ تَعْبُدَ اللهَ كَأَنَّكَ تَرَاهُ، فَإِنْ لَمْ تَكُنْ تَرَاهُ فَإِنَّهُ يَرَاك."

[الْمَصْدَرُ: صَحِيحُ الْبُخَارِيُّ ٥٠]

'"An Abi Hurairah (ra): (Jibreel (as)) Qala: "Fa akhberni 'an al Ihsan. Qala ﷺ: An Ta'bud Allaha, Ka annaka tarahu, fa in lam takun tarahu fa innahu yarak." [Sahih Bukhari 50]

"Narrated by Abi Hurairah: (Archangel Gabriel (as)) said, Now, tell me about Ihsan (Spiritual Excellence)." The Prophet Muhammad (pbuh) replied, "It is to worship/serve Allah (AJ) as though you behold/see Him; and if you don't behold/see Him, (know that) He surely Sees you." *[Source: Authentic by Bukhari 50]*

If your Lord sees you, everybody who's associated with your Lord also sees you. If you govern your life with somebody seeing you day and night, day and night – from how you sleep, how you walk, how you talk, how you interact – that camera is never OFF. If you govern your life with that camera and that sincerity, you should reach sincerity with no problems.

Shaykhs Connect to the Face of Their Shaykhs, All the Way to Prophet ﷺ

We've described before in the book, 'A Timeless Reality,' *inshaAllah*. Get the copy of the book of 'A Timeless Reality'. It describes that the meditation is one level of meditating, connecting, connecting until Allah ﷻ give a permission that they begin to connect with the face. The face of their shaykh begins to dress them because through the face is the satellite. Their face is a dress from the shaykh's face, from the shaykh's face, from the shaykh's face, all the way to the highest of *awliyaullah* whom receiving from Prophet ﷺ.

Even if you have a vision of Prophet ﷺ, it's a Muhammadan dress from the shaykhs. As each of the shaykhs have a *shekl* (face) and a form that looks like *Muhammadun Rasulallah* ﷺ and they're *Muhammadiyoon*. The *Ghawth* and the highest of these *awliya* take directly from the reality of Prophet ﷺ, direct image. Everyone else is a satellite image of the Muhammadan dress, down towards creation.

The Muhammadan Face Sends You Nazar to Bring You Up

That's because of the voltage. For us to understand, that when somebody comes and think, 'Oh, I'm having the visions of Prophet ﷺ,' and they think they're tapping into 10 million watts and they haven't exploded yet, they must be super powerful. No! That, those are reflections coming down to them to bring them towards guidance. Those reflections are the reflections from their Muhammadan shaykhs that are in the *Muhammadiyoon* image that's sending them a *nazar* to bring them up.

But as they become stronger and stronger in their spirituality in which the energy overwhelms their body, they become overheated and they have many effects on their physicality because of the amount of that energy. When they progress into that energy, then the higher level Muhammadan face is then dressing them, dressing them, dressing them. So, everything is being transferred from that which doesn't perish which is the *Wajhi hil Karim* (Holy Face of the Most Generous) – is the face and the essences that are dressing from the face.

$$﴿٨٨﴾ \text{ ... } ^{ﹾ}\text{وَجْهَهُ } \text{إِلَّا} \text{ هَالِكٌ } \text{شَيْءٍ} \text{ كُلُّ}...$$

28:88 – "...Kullu shayin halikun illa wajha" (Surat Al-Qasas)

"...Everything (that exists) will perish except His holy Face..."
(The Stories, 28:88)

There are seven faces on this Earth that represent the seven continents. They take and they give onto this Earth, its power and its dressing for *awliyaullah* to take from that, *inshaAllah*. So, there's a whole power structure in which Allah ﷻ has put into place, *inshaAllah*.

231

Connect Through Your Heart, Not Your Mind

Our life is to connect; connect with the shaykh, ask to reach to that light, to that *faiz* (downpouring blessings), the energy and their stages. So, not my imagination – not somebody imagining through their mind. Because we also  have many people whom are watching that are not well. They imagine in their mind that they're connecting, but that's not it. The mind is a dangerous place to use. I think that there's a commercial about the mind is a dangerous thing to lose, yes. So the mind is definitely, this is not a part of the mind. This is a part of the heart.

That when you make that connection and the visualization is through the soul. That, that face is dressing and they feel the energy of the dress. They feel the sweating, they feel the heat. So, these are established energies upon the soul. The character is very soft. The character has a lot of fear because of the Divinely Presence and the energy that's coming upon it. So, there are many signs for people whom have been dressed by these realities, *inshaAllah*. The rest is just people being confused in their mind. It's not easy to achieve and a great struggle has to occur, *inshaAllah*.

Subhana rabbika rabbal 'izzati 'amma yasifoon, wa salaamun 'alal mursaleen, walhamdulillahi rabbil 'aalameen. Bi hurmati Muhammad al-Mustafa wa bi siri Surat al-Fatiha.

Be in the Presence of the Holy Face
Five Times a Day in Salah

Reciting Kalima (Testimony of Faith) Purifies the Soul

Alhamdulillah, that is the reality of the movement of energy and for us it makes every common sense. That anyone trying to reach to Allah's majestic Might and Grace, how could they possibly think that they just receive directly from Allah that Might and that Majesty? The reality of that *tawheed* (Oneness) is that Allah sends everything to the reality of *Muhammadun Rasulallah* because *tawheed* represents Oneness. The *kalimah* (testimony of faith) is an expression that purifies and takes away all sins and recalibrates the servant back to Oneness. So, the immensity of the *kalimah* that we recite all the time, "*Ashhadu an la ilaha illAllah, wa ashhadu anna Muhammadan 'abduhu wa habibuhu wa Rasuluhu*."

أَشْهَدُ أَنْ لَا إِلَهَ إِلاَّ الله وَأَشْهَدُ أَنَّ مُحَمَّدًا عَبْدُهُ وَرَسُولُهُ

"*Ashhadu an la ilaha illallah, wa ashhadu anna Muhammadan 'abduhu wa Rasulu.*"

"*I bear witness that there is no god but Allah, and I bear witness that Muhammad is the messenger of Allah.*"

It immediately recalibrates the soul, the *nafs* (ego), and the servant back to the grace of Allah ﷻ. The immensity of that power is the ocean of forgiveness. Because as soon as the *kalimah* is recited, Allah ﷻ washes and purifies the soul and the body, the *nafs* and the ego from its sins and its badness. That's the amount of that power in that expression.

Everything We Do is to Show Our Love for Allah ﷻ – That's Tawheed

Its real understanding is our everyday life. That, *La ilaha illAllah* is a continuous flow to the reality of *Muhammadun Rasulallah* ﷺ. The pursuit of that love and the *ishq* and the real love for Allah ﷻ is the movement towards the reality of *Muhammadun Rasulallah* ﷺ. So, this is reiterating always this ocean of *tawheed*. That people think, 'Oh, you think your shaykhs have power. Oh, you people love Prophet ﷺ too much.' Again never understanding that, no, everything we do is actually our immense expression and love for Allah ﷻ. But they're not getting it. They're thinking there's two or three. Say, 'No, no. It's only but One.' Allah ﷻ is directing those whom love that, 'If you want Me and you love Me, *fattabi'uni.*'

قُلْ إِنْ كُنْتُمْ تُحِبُّوْنَ اللَّـهَ فَاتَّبِعُوْنِيْ يُحْبِبْكُمُ اللَّـهُ ... ﴿٣١﴾

3:31 – "Qul in kuntum tuhibbon Allaha fattabi'uni, yuhbibkumullahu…" (Surat Ali 'Imran)

"Say, [O Muhammad], "If you should love Allah, then follow me, [so] Allah will love you …" (Family of Imran, 3:31)

It means don't direct yourself to Me. You're not going to find Me. You should find Me in the one whom is reflecting all My realities, all My grace, and all My blessings to the best that creation can reflect.' Not to Allah's ﷻ reality; He's *La Sharik* (no partner) – there's nothing like unto Allah ﷻ. But for the best of what we can understand. The most purified of what we can understand in this world of creation that encompasses everything from the heavens to the Earth, Allah ﷻ made the reality of *Muhammadun Rasulallah* ﷺ.

Muhammadun Rasulallah ﷺ Has Been Taught By the Mighty Power

Then gave for us every seal throughout Qur'an, *"Khuluqul 'azheem,"* that, 'You are of a magnificent character.'

$$ وَإِنَّكَ لَعَلَىٰ خُلُقٍ عَظِيمٍ ﴿٤﴾ $$

68:4 – *"Wa innaka la'ala khuluqin 'azheem."* (Surat Al-Qalam)

"Truly, You (O Muhammad!) are of a magnificent character."
(The Pen, 68:4)

Allah ﷻ calls nothing magnificent other than what Allah ﷻ has made. So, giving for us an *isharah* (sign) that, 'I have perfected this reality' and *"Allama shadeedul quwa"* – 'And he has been taught by somebody immense in power.'

$$ وَمَا يَنطِقُ عَنِ الْهَوَىٰ ﴿٣﴾ إِنْ هُوَ إِلَّا وَحْيٌ يُوحَىٰ ﴿٤﴾ عَلَّمَهُ شَدِيدُ الْقُوَىٰ ﴿٥﴾ $$

53:3-5 – *"Wa ma yantiqu 'anil hawa.*
(3) In huwa illa wahyun yooha. (4)
'Allamahu shadeedul Quwa. (5)"
(Surat An-Najm)

235

"Nor does he (Prophet Muhammad (s) speak from [his own] desire. (3)
He is not but a revelation revealed. (4) He was taught by one Mighty in
Power. (5)" (The Star, 53:3-5)

Throughout Holy Qur'an Allah 'ﷻ is continuously giving us and pointing
to us that this light of *Muhammadun Rasulallah* ﷺ, not like you and
other creation. This creation is of an immense purity. This creation of
immense lights, immense reality. When you direct from Allah's 'ﷻ love,
He directs the servant towards that reality. Now you know you've been
guided.

Whom Allah 'ﷻ Guides is Truly Guided

Allah 'ﷻ describes, 'There
is no guidance, *"La
hadanAllah."* There is no
guidance except those
whom Allah 'ﷻ guides and
don't think that everybody
has been guided. It means
the guidance doesn't come
easy. People may accept Islam in billions, in trillions over the centuries
and beyond the amount and the count of understanding, but whom
Allah 'ﷻ guides is truly guided. It means that when Allah 'ﷻ want to grant
the servant guidance, He directs them to the love of Sayyidina
Muhammad ﷺ because that is the reflection of Allah 'ﷻ in this ocean of
creation.

...وَقَالُوا الْحَمْدُ لِلَّهِ الَّذِي هَدَانَا لِهَٰذَا وَمَا كُنَّا لِنَهْتَدِيَ لَوْلَا أَنْ هَدَانَا اللَّهُ ۖ لَقَدْ جَاءَتْ رُسُلُ رَبِّنَا بِالْحَقِّ... ﴿٤٣﴾

7:43 – "...Wa qalo Alhamdulillahi al ladhee hadana lihadha wa ma kunna linahtadiya lawla an hadana Allahu, laqad jaa at Rusulu Rabbina bil Haqqi..." (Surat Al-A'raf)

"... And they will say, Praise be to Allah, who has guided us to this [joy and happiness]; and we would never have been guided if Allah had not guided us. Certainly the messengers of our Lord had come with the truth..." (The Heights, 7:43)

Understand the Standard of Divinely Attributes Through Sayyidina Muhammad ﷺ

Through the reality of the soul of Prophet ﷺ, we learn what generosity is, what love is, what laws are, what compassion is; all of these realities are reflecting to us from a standard that we can understand. Imagine trying to understand compassion from Allah's ﷻ standard. It would be utterly unachievable and everybody would say, 'Well, you know, that's God and there's no way for us to do anything and forget about it.' Everything would be of a ridiculous nature. What is mercy? What is generosity? Are you comparing yourself with God's Divine generosity? That can never be understood, the extent of that generosity. So, it means that the names and attributes, they must be mirrored and reflected onto something created. It can't be just anything. It has to be the most perfected for Allah ﷻ is perfect.

Allah ﷻ Wants to Be Known By the One Whom He Has Perfected

When Allah ﷻ wants to be known, He's not going to be known by something broken, something slightly imperfect. Allah ﷻ is going to be known by that which He has perfected and as a result stamped, *"Khuluqal 'azheem."*

وَإِنَّكَ لَعَلَىٰ خُلُقٍ عَظِيمٍ ﴿٤﴾

68:4 – "Wa innaka la'ala khuluqin 'azheem." (Surat Al-Qalam)

"Truly, You (O Muhammad!) are of a magnificent character."
(The Pen, 68:4)

Allah ﷻ praising Himself. That, 'I have made a magnificent character.' These are the dialogue because we don't read Qur'an thinking ourself is there. At a level higher, we read Qur'an as a dialogue between Allah ﷻ and Sayyidina Muhammad ﷺ because I negated myself at the door, *"La ilaha illa anta Subhanaka, innee kuntu minazh zhalimeen."* 'Ya Rabbi I'm not interested in knowing about myself. I'm asking to be nothing.'

﴿٨٧﴾ ...لَا إِلَٰهَ إِلَّا أَنتَ سُبْحَانَكَ إِنِّي كُنتُ مِنَ الظَّالِمِينَ

21:87 – "...La ilaha illa anta Subhanaka, innee kuntu minazh zhalimeen." (Surat Al-Anbiya)

"...There is no god/diety except You; Glory to you: Indeed I have been of the wrongdoers/Oppressor to Myself!" (The Prophets, 21:87)

As a result, the beatific dialogue of Allah ﷻ on how He guides and praises the reality of Sayyidina Muhammad ﷺ. That, 'You are of a magnificent character,' (Holy Qur'an, 68:4). Allah ﷻ is praising that what He has created, He's very happy with. As a result, these beatific realities to perfection is reflecting out. We say again because if somebody understands that, then they begin to understand what is the immensity of *tafakkur* (contemplation).

Your Salah is a Means, Not the End Goal

Anybody who's not practicing their *tafakkur*, then how are they trying to achieve the light and the love of Allah ﷻ? Through the actions? Through their prayers? Through the *zakah* (charity)? All of these, all of these actions are but a minute

reality in the perfection and the cleansing of their mirror. Your *salah* (daily prayers) is a means in which to purify your mirror. It means we said that it's a means, it's not the end. When we ask Muslims to meditate, they say, 'Ya Shaykh, we don't need to, we make *salah*.' You were wrong. Your *salah* was a means to something, you didn't get there.

239

Is Your Salah Like Ringing a Doorbell and Running?

We described many times before when we were children or other people were children, I can't describe things bad for myself. But when kids were small they would go ring doorbells on people's doors 'ding, ding' and then run. You ring the doorbell and then run. Those naughty kids, I don't know why they did that, but every time they would ring a doorbell and then run. That's everybody's *salah*.

99.9% of people who pray, they pray like a child ringing a doorbell and running, right? You did all these movements as if you achieved something. Then as soon as its finished, *as salaam alayk, as salam alayk* [ending with last part of prayer] and run. What, what happened? What was the point of this prayer? It was something you had to do to get rid of and finish it and you did it? And they think that's enough. But that that was not the purpose of *salah*. That they gave their five bucks to somebody, 'I did my charity and that was it.' That was not the purpose of their *zakah*.

You Say Shahadah to Prepare for Salah

It means that all of this was in order. One – you had to testify so that bring yourself into Oneness and that you're nothing. When you're nothing, there is nothing but Allah 🕋 and Muhammadun Rasulallah 🕌. That doesn't mention me and you in there. But that there's nothing but Allah 🕋 and that Prophet 🕌 is the messenger of Allah 🕋, representing Allah 🕋. He's the *imam* and the way to Allah 🕋.

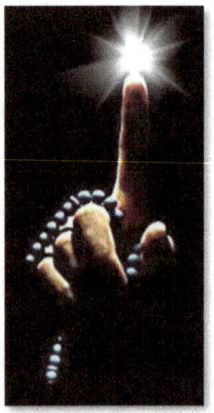

Then you begin on everything you're doing [5 Pillars of Islam]. Then you're going to make your *Shahadah* (testimony of faith) and then *salah*. Then you make *Zakah*. Why? Because *zakah* means now cleanse yourself. Your *zakah*, you have to wash and make *wudu* (ablution). Now your inner *zakah*, you have to pay, you have to give an alms. You have to purify from what you made and take it off of you, take the burden and the badness off of you.

We Give Salaams to Prophet ﷺ in Present Tense During Salah

The *salah* was to communicate with Allah ﷻ. It was to park your

physicality, discipline it by its movements and the energy that Allah ﷻ is providing in the movement. As soon as they make their *'attahiyat*, make their *shahadah*, and give *salaams* (last part of prayer), their soul is supposed to be in Divinely Presence and communicating with the Divinely Presence. It means that they sit in there after their *'attahiyat*. They say *"Assalamu 'alayka ayyuhan Nabi"* is that Allah ﷻ saying, 'Before you go anywhere, remember that you're giving

Prophet ﷺ in your prayers, before you closed your prayers, you're giving *salaams* in present tense.' How could you go anywhere? How could you move? You gave *salaams* in present tense to the reality and the soul of Sayyidina Muhammad ﷺ.

Then now you visualize Prophet ﷺ is right in front of you in your *salah*

and all *'Ibadullahis saliheen* (the righteous servants of Allah ﷻ) are all around. Allah ﷻ, before you left the *salah* you're saying, *"Assalamu 'alayka ayyuhan Nabi."* Oh, Prophet ﷺ is right in front of me and *"Salaamu alaykum 'ibadullahis saliheen"* because they're all with Prophet ﷺ. They don't leave Prophet ﷺ alone for a second, not even for a fraction of a second.

التَّحِيَّاتُ لِلَّهِ وَالصَّلَوَاتُ وَالطَّيِّبَاتُ. السَّلَامُ عَلَيْكَ أَيُّهَا النَّبِيُّ وَرَحْمَةُ اللَّهِ وَبَرَكَاتُهُ، السَّلَامُ عَلَيْنَا وَعَلَى عِبَادِ اللَّهِ الصَّالِحِينَ، أَشْهَدُ أَنْ لَا إِلَهَ إِلاَّ اللَّهُ وَأَشْهَدُ أَنَّ مُحَمَّدًا عَبْدُهُ وَرَسُولُهُ.

"Attahiyatu Lillahi wa salawatu wat tayyibatu. Assalamu 'alayka ayyuhan Nabiyu ﷺ, wa rahmatullahi wa barakatuhu. Assalamu 'alayna wa 'alaa 'Ibadulllahis saliheen. Ashhadu an la ilaha illallahu wa ashhadu anna Muhammadan 'abduhu wa Rasuluhu."

"All the best compliments and the prayers/praising and the pure/good things are for Allah. Peace and Blessings be upon you, O' Prophet (pbuh)! Peace be on us and on the righteous servants of Allah. I testify that there is no deity but Allah (AJ), and I testify that Prophet Muhammad (pbuh) is the servant and Messenger of Allah (AJ)."

How you could leave? Where are you going? It means that you have an audience now. So, then we can see that 99.9% of the people, they ring the doorbell and ran which could be quite annoying because you're in that audience and you got up and left.

Tafakkur Teaches Us to Make Our Connection Real

What then *tafakkur* is teaching people? That you are supposed to be connecting and you want the energy and that reality to be dressing you. You don't really know what we're saying in *salah* and we really don't know who we're facing. But when we begin to really understand and meditate, this is the month of the reality of a mirror [Dhul Qi'dah, 11th lunar month]. That what Allah ﷻ gave to us of the immensity of our prayer. That's not in the middle of a mosque to do this or in middle of a big crowded *jama'ah* (congregation), you start to sit and identify yourself. Because whatever we teach, it's very private.

That's why the shaykhs, they pray very fast in front of people. This is not something to gain the attention of people and all of a sudden making your every sort of significant connection in a crowded *jama'ah*. But these are the personal and intimate relationship with Sayyidina Muhammad ﷺ and with Allah ﷻ, Most High. It's usually best done after *'Asr* (Afternoon prayer) when you're by yourself, at *Fajr* (Dawn prayer) when you pray by yourself.

Salah is the Greatest Gift to Us Because We Face Sayyidina Muhammad

The concept and the understanding of this mirror is immense. That *La ilaha illAllah* is reflecting to *Muhammadun Rasulallah* . Then Allah grants us that, 'I want them to make the real *salah*,' and Allah gave the words. Prophet did not come up with these words for *salah*. That the words and the recitations were told to him . This is the way Allah wanted the prayers and the words in the prayers to be recited, in the order that it is recited because it is a dialogue between Allah and Prophet . This is the greatest gift to the nation that, 'I am a hidden treasure and I'm going to put into your *salah* that you are a nation in which every time you pray – you don't understand where your soul is but you should understand from the words that you're reciting – you are in the presence and facing Sayyidina Muhammad in every *salah*.

Imagine then the world of souls. That this immense soul and there's trillions and trillions and trillions of souls. As soon as they go, '*Allahu Akbar*' (Allah is the Greatest) and they begin to pray, their souls are all in that audience. How big is that face facing all these souls? Something can't be imagined. Are you facing the soul from the ground? Or you're facing from face to face? Or are they held in a hand that faces the soul of Sayyidina Muhammad ?

Contemplate the Words of Salah to Understand the Blessing of Wajhi hil Kareem

It means that we can't even understand. What Allah ﷻ gave to us of an immense gift that, 'If they would just sit and contemplate the words of their *salah*, they would understand what gift I gave to this nation.' That as soon as they're in their prayer and they're giving *salaams* to  Prophet ﷺ. It means all these realities and all these months that have been taught is that when you're praying, the holy face of Sayyidina Muhammad ﷺ is there. Because anytime you give *salaams* you have to be face to face to somebody. You can't give *salaams* in present tense to the back of somebody's head. Allah ﷻ has the holy face, *Wajhi hil Karim* (the Holy Face of the Most Generous) facing you in your *salah*.

That's why anyone come to debate and say, 'What you're talking about?' First thing is that first, go read the words of your *salah* and tell me what you understood from them. You're saying, *"Assalamu 'alaiyka ayyuhan Nabi."* That the face, the holy face of Sayyidina Muhammad ﷺ is facing you. That's the gift Allah ﷻ gave. That, 'My Divinely mirror, you are praying in the presence of that mirror.' That face is the face that dresses you. That face is the face that blesses you. That face is the face that puts every *tajalli* (manifestation) upon your reality and takes every badness away from you.

All Prophets Perfected Their Faith on the Night of Isra wal Mi'raj

Then Allah ﷻ, 'I would have not sent that reality except that it is a mercy to all of creation – *Rahmatal lil'alameen*, that he's a mercy to all of creation.'

$$\text{وَمَا أَرْسَلْنَاكَ إِلَّا رَحْمَةً لِّلْعَالَمِينَ ﴿١٠٧﴾}$$

21:107 – "Wa maa arsalnaka illa Rahmatal lil'alameen."
(Surat Al-Anbiya)

"And We have not sent you, [O Muhammad (pbuh)], except as a mercy to the worlds/creation." (The Prophets, 21:107)

The greatest nation is the nation that was given this mirror. The greatest nation is the nation that was given the mirror and the *salah* to say and to be in the presence of the holy face of Sayyidina Muhammad ﷺ. It means what a gift Allah ﷻ gave to this nation. Then Allah ﷻ perfected the faith of all other prophets, only in the *Isra wal Mi'raj* (Night Journey and Ascension). So that all nations would come to that reality.

Imagine on *Isra wal Mi'raj*, why then the Prophet ﷺ was taken all the way to Jerusalem, where 124,000 prophets were then brought in their

physicality to be present with Prophet ﷺ? They were resurrected and brought into his holy presence and Allah ﷻ gave them the Muhammadan *salah*. Then they prayed and said, *"Assalamu 'alayka ayyuhan Nabi."* In his physical presence, they gave their *shahadah*, they gave the *salaams*, and the light of Prophet ﷺ dressed all the messengers and all the prophets of Allah ﷻ. As a result, all their nations are under the nation of Muhammadun Rasulallah ﷺ.

The Highest Khidmat is to Do Da'wah and Spread Knowledge

Rabbil Mumineen wa Rabbil Kafireen wa Rabbil 'aalameen (Lord of the believers and unbelievers and all worlds), that there is nothing under or outside of the nation of Sayyidina Muhammad ﷺ. The nation that has accepted Islam and the nation that is not accepted yet. And it's responsibility for us to do *da'wah* (religious propagation) to that nation. That's why the highest, highest *khidmat* (service) in our life, as a Muslim, is to do *da'wah*. There is no Muslim who can come into the world and say, 'I'm not doing *da'wah*.' Your wasted life. Your life is to propagate the religion of Islam and propagate the love of Sayyidina Muhammad ﷺ. This is the highest purpose of our existence.

We're not here to accumulate wealth. We're not here to accumulate degrees and bachelors and law and all these different degrees. We're not here to accumulate whatever we want from *dunya* (material world). Allah ﷻ gave us an existence to come and worship.

وَمَا خَلَقْتُ الْجِنَّ وَالْإِنسَ إِلَّا لِيَعْبُدُونِ ﴿٥٦﴾

51:56 – "Wa ma khalaqtu aljinna wal insa illa liya'budoon."
(Surat Adh-Dhariyat)

"I did not create jinn and humans Except to worship Me."
(The Winnowing Winds, 51:56)

The highest form of worshipness is *khidmat*. That seek out knowledge. When you find that knowledge that teaches who you are and where you came from, you now begin to understand your purpose. It means that these souls will be brought back to *Muhammadun Rasulallah* 鄉. Our life has a meaning and a purpose when we dedicate it to *da'wah*, when we dedicate it to propagating the message, the beatific message and the love of Sayyidina Muhammad 鄉. That's why then you spread the teachings.

The Shaykh is the Maestro of an Orchestra

The reward that you get for doing these *khidmat*, coming and reciting. The gentlemen who are opening the center all the time, servicing the center. People all over Pakistan, *mashAllah*, entire we have like six or seven orphanages, thousands of wells by now. All these people whom are doing what they have to do and the untold hundreds that are behind the scenes supporting.

The shaykh, his job is like the maestro of an orchestra. They inspire people to rise that, 'Come to who you really are.' You know, those two feet of yours, if you use it in Allah's 's way you'll be astonished that who you are and what Allah 's wrote for you. Then the maestro is moving, everybody is playing and playing the role that they promised Allah 's that they would play.

People can look back and see this is astonishing. How this little group they are like ants that are everywhere, doing everything that they can. Why? So, that when you go back to your *salah* and you're in your prayer and say, 'I don't really know if I have anything to offer. *Ya Assalamu 'alayka ayyuhan Nabi*. Forgive me my wrongs and give me *himmah* and a dress to do more.' The shine of the holy face of Sayyidina

Muhammad ﷺ to dress your soul because you fed people, you helped people. You put a smiling face on an orphan. Or you took your *rizq* and your sustenance that, 'Oh I'm so busy, I don't have time to do that but I want to share in what you're doing. I want to share in helping you to propagate your message, for your food to go out, your orphanages to be fed.'

It's Allah's ﷻ Love That Allows Us to Be of Service and Gain More Blessing

So, that when you sit in your *salah* you think, '*Ya Rabbi*, I have nothing. *Assalamu 'alayka ayyuhan Nabi*'. Let the light of Prophet ﷺ to dress us and to bless us. You go into *sujood* (prostration) and ask, '*Ya Sayyidi, ya Rasulul Kareem* (The Most Generous Messenger), take away difficulty from me, hardship from myself, from my family and those whom I love and my community. That your *nazar* (gaze) be upon me. That your dress and the *himmah* (zeal) to be dressed upon me and take away obstacles from my path.'

That my *ajr ul 'azim* (immense reward) – that Allah ﷻ give me a great, a great ability and great gifts and lights that Allah ﷻ reward because everything is a gift from Allah ﷻ. That don't think you pick up, you

know, 500 dishes because you were clever. Allah ﷻ loves you and says that, 'No, no, no, I don't want this for these people. I want him to pick it up because I'm going to now reward him greatly for what he's doing.' So, it means these things are not coming to us by chance and good luck and good fortune. It's Allah's ﷻ dressing for us. When He loves us, He wants to give us more. More what? Good deeds. 'I want to write a lot on your account.' That, '*Ya Rabbi*, open for us what's hidden, open for us what's closed.'

Prophet ﷺ is the Key That Unlocks Heavenly Realities

The foods that we can give away, the people that we can help, the support that needs to be done. All of these and the time that we take for sitting for *zikr* and for *salah*. So that when you're in your *salah*, "*Assalamu 'alayka ayyuhan Nabi.*" That Prophet ﷺ begin to reflect immense lights and those are the lights of Allah ﷻ. That's from the ocean of *La ilaha illAllah*. When Allah ﷻ begin to dress because the switch, when we don't understand that Prophet ﷺ is a key, is a

Miftah ur Rahmah (The Key of Mercy). Allah ﷻ is a lock and Allah's ﷻ expecting that Prophet ﷺ to activate. Why he's not activating in your *salah* and shining upon you? Everybody thinking they're going to get it directly. The real *tawheed* is from *La ilaha illAllah* to the ocean of *Muhammadun Rasulallah* ﷺ. As a result, that reflection begin to dress the souls, bless the souls.

Allah ﷻ Gave the Gift of Salah to the Nation of Sayyidina Muhammad ﷺ

When they begin to feel that and understand that, then they understand what Allah ﷻ gave to them from their shaykhs and their guides. The shaykh and the guide that understands and teaches this reality is teaching that when you sit and connect, you're asking from that light of *Muhammadun Rasulallah* ﷺ to begin to reflect.

Every time they make their *salah*, they're asking from that light that, 'Dress me, bless me.' And spend just a few minutes in that light, in that dress.

Go into *sujood* (prostration) and cry and ask Allah ﷻ for help, for Prophet ﷺ to give help and support and *madad*. Then the *salah* becomes real. Not every time, in the middle of the day, you're busy and you can't do that. But at the times you can, you understand that this *salah* is the greatest gift that Allah ﷻ can give. Allah's ﷻ giving a gift that he gave to no nation because that gift has to be *Muhammadun Rasulallah* ﷺ. How could it be any other nation? That, 'I'm going to give to you My key and in your prayers you'll be facing that key and from that holy face comes my Divinely lights upon your nation.' Then you understand how blessed your nation and our nation is and the nation of Sayyidina Muhammad ﷺ.

Subhana rabbika rabbal 'izzati 'amma yasifoon, wa salaamun 'alal mursaleen, walhamdulillahi rabbil 'aalameen. Bi hurmati Muhammad al-Mustafa wa bi siri Surat al-Fatiha.

The Station of Excellence is to Know That the Holy Face Sees You in Salah

عَنْ أَبِي هُرَيْرَةَ رَضِيَ اللهُ عَنْهُ: (جِبْرِيلُ عَلَيْهِ السَّلَامُ) قَالَ: فَأَخْبِرْنِي عَنِ الْإِحْسَانِ.
قَالَ ﷺ: "أَنْ تَعْبُدَ اللهَ كَأَنَّكَ تَرَاهُ، فَإِنْ لَمْ تَكُنْ تَرَاهُ فَإِنَّهُ يَرَاكَ."
[الْمَصْدَرُ: صَحِيحٌ الْبُخَارِيُّ ٥٠]

"'An Abi Hurairah (ra): (Jibreel (as)) Qala: "Fa akhberni 'an al Ihsan. Qala ﷺ: An Ta'bud Allaha, Ka annaka tarahu, fa in lam takun tarahu fa innahu yarak." [Sahih Bukhari 50]

"Narrated by Abi Hurairah: (Archangel Gabriel (as)) said, Now, tell me about Ihsan (Spiritual Excellence)." The Prophet Muhammad (pbuh) replied, "It is to worship/serve Allah (AJ) as though you behold/see Him; and if you don't behold/see Him, (know that) He surely Sees you." [Source: Authentic by Bukhari 50]

Who Are You Facing in Your Salah?

This purification and this *madad* (support) and everything that has been building up, they're all beads on a *tasbih* (prayer beads). So, in previous talks about the importance of the *madad*, the importance of the *bay'ah* (pledge of allegiance) as a completion of Islam, the importance of all these practices leads up to the importance of who you're facing in your *salah*

253

(daily prayers). That the purification, how to receive this light from Prophet ﷺ, how to see Prophet ﷺ and if you don't see him, know that he sees you. This is our opening for that *taqwa* (consciousness). Because maybe Allah ﷻ is a bit too much for people to understand, but to know that we want to see Prophet ﷺ and this is from Allah ﷻ teaching us our *salah*. That *"Assalamu 'alayka ayyuhan Nabi"*; I want it to be real.

التَّحِيَّاتُ لِلَّهِ وَالصَّلَوَاتُ وَالطَّيِّبَاتُ. السَّلَامُ عَلَيْكَ أَيُّهَا النَّبِيُّ وَرَحْمَةُ اللَّهِ وَبَرَكَاتُهُ، السَّلَامُ عَلَيْنَا وَعَلَى عِبَادِ اللَّهِ الصَّالِحِينَ، أَشْهَدُ أَنْ لَا إِلَهَ إِلَّا اللَّهُ وَأَشْهَدُ أَنَّ مُحَمَّدًا عَبْدُهُ وَرَسُولُهُ.

"Attahiyatu Lillahi wa salawatu wat tayyibatu. Assalamu 'alayka ayyuhan Nabiyu ﷺ, wa rahmatullahi wa barakatuhu. Assalamu 'alayna wa 'alaa 'Ibadulllahis saliheen. Ashhadu an la ilaha illallahu wa ashhadu anna Muhammadan 'abduhu wa Rasuluhu."

"All the best compliments and the prayers/praising and the pure/good things are for Allah. Peace and Blessings be upon you, O Prophet (pbuh)! Peace be on us and on the righteous servants of Allah. I testify that there is no deity but Allah (AJ), and I testify that Prophet Muhammad (pbuh) is the servant and Messenger of Allah (AJ)."

Be of Service and Charitable to Make Your Salah Real

I want to see Sayyidina Muhammad ﷺ, the generous face that the Divine allows us to see. I want to see that. I want my *salah* to be real. Well, how am I going to see that? How am I going to be dressed by that? That becomes then all of the reasons for purifying ourselves, cleansing ourselves, living a life of *khidmat* and service and donating and giving our time. Whether we donate our time, our wealth, our life – whatever it is that we're going to donate in that way, it's the way of purification to reach towards that holy face.

Our Khidmat is as Important as Our Obligatory Actions

It means giving in Allah's ﷻ way is not something we can imagine. And no matter what we do, we didn't accomplish anything of our predecessors in the way in which they gave from themselves, their lives, their families. They gave everything in the sacrifice in the way of Allah ﷻ and Allah ﷻ is the best of those to keep a *hisaab* (account). It means Allah ﷻ gives the reward. Allah ﷻ knows exactly what was given and what Allah ﷻ wants to open for the servant.

These openings are the reality of how to reach to that reflection. Our *khidmat* (service) and the only thing that has a value because we don't place a value on our actions. We don't think, 'Oh my *salah*, my prayer is so amazing. Allah ﷻ will open everything because of my *salah*.'

But *awliyaullah* (saints) come and teach us – no, whatever is opening is this *khidmat* of the servant. It means their willingness to serve with their life, with their wealth, with their time, with their possession. They lived a life of service. That service was the purification. That service was the cleaning of their souls. We said what we want to achieve is not an energy that we can achieve to rise to reach it, but the reflection and the purification of the reflection. So, it means our life is our *zikr* (Divine remembrance), our *tazkiyah* (purification), our cleansing. All of our service that we're doing for why? Because then the soul becomes purified, purified, purified until it becomes so purified it begins to reflect that which it loves.

Being Muhammadiyoon is to Reflect the Light of Sayyidina Muhammad ﷺ

It means then now they described the mirror is the holy face of Sayyidina Muhammad ﷺ. If that holy face begins to reflect upon the soul, his holy realities of what Allah ﷻ dressed the seven holy openings which we then

described is the reality of the 'Arsh and the throne. If those seven holy openings are continuously dressing upon the soul and the soul becomes so clean and so purified that it's a mirror reflecting that light. It means not only is it dressing the soul but then anyone who comes into the presence of that soul is being reflected to the lights of Sayyidina Muhammad ﷺ and that's what it means to become *Muhammadiyoon*. They reflect the light of Sayyidina Muhammad ﷺ and they are the satellites living upon this Earth and that's the purpose of their existence. Allah ﷻ raised them, purified them and said, 'From a realm that is unseen, you will manifest that light onto this Earth.'

So, it means then this way of purification, cleansing and all the practices that they're asking for us to do, it begins to reflect that holy face so that the soul can begin to witness and understand who they're facing in these realities and how to be dressed by these realities. As a result, it reflects out to all of creation, these realities. That's why their souls are blessed. That's why that Muhammadan light, when it reflects from them, is the source of *rizq* (sustenance), is the source of bounty. It's the source of *rahmah* (mercy). It's the source of every grace from Allah ﷻ is reflecting like a mirror off of their souls to everything, to every environment that that light is touching. It's touching from the holy face of Sayyidina Muhammad ﷺ; immensity that can't even be understood.

Wajhi Hil Karim Revives the Souls Who Strive to Purify Themselves

It means that's why then these teachings are give your time, give from your possessions, do whatever you can for *zaki* and perfection and cleanliness of the soul and of the character. Then the *muraqabah* (spiritual connection) to understand what is it that you are and who is it that you're facing and how to receive that *tajalli* (manifestations) so that the *salah* can be real and the heart can become open and alive.

Muhyil qulub (reviver of hearts), the one whom opens and revives the heart. How he revives the heart? Why there all these expressions were coming? Because like the beads that people don't put together. Why the name of Prophet ﷺ in the *nasheed* that all thousands of *tariqah jama'ahs* (communities) are reciting? '*Muhyil qulub.*' How he's *muhyil qulub*? Because by the love and the *salawat* of Sayyidina Muhammad ﷺ and what we described last night, that in five times a day, Allah ﷻ wants his holy face looking at his nation.

يَا مُحْيِي الْقُلُوبِ، سَلَامٌ عَلَيك يَا مَاحِي الذُّنُوبِ ، سَلَامٌ عَلَيك
يَا مُحْيِي الْقُلُوبِ، يَا مَاحِي الذُّنُوبِ ، سَلَامٌ عَلَيك

Ya Muhyil qulubi, Salaam 'Alayk
Ya Mahidh dhunubi, Salaam 'Alayk
Ya Muhyil qulubi, Ya Mahidh dhunubi, Salaam 'Alayk

O the reviver of the hearts, O the eraser of the sins, Peace be upon you

So, all their *salah* (prayer) is in the presence of that holy face. From *nur* (Light) and *hay* (Ever-living), from the holy eyes of that beloved face, he is dressing his nation with lights and *Bahrul Hayat* (Ocean of Ever-living), from *Rahman* (Most Compassionate) and *Raheem* (Most Merciful) are dressing these souls. Every time they make *salah*, whether they are making their *sunnah* prayers or *fard* (obligatory) prayers, their *salah* are all in the presence of that face ﷺ. That's why, as a result, every time they enter into *salah*, the beloved face of Sayyidina Muhammad ﷺ, *Wajhi hil Karim* is dressing their souls and reviving, reviving their souls.

Prophet's ﷺ Soul Sends Ten Salawats Upon Us When We Send One

Now imagine if they understood that and they made their *salawats*. So, people whom say, 'Oh, we don't have to do *salawats*.' See how far they are away from real Islam. You don't even know who you're facing. You're not understanding even the words in your *salah*. If you understood who you were facing then you would understand how powerful the *salawat* is, *"Allahumma salli 'ala Sayyidina Muhammadin wa 'ala aali Sayyidina Muhammad."*

اَللَّهُمَ صَلِّ عَلَى سَيِّدِنَا مُحَمَّدٍ، وَّعَلَى آلِ سَيِّدِنَا مُحَمَّدْ

"Allahumma salli 'ala Sayyidina Muhammadin wa 'ala aali Sayyidina Muhammad"

"O Allah! Send Peace and blessings upon Muhammad and upon the Family of Muhammad (Peace be Upon him)"

What Prophet ﷺ gave back, 'As soon as you make a *salawat* upon me, Allah ﷻ sends my soul to make ten *salawats* upon you.'

عَنْ أَنَسِ بْنِ مَالِكَ رَضِيَ اللهُ عَنْهُ، قَالَ:
قَالَ رَسُولُ اللهِ ﷺ: "مَنْ صَلَّى عَلَيَّ صَلَاةً وَاحِدَةً، صَلَّى اللهُ عَلَيْهِ عَشْرَ صَلَوَاتٍ،
وَحُطَّتْ عَنْهُ عَشْرُ خَطِيئَاتٍ، وَرُفِعَتْ لَهُ عَشْرُ دَرَجَاتٍ"

"'An Anasin ibn Malik (ra) qala: Qala Rasulullah ﷺ: Man Salla 'alaiya Salatan wahidatan, Sallallahu 'alayhi 'ashra Salawatin, wa Huttat 'anhu 'ashru khaTeatin, wa ruf'at lahu 'ashru darajatin."

Prophet Muhammad (pbuh) said: "Whoever sends blessings [Praises] upon me, God will shower His blessings upon him ten times, and will erase ten of his sins, and elevate [raise] his [spiritual] station ten times." [Hadith recorded by Nasa'i]

Sayyidina Abu Bakr as Siddiq ؓ Witnessed the One Who Held His Soul in His Hands

See now all these beads begin to come together. 'Why send my soul is because you're facing my holy face and as soon as you make *salawat*, my face begins to dress your soul.' So, people want to understand – just for us to have a perception that where is all of this? Imagine a room for us to just understand where the holy face of Prophet ﷺ is and all the souls are there and every time they enter into their *salah* (prayer), that face is shining upon their soul. So, it's something that can't be even imagined.

That *Abu Arwah*, the father of souls, the one whom is in the presence of all their souls is this beloved face dressing and blessing their reality. So *alhamdulillah*, and holy companions, Sayyidina Abu Bakr as Siddiq ؓ, all of them gave us hints for them. Anytime there is an oath, a testimony of oath from Sayyidina Abu Bakr as-Siddiq ؓ, what his oath was? 'I swear by the one whom holds my soul in his hand.' It means he's giving a station that when he prays, he witnessed. He witnessed the one who holds his soul in his hands and from there, he is looking at the beloved face of Sayyidina Muhammad ﷺ.

عَنْ أَبِي هُرَيْرَةَ رَضِيَ اللَّهُ عَنْهُ، أَنَّ رَسُولَ اللَّهِ ﷺ قَالَ: " فَوَالَّذِي نَفْسِي بِيَدِهِ لاَ
يُؤْمِنُ أَحَدُكُمْ حَتَّى أَكُونَ أَحَبَّ إِلَيْهِ مِنْ وَالِدِهِ وَوَلَدِهِ."
[صَحِيحُ الْبُخَارِي، كتاب ٢، حديث ١٤]

'An Abi Hurairah (ra), anna Rasulallahi ﷺ qala: "Fawal lazi nafsi bi yadihi, la yuminu ahadukum hatta akoona ahabba ilayhi min walidihi wa waladihi." [Sahih Al Bukhari, Kitab 2, Hadith 14]

Narrated by Abi Hurairah (ra), that the Messenger of Allah (pbuh) said: "By Him in Whose Hands is my soul, none of you will have faith till he loves me more than his father and his children."
[Authentic by Al Bukhari, Book 2, Hadith 14]

The Generous Face is Holier Than the House of Stones

All worshipness is for Allah ﷻ. All worshipness is for Allah ﷻ. You pray, we pray to Allah ﷻ. People say, 'Oh, because you said the face thing, is this like a partner?' *Astaghfirullah!* Don't people understand that you were facing the Ka'bah? So, you were facing stones and you were happy with that. Everybody comes and they face this house of stones, the ancient house of stones and they're happy with that.

When *awliya* (saints) come and elevate the understanding and say, 'Why house of stones? The owner of these stones, his face is more holy ﷺ.' What did it change? You were bowing down in the presence of stones so you bow down in the presence of this holy face. All worshipness is for Allah ﷻ. Nothing changed, just the description of your Ka'bah changed, become much more holier. We begin to understand the Ka'bah was a sense to bring me into *tawheed* (oneness). The Ka'bah was a symbol. Activate your heart because the Ka'bah represents your heart. Everybody come to one. We have to have one heart, not multiple hearts. We have one heart. 'I created no man with two hearts.'

مَّا جَعَلَ اللَّـهُ لِرَجُلٍ مِّن قَلْبَيْنِ فِي جَوْفِهِ ۚ ... ﴿٤﴾

33:4 – "Ma ja'ala Allahu lirajulin min Qalbayni fee jawfihi..."
(Surat Al-Ahzab)

"Allah has not made for a man two hearts in his interior..."
(The Combined Forces, 33:4)

Three Stations of Faith: Islam, Iman, Maqamul Ihsan

So, the Ka'bah was the symbol of one heart. *"La ilaha illAllah."* This was your first level and first *maqam* (station), Islam. What *Maqamul Iman* (station of faith) is that Prophet ﷺ describe, 'You have to love me more than you love yourself'.

عَنْ أَنَسِ بْنِ مَالِكٍ رَضِيَ اللهُ عَنْهُ قَالَ، قَالَ رَسُولُ اللهِ ﷺ، " لاَ يُؤْمِنُ أَحَدُكُمْ حَتَّى
أَكُونَ أَحَبَّ إِلَيْهِ مِنْ وَالِدِهِ وَوَلَدِهِ وَالنَّاسِ أَجْمَعِينَ."
[صَحِيحُ مُسْلِمْ، حديث ٤٤، وَالْبُخَارِي، كِتَابُ الْإِيْمَانْ، حديث ١٥]

'An Anas ibn Malik (ra) qala, qala Rasulullahi ﷺ, "La yuminu
ahadukum hatta akona ahabba ilayhi min walidihi wa waladihi wan
nasi ajma'yeen."
[Sahih Muslim, Hadith 44, wa Al Bukhari, Kitabul Iman, Hadith 15]

Narrated by Anas son of Malik (ra) that Prophet Muhammad (pbuh)
said: "None of you will have faith till he loves me more than his father,
his children, and all mankind."
[Authentic by Muslim, Hadith 44 & by Al Bukhari, Book of Faith,
Hadith 15]

That became the station of faith. If I love Prophet ﷺ more than I love myself, then my heart is filled with the love of Prophet ﷺ. It means now my station and my *qiblah* (direction of prayer) is the love of Prophet ﷺ. My heart has to be filled with *Muhammadun Rasulallah* ﷺ. Then what was *Maqamul Ihsan* (station of moral excellence)? Worship as if you see your Lord and if you don't see your Lord, know that your lord sees you. It means that this now is *Maqamul Ihsan*. That when you pray, your *Rab* (lord) is seeing you and if you don't, see the face of Prophet ﷺ.

قَالَ ﷺ : " أَنْ تَعْبُدَ اللهَ كَأَنَّك تَرَاهُ، فَإِنْ لَمْ تَكُنْ تَرَاهُ فَإِنَّهُ يَرَاك."
[المَصْدَرْ: صَحِيحْ اَلْبُخَارِيْ ٥٠]

Qala ﷺ: "An Ta'bud Allaha, Ka annaka tarahu, fa in lam takun tarahu fa innahu yarak." [Sahih Bukhari 50]

The Prophet Muhammad (pbuh) replied, "It is to worship/serve Allah (AJ) as though you behold/see Him; and if you don't behold/see Him, (know that) He surely Sees you." [Source: Authentic by Bukhari 50]

If You are Not Seeing the Holy Face in Salah, Know That He Sees You

"Assalamu 'alaika ayyuhan Nabi." I don't know if people are understanding the prayers and people who want to get agitated by everything. These are the words of the prayers. *"Assalamu 'alaik ayyuhan Nabi ﷺ,"* means then you're facing. If you are not seeing the face, then know that that holy face ﷺ is seeing us and live your life in accordance to that understanding, that Prophet ﷺ is watching me.

التَّحِيَّاتُ لِلَّهِ وَالصَّلَوَاتُ وَالطَّيِّبَاتُ. السَّلَامُ عَلَيْكَ أَيُّهَا النَّبِيُّ وَرَحْمَةُ اللهِ وَبَرَكَاتُهُ،
السَّلَامُ عَلَيْنَا وَعَلَى عِبَادِ اللهِ الصَّالِحِينَ، أَشْهَدُ أَنْ لَا إِلَهَ إِلَّا اللهُ وَأَشْهَدُ أَنَّ مُحَمَّدًا
عَبْدُهُ وَرَسُولُهُ .

*"Attahiyatu Lillahi wa salawatu wat tayyibatu. Assalamu 'alayka
ayyuhan Nabiyu* ﷺ*, wa rahmatullahi wa barakatuhu. Assalamu 'alayna
wa 'alaa 'Ibadulllahis saliheen. Ashhadu an la ilaha illallahu wa
ashhadu anna Muhammadan 'abduhu wa Rasuluhu."*

*"All the best compliments and the prayers/praising and the pure/good
things are for Allah. Peace and Blessings be upon you, O' Prophet
(pbuh)! Peace be on us and on the righteous servants of Allah. I testify
that there is no deity but Allah (AJ), and I testify that Prophet
Muhammad (pbuh) is the servant and Messenger of Allah (AJ)."*

We Must Give to Others From What Allah ﷻ Has Given Us

I govern myself. I do what I
can. That then goes back to
why we do charity, why we do
khidmat, why we do service,
why we do all these things is
why? Because Allah ﷻ said,
'They feed people.' Not for
any money that somebody's
going to give. They don't
come to the door and say, 'Okay, now give me ten dollars like I brought
you a dinner for free.'

إِنَّمَا نُطْعِمُكُمْ لِوَجْهِ اللَّهِ لَا نُرِيدُ مِنكُمْ جَزَاءً وَلَا شُكُورًا ﴿٩﴾

*76:9 – "Innama nut'imukum liWajhillahi la nureedu minkum jazaa an
wa la shukora." (Surat Al-Insan)*

*"(Saying), We feed you for the sake of the Holy/divine Face alone: We
wish not from you reward or gratitude." (The Human, 76:9)*

They feed people but for the sake of the holy face. It means this *khidmat*, this service that the shaykhs are encouraging people, 'Please go out and be of service.' Do good things and good deeds. Give from what Allah has given to you. Why? So that the holy face begins to activate its *nazar* (gaze) upon the soul and begins to look to that one with a special light and that light begin to dress them like what we talked about last night.

The Seven Essences of the Holy Face

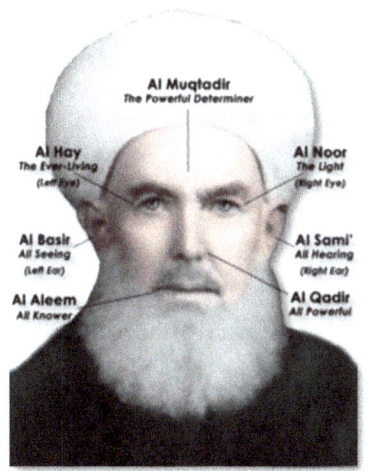

The seven essences from the reality of the face; each time Prophet will begin to activate. From the two ears, *As Sami'* (All Hearing), *Al Basir* (All Seeing). From the *sifat* (attribute) of *As Sami'* means the one whom hears, this is a Divine attribute. *Al Basir*, the one whom sees. It means that when Prophet begin to activate with *nazar* (gaze), when his *nazar* comes upon the soul of the individual because it can be three people praying and only one receive that special *tajalli* (manifestation).

Like a laser, it comes. That's why each one's state and *haal* (spiritual state) is individual to themselves because of the *nazar* of what Prophet is sending. If he sends *sifat al Sami'*, it means that he's sending a light that enables the soul to begin to push its speech onto the personality and the body of the individual. They begin to hear what Allah describes from *Hadith al Qudsi* (Holy Hadith), 'I become the hearing in which you hear.'

عَنْ أَبِي هُرَيْرَةَ رَضِيَّ اللهُ عَنْهُ قَالَ، قَالَ رَسُولُ اللهِ ﷺ : إِنَّ اللهَ تَعَالَى قَالَ: "...وَلَا يَزَالُ عَبْدِي يَتَقَرَّبُ إِلَيَّ بِالنَّوَافِلِ حَتَّى أُحِبَّهُ، فَإِذَا أَحْبَبْتُهُ كُنْتُ سَمْعَهُ الَّذِي يَسْمَعُ بِهِ، وَبَصَرَهُ الَّذِي يُبْصِرُ بِهِ، ..."

[حَدِيثُ الْقُدْسِيِّ – اَلْمَصْدَرُ: صَحِيحُ الْبُخَارِي – رقم:٦٥٠٢]

'An Abi Hurairah (ra) qala, Qala Rasulullahi ﷺ *: InnAllaha ta'ala qala: " ..., wa la yazaalu 'Abdi yataqarrabu ilayya bin nawafile hatta ahebahu, fa idha ahbabtuhu kunta Sam'ahul ladhi yasma'u behi, wa Basarahul ladhi yubsiru behi, ..."*
[Hadith Qudsi, Sahih al Bukhari, Raqam: 6502)

Narrated by Abu Hurairah (ra) that: the Messenger of Allah (pbuh) said that: Allah the Almighty said: "...My servant continues to draw near to Me with voluntary acts of worship so that I shall love him. When I love him, I am his hearing with which he hears, his seeing with which he sees..." [Holy Hadith, Authentic by al-Bukhari, # 6502]

Allah ﷻ Dresses Us Only Through Sayyidina Muhammad ﷺ

Allah ﷻ does nothing to the servant except dressing first through Sayyidina Muhammad ﷺ. It means the holy face has to begin to send *sifat al Sami'* (attribute of All Hearing) so that the servant begins to hear. Like a light and a laser that keeps coming and keeps dressing, can be dressing over years of their life. *Sifat al Sami'* so that they hear what Allah ﷻ wants them to hear because we said it's all from Allah ﷻ.

From *"La ilaha illAllah"* coming to *"Muhammadun Rasulullah* ﷺ*,"* that Divinely face begins to dress the soul.

Sifat al Basir. Sami al Basir are locks on the ears. So, anyone who wants to hear and see, what's then your most important faculty? These are the attributes on ears. So, unless you achieve *"Sam'ina wa ata'na,"* that, 'We hear and we obey.' Not we hear and we argue, not we hear and we debate but that we hear and we obey.

...سَمِعْنَا وَأَطَعْنَا غُفْرَانَكَ رَبَّنَا وَإِلَيْكَ الْمَصِيْرُ ﴿٢٨٥﴾

2:285 – "Sam'ina wa ata'na, ghufranaka Rabbana wa ilaykal masir."
(Surat Al-Baqarah)

"…We hear, and we obey: (We seek) Thy forgiveness, our Lord, and to Thee is the end of all journeys." (The Cow, 2:285)

'Hear and Obey' to Open Your Spiritual Hearing and Seeing

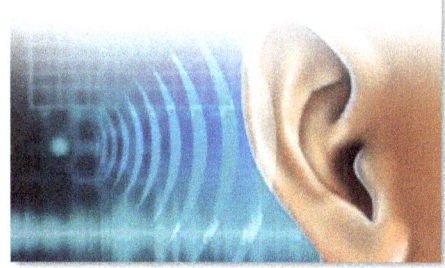

As a result, Allah ﷻ lifts the locks off their ears. Why? So that the light of *Al Sami'* begins to dress them so they cannot see and they cannot hear if there are locks on their ears. So, they practice in the *tariqah,* *"Sam'ina wa ata'na"* – 'I hear and I obey.' *Tamam,* the Turkish, they say *tamam,* finished, *khalas,* it's okay. We heard it, it's done. It's not a teaching – I'll debate it, maybe think about it, maybe send a comment arguing about it. I took a path in which to hear and obey. As a result of that practice in life, the light of Prophet ﷺ from his holy ears in this world of light begins to dress their ear and their soul so that they hear. The holy light of *Al Basir* (All Seeing) and the people of vision dressing their heart to begin to see.

Safeguard Your Tongue From Lies and Shaitan

'Alim (All Knowing), *Al Qadir* (All Powerful), that when Prophet ﷺ, 'Safeguard your mouth. Safeguard your mouth so my *sifat al-'Alim* (attribute of The All-Knowing) can begin to dress your heart.'

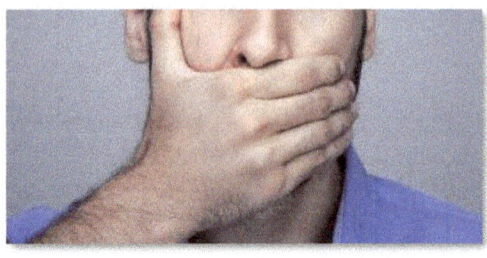

عن عُقْبَةَ بن عامر رضي الله عنه قال: قلت: يا رسول الله ﷺ ما النَّجَاةُ؟ قال:
"أَمْسِكْ عليك لِسَانَكَ، وَلْيَسَعْكَ بَيْتُكَ، وابْكِ على خَطِيئَتِكَ."
[صحيح – رواه الترمذي وأحمد]

'An 'Auqbati bin 'Amir (ra) qala, qultu: "Ya Rasulallah ﷺ maa annajatu?" Qala ﷺ: "Amsek 'alayka lisanaka, wal yasa'ka baytuka, wabki 'alaa khatiatika." [Sahih - Rawahu at Tirmidhi wa Ahmad]

Uqbah ibn 'Amir (ra) narrated, I asked: "O Messenger of Allah, what is salvation?" He (pbuh) replied: "Hold back your tongue, abide/stay in your house, and weep over your sin/wrongdoing."
[Authentic by at Tirmidhi wa Ahmad]

It means don't speak lies. Don't speak at all and don't speak anything from *shaitan* (satan). It means what? Safeguarding the mouth and that's why the *tariqah* (spiritual path) is based on *samt*, silence. Keep a path in life in which you're silent if you want Prophet ﷺ to begin to open *'Alim, Al 'Alim*. That's why the *tariqah* structure is based on this holy face. So, the student takes a practice that, 'I want my tongue to open,' safeguard your tongue. Don't talk. Don't lie. Don't spread falsehood. How can anything from that tongue be dressed from Prophet ﷺ that he take from his holy saliva to bless and moisten the tongue?

Control Your Tongue to Inherit from Lisanul Siddiqul 'Aliya

Then with their *salawats*, the beatific praising, their mouth becomes beatific, becomes fragranced with the light and the love of Prophet ﷺ.

 That's why the *nasheeds* (songs of praise) and the recitations and the reciters are immense warriors in Allah's ﷻ way. That by the power of the sincerity in the heart, when they recite, devils are running. These are the weapons of the heavens is recitation. Why? Because Prophet ﷺ fragranced their tongue. It means the tongue has an immense importance so speak the truth. Speak with good character, no yelling, no anger. As much as we can control the tongue, Prophet ﷺ is dressing a *sifat Al 'Alim* (attribute of All Knowing). Why we want to inherit from *Lisanul 'Aliya*. When Allah ﷻ says, 'The one whom We grant a wisdom has been granted My greatest gift. That I grant for you the tongue, *Lisanul 'Aliya*, the tongue most high.

وَوَهَبْنَا لَهُم مِّن رَّحْمَتِنَا وَجَعَلْنَا لَهُمْ لِسَانَ صِدْقٍ عَلِيًّا ﴿٥٠﴾

19:50 – " Wa wahabna lahum min rahmatina wa ja'alna lahum lisana Sidqin 'Aliya." (Surat Maryam)

"And We bestowed of Our Mercy on them, and We granted them lofty honour from/ on the tongue of truth." (Maryam, 19:50)

269

Did You Thank Allah ﷻ For Your Breath?

When the holy face wants to dress the servant from the oceans of power, *Al Qadir* (All Powerful) which is the *nafas* (breath) and the nose symbolizes the breath of power, the breath of *rahmah* (mercy). So, that when they are safeguarding their breath, they're conscious of their breath and say, 'Before I ask from anything, did I thank Allah ﷻ for my breath? Did I thank him from this power and this life He's given to me?'

As a result, when they meditate, they're breathing by *zikr* "*Hu.*" They meditate, they connect with the shaykh and ask that, 'Dress my breath.' As they're breathing, they visualize this fire of *Hu* that enters within them and that they push out the *zikr Hu*. Every time the *Hu* is coming and filling with lights and energy and every time, all the badness is repelling from the body because when this fire of energy comes in, it pushes out all the negativity. The more they safeguard their breath and understand the breath, then the holy breath and *sifat Al Qadir* begins to dress from the holy face upon their soul.

Serving the Shaykh Opens the Power of An-Nur and Al-Hay

Then we describe then from the right eye *nur* (Light) and left eye *hay* (Ever-living). That in their meditation and contemplation, every time their goodness and they're under the *nazar* (gaze) because of their efforts, their *khidmat*, their service, these holy eyes are now dressing. So your *khidmat* and service, the charity you give, the charity of your time, of your effort, your practices, whatever you're doing to be of service to the shaykhs, to the *tariqah*, to the way, what do you open?

So, when you serve the shaykh, it's the most powerful opening of *nur* and *hay* because the Prophet ﷺ loves the shaykh, is a representation of Sayyidina Muhammad ﷺ. It means then the gaze of Prophet ﷺ begins to open from *sifat ar-Rahman an-Nur*. Every time that servant is being dressed by the light of *nur* upon their eye, upon their being, and complete and perfect their light.

Activating Your Eyes is to Love Imam al-Hassan ؑ and Imam al-Hussain ؑ

From *sifat ar-Raheem*, the left eye, Prophet ﷺ is then dressing them from *Bahrul Hayat* (Ocean of Ever-living). That they are becoming eternal servants of Allah ﷻ and perfecting their character and their lights.

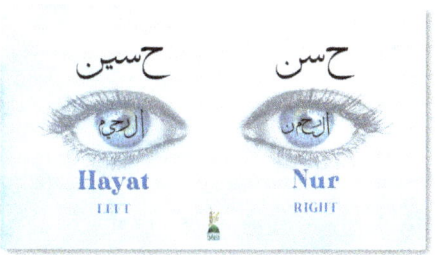

271

That's why the love of *Ahlul Bayt* (holy family of Prophet ﷺ) is so important. Because these two lights, from those lights Allah ﷻ created the soul of Sayyidina Imam al Hassan ؏, the right eye. The left light and left eye of Sayyidina Muhammad ﷺ, there's the creation of Imam al Hussain ؏. By loving these *Ahlul Bayt* means activating more of the immensity of these realities because these eyes of Prophet ﷺ described Imam al Hassan ؏ and Imam al Hussain ؏ *wa qurratol 'ain*.

إِلَى النَّبِيْ قُرَّةُ الْعَيْنِ   أَسْيَادِي الْحَسَّنْ وَالْحُسَّيْنِ

جَدُّكُمْ صَاحِبُ الْقُرْآنَ   يَا شَبَابَ الْجَنَّتَيْنِ

Asyadil Hassan wal Hussaini   *Ilan Nabi qurrato 'aini*
Ya shabaa bal janna'taini   *Jaddukum Saahibul Qur'ana*

Our Masters, Imam Hassan (as) and Imam Hussain (as),
They are the coolness of Prophet's (pbuh) eyes.
O the Youth of the Paradises,
Your grandfather (Prophet Muhammad (pbuh)) is the owner of the Holy
Qur'an.

Love the Two Imams ؏ More Than Yourself to Gain Real Hassanat

They were the beloved of those beatific eyes of Prophet ﷺ, his beloved grandchildren. They occupied the reality of that love and that *ishq*. So, then activating those eyes upon your life is to love his grandchildren more than you love yourself. Love Imam al Hassan ؏, Imam al Hussain ؏ more than we love ourself. That's the activation of those eyes. That's why Allah ﷻ, *"Fid dunya hasanat wa akhirah hasanat wa qinaa azaaban Naar."*

وَمِنْهُم مَّن يَقُولُ رَبَّنَا آتِنَا فِي الدُّنْيَا حَسَنَةً وَفِي الْأَخِرَةِ حَسَنَةً وَقِنَا عَذَابَ النَّارِ ﴿٠١﴾

2:201 – "Wa minhum mai yaqoolu rabbanaaa aatina fid dunyaa hasanatawn wa fil aakhirati hasanatanw wa qinaa azaaban Naar." (Surat Al-Baqarah)

"Our Lord, give us in this world [that which is] good and in the Hereafter [that which is] good and protect us from the punishment of the Fire." (The Cow, 2:201)

That's what they wanted. Allah ﷻ gave the clue in Holy Qur'an that, 'If you want *hassan* in life and you want the *hassan* of *akhirah* (hereafter) and you want protection from the fire, then love them. Be of service to them ﷺ. Remember them ﷺ, *alayhis salaam*.' It means these are immense beads that they come together like a beatific *tasbih*. Everywhere we look, Allah ﷻ is giving us these understandings, these blessings so that the *nazar* (gaze) and the light and the love of Prophet ﷺ, *inshaAllah*, to be dressing upon us, our families and our communities. By means of these lights is the perfection of our characters, *inshaAllah*.

Subhana rabbika rabhal 'izzati 'amma yasifoon, wa saluamun 'alal mursaleen, walhamdulillahi rabbil 'aalameen. Bi hurmati Muhammad al-Mustafa wa bi siri Surat al-Fatiha.

Fourth Power

Haqiqatut Tawassul

Reality of Conveyance

Directing to the Divinely Face to Open the Power of Conveyance

The 7 Eternal Flames are the 7 Eternal Attributes of the Holy Face

They dress the heart with what Allah ﷻ wants it to be dressed with. Throughout Bible also focuses on the holy face. 'Everything perishes but the Holy Face.' It's

that reality. Did you read the Book of Revelation? When John describes the Emerald Throne and the Seven Eternal Flames. He said, 'I saw the King seated upon the Throne and in front were Seven Eternal Flames.'

كُلُّ شَيْءٍ هَالِكٌ إِلَّا وَجْهَهُ ۚ {٨٨}

28:88 – "…kullu shayin halikun illa wajha" (Surat Al-Qasas)

"…Everything (that exists) will perish except His holy Face…" (The Stories, 28:88)

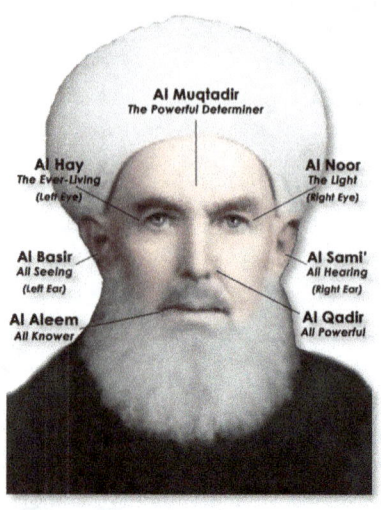

Al Muqtadir
The Powerful Determiner

Al Hay
The Ever-Living
(Left Eye)

Al Noor
The Light
(Right Eye)

Al Basir
All Seeing
(Left Ear)

Al Sami'
All Hearing
(Right Ear)

Al Aleem
All Knower

Al Qadir
All Powerful

These are the seven Divinely attributes that dress the Face. Those whom Allah ﷻ granted of His prophets because prophecy is based on the perfection of the face. They couldn't be a prophet unless Allah ﷻ perfected their face because the attribute of hearing has to be perfected. Otherwise, how you can be a prophet if you don't hear Allah ﷻ? As a result of guidance, guidance comes from *Nur* (Light), *al-Hayat* (Ever-living) has to come from their eyes. So then God perfected their eyes. The energy and the *qudra* (power) that they bring in to do what they have to do is through their breath.

It means when they breathe, they can ignite the energy of their soul from their breath. That's why all spiritual ways are based on the power of the breath because there is an energy and a force that makes everything to have an existence. The secret is *ruh* (soul). So rooted everything has a *ruh* in it that Allah's ﷻ *'Azimat* (Might) is making it all to exist. They reached a point in which that breath be unlocked for them. That when they breathe, they breathe that secret in

and they ignite their soul, like an energy that comes onto their soul immediately ignites.

1. Haqiqatul Juzba (Reality of Magnetism)

Our Souls are Hostages Under the Oppression of Our Bodies

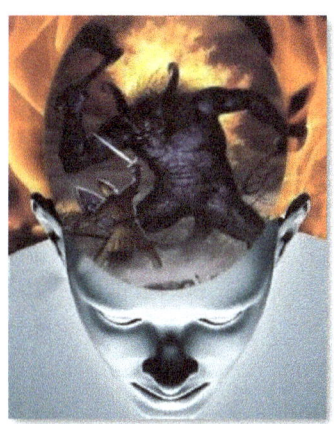

That's one of the realities of the *juzba* and the attraction. When you enter into a place, you enter into a Starbucks because of the energy you've been charged with in the *zikr* (Divine remembrance) and the associations. You enter a Starbucks; in reality if you could see, everybody in that room most likely their souls are deprived and starved like hostages because they're under the *zulumat* and the oppression of their body.

So, their body is like an oppressor, like a beast. Adam, the 'Compass' [Golden Compass] movie is like that. So, everybody is under the oppression of their beast. So, if you had eyes to see and you entered into one of these places like a coffee house or a mall, the beasts are controlling and the soul is deprived, ravaged, like a prisoner and they tortured him.

The Paradise Lights of Rijalullah Attracts the Souls of People

One of these *rijal* (people of maturity) or students of the *rijalullah* (men of God), as soon as they enter, the souls see their soul and understands this is not a deprived soul because the soul is not blind. It sees these are paradise

souls, paradise lights are shining from them. Immediately they feel attracted to that person and they push their body to go and to look at that person, look at that person. Why they're looking at the person? They're not looking at you because you're weird. They're looking because the soul is inspired that, 'Look at the face of that person.'

Souls Will Testify in the Grave for Seeing the Muhammadan Light

Why? Because when you enter into the *mawt* (death) and enter into the grave, the angels are going to ask, 'What was your religion? Who was your prophet?' All, all of that. [Angels ask] 'Have you seen a Muhammadan?' They say, 'What?' Immediately, the soul will testify, 'I've seen. I've seen. I've seen. I've seen that light.' Because the soul doesn't lie. The ego is the one who is going to be lying. The soul is going to say.

That's why Mawlana Shaykh ق said many times that the face of *awliya* (saints), it's enough if you passed their face. It's enough for them to see the face and their soul will call upon them. The soul will testify to the truth that, 'This is *La ilaha illAllah Muhammadun Rasulallah* ﷺ. These are the light of Sayyidina Muhammad ﷺ.' At that time, the angels said that, 'You have spoken the truth.' It means then *Nurul Muhammad* ﷺ (Light of Prophet Muhammad ﷺ) comes to intercede. That, 'Did you see my light?' Say, 'Yes.'

Children Can See the Lights From Heaven Inside Pious People

That's why they're staring. They're not staring because they think you're weird. They're staring because they're attracted to this light because they are deprived of it. You see it the most in the little  children because little children are innocent. So, when we go out it's like they're looking at Santa Claus. They just have this smile on them. You know, when they just can't stop looking. The parents are wondering, 'Why is he looking at you like that?' It's because he came from paradise, they're innocent. They know the light that they're seeing and they're not seeing that in this material world.

That's the *juzba* – that's the attraction. Their souls are attracted to these lights and to these energies. That's why people begin to converse with you and talk with you because they see that light. Now you fine-tune that more and more and more, they can bring an entire city into their associations because the energy they're emitting brings all people.

3. Haqiqatut Tawajjuh
(Reality of Directing to Divinely Face)

You Must Be Trained With Strong Practices to Enter the World of Souls

Then through the training, *tawajjuh*. 'Everything perishes but the Face.' (Holy Qur'an, 28:88) As soon as they train and make their *tafakkur* and their contemplation and continuously, 'I'm nothing, I'm nothing, I'm nothing.' When you're operating from your soul, Allah ﷻ then says, begin to teach you, 'Enter into the world of souls. Enter into the association of the world of souls.'

You saw in Lord of the Rings [movie], every time he put the ring on, he entered into the *arwah* (soul) but he wasn't able to carry the world of souls. Because also there are the world of *shayateen* (devils). You have to pass through their dimension. It's not easy to open the eye of the servant if his practices are not strong. As soon as you open the eye, it's the eye of everything. Every *shaitan* (satan), every *jinn* (unseen being), everything you can imagine is just sitting there waiting in this dimension.

Without Strong Energy, Spiritual Openings Can Be a Ticket to the Mental Hospital

Your practices have to be strong, belief has to be strong. The energy emanating from that servant has to be strong so that those beings have no interest in coming near that person. Because the energy is not there, you end up in a

mental hospital. That's why the people in a mental hospital most of them you hear, that's true. They say 'I'm seeing them; they're coming every night attacking me.'

These poor people, yes, this is what happens either through the drugs or trauma, it broke these *hijabs* (veils). So the drugs can break the *hijab*. When people who are taking too many excessive drugs, they break their *hijab* and begin to see all the demons running. People running into the wall and hiding into their ceiling. It's the *jinn* world. Or through very traumatic abuse – again where you've fragmented their hardware, and everything now is corrupt and they start to see every *jinn*.

Control Your State and Be From Ahlul Basirah

Because that state is only through their perfection, when they're perfecting themselves, building themself and the shaykh is slowly, slowly testing them. That they give you little bit to see, keep your practices. Don't go cuckoo and negate; be nothing, be nothing, be nothing. As soon as it make you to be crazy, they'll stop and close the whole thing, it stops. That whole *tawajjuh* then is a whole reality that Allah ﷻ, 'You have to be from *Ahlul Basirah*. People who operate from their heart not from the physical realm but through their spiritual realm, through their spiritual connection.'

4. Haqiqatut Tawassul (Reality of Conveyance)

Those Without a Connection Only Pray Through Their Mouth

Then the *tawassul* that they convey. If you are in their associations, and you merely mention their names and it's in their presence, like a bell. As soon as you mention their names, your praying is in their presence. 'You just mention the name, we understand what that person wants. Leave it in heart, it's none of your business.' Those are the real ones.

The fake ones, they keep talking and making *du'as* (supplications) and they just keep using their mouth. It's not them that has any ability to do. Right? So fake one talks a lot in the material world. They make  *du'as* for half an hour. The one who heard you he could've heard you in two seconds, what's the other half hour for? Because you don't know who you're talking to so you're just putting out all sorts of different *du'as* and hoping they make a difference.

Asking With Humility Resolves Half of Your Problem

But *rijalullah*, they merely mention the names of the shaykhs and mention the name of Prophet ﷺ, it's finished. They've taken the case. They heard exactly what that person's asking and they don't even need to know what you're asking. Allah ﷻ already knows His creation but the fact that you are coming to that door and knocking on that door – half of the claim is now resolved because Allah ﷻ wants humility.

The servant's coming and, 'One of My Servants, humbly that accepting to be nothing. I know the condition I put him in.' So, it means their claim already been heard, half their problem has been taken. Now these *rijal*, they inspire the person to do good deeds and good actions so that Allah ﷻ will be pleased. If Allah ﷻ is pleased, He may take the other half of the problem away. It's different than somebody just keep sitting there for half an hour and say this, say that, say this, say that. That's the *tawassul* because they're immediately able to convey.

5. Haqiqatut Tayy
(Reality of Folding Time and Space)

Those With Haqiqatut Tayy Can Move Through Time and Space

Haqiqatut Tawassul, Haqiqatut Tayy – the ability to move through space and time. If the star is completing, then these are the completions of a guide. It means the reality, the *haqqaiq* of *Tayy* – of moving through space and time. They can be anywhere at any time. Physically, they can move and be in many places at the same time, but that permission is very rare. Spiritually, they can be any place at the same time.

The Shaykh's Soul Can Be Present Anywhere Through His Gaze

This is the reality of light. It has particle, it has wave. You only see the particle, but everything must have a wave reality. So one whom Allah ﷻ gives command over himself means he has command over that reality. He has command over that reality that you see the particle, you see the form of that person, of that shaykh. At the same time the shaykh is operating on a wave.

It means through his *nazar* he's at *Rauza e Sharif* (holy burial chamber) with Prophet ﷺ. With his *nazar* same time he's at Holy Ka'bah. With the *nazar* he's at the *maqam* (station) of all his shaykhs. Like a television with a digital signal, not analogue signal. Digital because each channel is

defined and perfected because their light in all of them. It's not by imagination but their light in all of those stations receiving the *faiz* (downpouring blessings) from those associations and coming back onto their physicality. So it means they are always accompanying their shaykh, their *arwah* – their soul always with their shaykh, being dressed by it, blessed by it. Every *tajalli* (manifestation) that the shaykh is encountering and rising is sending that emanation upon them. They can be anywhere at any time from the power of the soul.

Those Who Make Contracts With Jinn for Power Will Be Severely Punished

Because from the book, from the one who had knowledge of the book said, 'I can bring it.' It is Allah's ﷻ *daleel* (proof) in Qur'an. When Sayyidina Sulaiman عليه السلام said, 'I want the throne.' The *jinn*, because the *jinn* has a power too; that's why he can play with people, he can move you back and forth through space and time. That's what we said was the Mandela

Effect. *Jinn* now are taking people through different dimensions.

Those who give themself to these *jinn* and make their contract and, 'They sold themselves for a small price' Allah ﷻ give in Qur'an. They sell themselves to devils for a small price to the extent of their soul will be punished.

$$
\text{أُولَٰئِكَ الَّذِينَ اشْتَرَوُا الْحَيَاةَ الدُّنْيَا بِالْآخِرَةِ ۖ فَلَا يُخَفَّفُ عَنْهُمُ الْعَذَابُ وَلَا ﴿٨٦﴾ هُمْ يُنْصَرُونَ}
$$

2:86 – "Ulaaa'ikal lazeenash tarawul hayaatad dunyaa bil aakhirati falaa yukhaffafu 'anhumul 'azaabu wa laa hum yunsaroon."
(Surah Al-Baqarah)

"Those are the ones who have bought the life of this world [in exchange] for the Hereafter, so the punishment will not be lightened for them, nor will they be aided." (The Cow, 2:86)

Those With Knowledge of the Book Can Be Present in All Dimensions

But whom Allah ﷻ gave the knowledge of the book, that was a gift from Allah ﷻ. He [with the knowledge of the book] said, 'I bring it to you before your eye blinks. It will be replicated and brought right in front of you.'

$$
\text{قَالَ يَا أَيُّهَا الْمَلَأُ أَيُّكُمْ يَأْتِينِي بِعَرْشِهَا قَبْلَ أَن يَأْتُونِي مُسْلِمِينَ ﴿٣٨﴾ قَالَ عِفْرِيتٌ مِّنَ الْجِنِّ أَنَا آتِيكَ بِهِ قَبْلَ أَن تَقُومَ مِن مَّقَامِكَ ۖ وَإِنِّي عَلَيْهِ لَقَوِيٌّ أَمِينٌ ﴿٣٩﴾ قَالَ الَّذِي عِندَهُ عِلْمٌ مِّنَ الْكِتَابِ أَنَا آتِيكَ بِهِ قَبْلَ أَن يَرْتَدَّ إِلَيْكَ طَرْفُكَ ۚ فَلَمَّا رَآهُ مُسْتَقِرًّا عِندَهُ قَالَ هَٰذَا مِن فَضْلِ رَبِّي ۖ ... ﴿٤٠﴾}
$$

27:38-40 – "Qala ya ayyuha almalao ayyukum yateenee bi'arshiha qabla an yatoonee muslimeen. (38) Qala 'ifreetun mina aljinni ana ateeka bihi qabla an taqooma min maqamika wa inni 'alayhi laqawiyyun ameen. (39) Qala alladhee 'indahu 'ilmun minal kitabi ana ateeka bihi qabla an yartadda ilayka Tarfuka, falamma raahu mustaqirran 'indahu qala hadha min fadli rabbi…(40)"
(Surat An-Naml)

"[Solomon] said (to his own men), "O Chiefs! which of you can bring me her throne before they come to me in submission? (38) Said An 'Ifrit, of the Jinns, I will bring it to you before you rise from your place/council, and indeed, I am for this (purpose/task) strong and trustworthy. (39) Said one who had knowledge of the book: "I will bring it to you within the twinkling of an eye!" Then when (Solomon) saw it placed firmly before him, he said: "This is by the Grace of my Lord!…(40)"
(The Ant, 27:38-40)

Awliya Receive the Charge Wirelessly From Heaven and Other Dimensions

That's bringing a throne, that's not even describing the power of how 'he' can move through space and time. So it means that knowledge, that's *Haqiqatut Tayy*, that they can fold and move into a different dimension. Even faster the soul can be in all dimensions and their souls in the paradise realities. Every association their soul is in paradise realities, being dressed by that reality and emanating from that reality onto the physical plane. Right?

It's charged, the wireless charging. As soon as it charges in that dimension, all of that energy is coming onto that physicality. So wherever that physicality is going, that's the source of its *faiz* because Allah ﷻ opens these associations and rooms that, 'Come into My paradises. Come into the association of the *Diwan ul Awliya*, the association of all the *awliya* and the association of Prophet ﷺ.' If Allah ﷻ opened that reality, that's the source of your *faiz*, because your soul is there. It means wirelessly sending to you wherever you are. It's tremendous emanation, tremendous blessing.

Awliya Experience the Manifestation of Holy Nights From Their Soul

That's why when they come to the shaykh and say, 'Oh the *Laylatul Qadr* (Night of Power) was this day Shaykh' or 'This was this day' and 'This was that day.' They're not people who looking at a calendar; they're experiencing it directly from their soul. When Allah ﷻ opens, He's opening it upon their [saints] association, not opening it to the people of *dunya* (material world). It opened first in their association, they experience that, and then it begin to emanate upon Earth and upon the normal souls that didn't achieve those *darajats* (spiritual ranks).

6. Haqiqatul Irshad (Reality of Guidance)

All Powers of the Heart are Granted to the Servant for Being of Service to Allah ﷻ

As a result of *Haqiqatut Tayy* (Reality of Folding Time and Space), then Allah ﷻ opens *Haqiqatul Irshad.* Because all these five powers of their heart is ignited, then the last power Allah ﷻ give that, 'You are being given the permission of guidance.' Because you'll be using all these gifts that Allah ﷻ granted upon the heart and the soul for what? For guidance. That's why they didn't leave when Allah ﷻ offered, 'You want to leave the *dunya*?' They said, 'No, that I want to be of service, *Ya Rabbi.*' Then, 'Now you have then that authority of guidance.'

Subhana rabbika rabbal 'izzati 'amma yasifoon, wa salaamun 'alal mursaleen, walhamdulillahi rabbil 'aalameen. Bi hurmati Muhammad al-Mustafa wa bi siri Surat al-Fatiha.

Reality of Tawassul Opens When the Guide is Connected to the Holy Face

Direct Yourself to the Divinely Face in Contemplation

With this immense ocean of abundance and the immense realities of their *tafakkur* and their contemplation, what's the next that opens? *Haqiqatut Tawajjuh* (Reality of Directing to Divinely Face). The reality of the *tawajjuh* is the conveyance and focusing onto the face. *Tawajjuh* is the face and *Haqiqatul Tawassul* (Reality of Intercession) that coming after is how they are going to convey. So, *Haqiqatul Tawajjuh* is a connection to the face.

It means again, the reality of guidance can't be achieved without these realities. That's why the *turuqs* teach step by step. So, that when somebody say, 'Oh, this is a *Shaykh ul Irshad*. This is a shaykh, he has five *tariqahs* in his control.' One, Naqshbandiya is immensely difficult to achieve more or less saying that you are controlling five *tariqahs* under your belt. It doesn't make any sense when these people talk like that.

Have Love and Respect for Muhammadan Guides

It means this *haqiqat* now, this reality of *tawajjuh* is that in their *tafakkur* and in their contemplation, not only they learn how to connect and connect, connect, connect, but Allah ﷻ taught to them, inspired within them, connect to that which is not perishing. Everything will perish but the Divinely Face.

$$\ldots \text{كُلُّ شَيْءٍ هَالِكٌ إِلَّا وَجْهَهُ} \ldots \{٨٨\}$$

28:88 – "...Kullu shayin halikun illa wajha..." (Surat Al-Qasas)

"...Everything (that exists) will perish except His holy Face..."
(The Stories, 28:88)

So that in their meditation, they continuously reach a state that, 'I am

nothing. I'm nothing. That I don't want to exist. I don't want to be anything in your presence. That I'm nothing, I'm nothing.' That's why the loyalty, the reverence, the respect. All of the *tariqah* was based on manners because these are in their official capacity. These are the Muhammadan representatives. It's a respect for the love of Sayyidina Muhammad ﷺ. That's why we said this is all based on love and *muhabbat*. This is not based on *'aqel* (intellect) and brain.

The Heavenly Satellites From the Divinely Face of Prophet ﷺ to Awliya

When they want to reach the *tawajjuh* and the Divinely Face, the power that coming from the Divinely Face, means that in their meditation that they reach to a state of annihilation. That, 'I'm nothing, I'm nothing, I'm nothing. Just dress me from Your Divinely lights and Divinely oceans, *ya Rabbi.*' Then in their meditation, they begin to be dressed by the face of the shaykh.

There are seven attributes that are dressing. Their face is dressed from the face of their shaykh all the way up to the face of Sayyidina Muhammad ﷺ. The holy face of Sayyidina Muhammad ﷺ is dressed by the Face of Allah's ﷻ Divinely Face, Divinely attributes and names and essences.

It means that Allah's ﷻ Divinely essences are dressing the face of Sayyidina Muhammad ﷺ. That Prophet ﷺ is dressing the *awliya*. Then from satellites, we've described before, dresses the face of the *Ghawth*. The *Ghawth* dresses the shaykhs below, then the shaykhs dress below them, shaykhs dress below. Then this network of satellites is dressing upon the face.

The 7 Divinely Essences That Dress the Holy Faces of Awliya

Their face is the only thing that can capture that energy and that power.

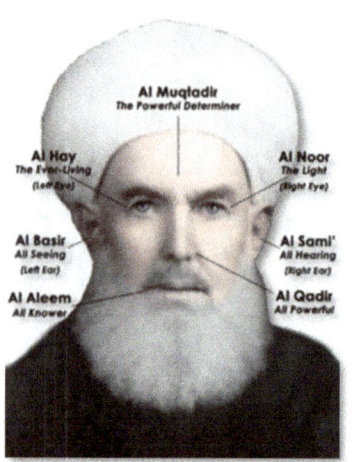

As a result, Allah ﷻ dresses from seven essences, seven openings. That from one [right ear], two [left ear], three [right eye], four [left eye], five [nostrils], six [tongue], seven [forehead]. So, the two ears, two eyes, nostrils, tongue, and forehead; the seven points dressing their face. These are the eternal attributes that dress their face. As a result, Allah ﷻ dressing from the face of the shaykh to the face of the student. They are in the reality of the *tawajjuh* and what's being conveyed to them of energies, of lights and realities dressing upon their soul, dressing upon the different essences that are dressing upon that reality.

That's in the *Lataif ul Qalb* which shows a picture of the face of Shaykh Daghestani ق, the attribute of Allah ﷻ associated with that. That Allah ﷻ dressing the ear of Prophet ﷺ in the World of Light with that *Ismullah* (Name of Allah ﷻ) and that, that light and that *Ismullah* dressing Prophet ﷺ dresses the *awliyaullah*. So, then those essences are reflecting upon the student to make them to be raised and dressed by the immensity of those lights and the blessings of those lights.

Oceans of Eternity Dress Saints with Hidayat and Wadud

As a result of that connection, they are in the reality of *tawassul* which is the reality of intercession and the conveyance of prayers. So, they're all now interconnected. So, we want the *juzba* to have the connection. We want the *faiz* and the lights and Divine emanation to dress us. Then they train on how to connect with the face. How to receive the emanations from the Face and that becomes from the oceans of eternity and they become from the oceans of *al Hayat*, of Allah's ﷻ oceans of eternity.

هو	
Hu	
و	ه
Waw	*Ha*
ودود	هداية
Wadud **(The Most Loving)**	*Hidayat* **(Guidance)**

*Note: Please read English from right to left to coincide with Arabic.

Those essences, those realities are from Allah's ﷻ oceans of eternity making that servant to be from the real and the reality of Hu-men. It means that they are now in the oceans of guidance of '*Hu*' where Allah ﷻ give them *hidayah* (guidance) and real *hidayah* and dressings and that they are being dressed from Allah's ﷻ ancient oceans of *Al Wadud* (The Most Loving). We described before the people of *Hu*, they are an ancient reality of Divinely love and they're eternal. That the lights that dressing upon them is from Allah's ﷻ oceans of eternity. So, this network of satellite dressing them, making them to reach towards their eternal reality.

By Connecting to the Holy Face, the Reality of Conveyance is Established

So, when the shaykh is connecting to the face of his shaykh then he is now under that *tajalli* (manifestation), under the immensity of lights and blessings that coming upon them. At the same time, Allah ﷻ opened for them now the reality of *tawassul*, 'Convey what you need to convey.' If Allah ﷻ opening for  the servant that, 'You connected to the Divinely Face, to the holy face and to the face of the *awliyaullah*, then convey what you need to convey.' That opens for them the reality of *tawassul*. *Haqiqatut Tawassul*, the reality of conveyance. Right? So, that they're meditating, they're connecting. At that reality, they can begin to convey what needs to be conveyed of *du'as*, of askings, of whatever needs to be asked.

Allah ⸢ ⸣ Ordered Us to Seek a Wasila and a Means to Approach

When people say that, 'Why do they go to these people to ask? You can make *du'a*. Oh Allah ⸢ ⸣ ...' Yeah, everybody can make *du'a* but when Allah ⸢ ⸣ want to open these realities, these are realities that are not understood. People can live thousand lifetimes and not achieve these realities. But when Allah ⸢ ⸣ open for these servants these realities, then Allah ⸢ ⸣ gives them a means in which to approach. A *tawassul* means 'a means in which to approach.' Allah ⸢ ⸣ says in Qur'an, 'Seek, seek a *tawassul* to Us. Seek a means in which to approach Our Divinely kingdom.'

يَا أَيُّهَا الَّذِينَ آمَنُوا اتَّقُوا اللَّـهَ وَابْتَغُوا إِلَيْهِ الْوَسِيلَةَ وَجَاهِدُوا فِي سَبِيلِهِ لَعَلَّكُمْ تُفْلِحُونَ ﴿٣٥﴾

5:35 – "Ya ayyuhal ladheena amanoo ittaqollaha wabtagho ilayhi alwaseelata wa jahidoo fee sabeelihi, la'allakum tuflihoon."
(Surat Al-Mayidah)

"O you who believe! Have consciousness and seek the means of approach unto Him, and strive in his cause: that you may prosper/succeed."
(The Table Spread, 5:35)

Allah ﷻ Shows the Necessity of Tawassul in All We Do

Some people have to use a mobile phone to call for help. So, anyone who says, 'Oh that's *shirk* (polytheism). You only rely on Allah ﷻ,' they're liars. Because they need a mobile phone to call the Triple A and tow truck and police if they feel a burglar's coming. That is a *tawassul*.

All of *hajj* (pilgrimage) is *tawassul* – seeking a means and a blessing. You're trying to kiss the Ka'bah because you want to be closer to the heavens. You have to go to the *maqam* (station) of Sayyidina Ibrahim ﷺ to get the *barak* and *tabarak* of Sayyidina Ibrahim ﷺ. You go to *zamzam* to get from the dress of what Allah ﷻ dressed upon these waters that are on Earth but dressed from paradise. So, everything in our life is the reality of *tawassul*.

That's why Allah ﷻ says that, 'Seek a means in which to approach Me.' (Holy Qur'an, 5:35) Not the arrogant just say that, 'God is with me.' Allah ﷻ said, 'No, you have to seek a means in which to reach towards God.' That you're just the milk but you want to become *ghee* or butter, you have a whole process of cleansing and stirring and trials and tribulation until you become *ghee*. They stir you up really good. Other than that, it's just milk. So, there's a whole process.

Awliyaullah Souls are Dressed With Immense Faith

As a result, Allah ﷻ opens that reality so it becomes two-way. They're connecting to the face to receive its immense blessings. At the same time Allah ﷻ is that if there's anything that needs to be conveyed at that moment, convey through that channel, which is rarely used because their level of belief is that, 'That face that gazes upon me knows entirely what my condition is.' That's the level of their faith. Rarely are they  required to enter into that connection to begin to convey unless a sudden emergency or something unforeseen. But in the oceans of submission that gives the understanding that that face watching them.

When people don't understand the faith of a shaykh, asking, 'How do you have like this? Why like this? Explain like this.' Their life is not to explain anything why and how things happen or what Allah ﷻ is conveying to them. But this process gives us an understanding. That they are souls in which they convey. They meditate, they contemplate and that their soul is in the presence of that face and that face knows every condition that that person's body is in. They don't need to say anything. They are nothing because their whole movement and breath is in that reality. That gives to them the immensity of their faith.

By Allah's ﷻ Permission, These Heavenly Knowledges are Opening

So, that spiritual world is not something that can be understood because people are living a physical world in which every moment they're scared. That they're worried, they're wondering, 'How it's going to happen? What's going to happen? What's going to happen like this? We're going to die. We're going to have to do this, do that.' That's because they're only using their physical connection. But when Allah ﷻ guides, that's why we said, 'There is no guidance unless Allah ﷻ guides.'

Because all of what we just described in the last two nights are all by permission and *'Izzatullah* (Allah's ﷻ Might and Magnificence). That's why it's insulting when people say, 'Oh, it's only Allah ﷻ.' Who you think opening all these realities to Allah's ﷻ Kingdom and Allah's ﷻ Presence?

...وَقَالُوا الْحَمْدُ لِلَّهِ الَّذِي هَدَانَا لِهَٰذَا وَمَا كُنَّا لِنَهْتَدِيَ لَوْلَا أَنْ هَدَانَا اللَّهُ ۖ لَقَدْ جَاءَتْ رُسُلُ رَبِّنَا بِالْحَقِّ... ﴿٤٣﴾

7:43 – "...Wa qalo Alhamdulillahi al ladhee hadana lihadha wa ma kunna linahtadiya lawla an hadana Allahu, laqad jaa at Rusulu Rabbina bil Haqqi..." (Surat Al-A'raf)

"... And they will say, Praise be to Allah, who has guided us to this [joy and happiness]; and we would never have been guided if Allah had not guided us. Certainly the messengers of our Lord had come with the truth..." (The Heights, 7:43)

You Have to Believe With Sincerity That Everything is From Allah ﷻ

It's not only Allah ﷻ that you say like that by tongue but you have to believe that when you say, 'It's only Allah ﷻ,' that you lived that way. That you understood that way. And that Allah ﷻ found sincerity in you and opened your heart to be magnetic, opened your soul and your body to be *juzba*

and to take these emanations. He opened your reality to connect to the Divinely Face, the heavenly face, the beatific face of *Wajhi hil Karim* (The Holy Face of the Most Generous) of Sayyidina Muhammad ﷺ, face of *awliyaullah*. Whatever face that Allah ﷻ is opening for that servant, these are by the Might and the Will of Allah ﷻ. That they achieved the immense oceans of *tawheed* (Oneness) and faith and sincerity. As a result, Allah ﷻ dress them and bless them and they can begin to convey through that connection.

Subhana rabbika rabbal 'izzati 'amma yasifoon, wa salaamun 'alal mursaleen, walhamdulillahi rabbil 'aalameen. Bi hurmati Muhammad al-Mustafa wa bi siri Surat al-Fatiha.

Fifth Power

Haqiqatut Tayy

Reality of Folding

Time and Space

Reality of Folding Time and Space and the Mandela Effect

The Concept of Dajjal is a Great Deceit

Awliyaullah (saints) come into our lives and remind us that the understanding of the Last Days and the concept of *Dajjal* is a great deceit. It is a tremendous deceit beyond any deceit that can be imagined. It's not translated as an anti-Christ because this is for

The Day when We will fold the heaven like the folding of a [written] sheet for the records. As We began the first creation, We will repeat it. [That is] a promise binding upon Us. Indeed, We will do it.

Al Quran 21:104
IslamicSayings.com 21.104

all the religions. All the world's going to be cast into a tremendous difficulty. That difficulty is beyond comprehension of what type of *fitna* Allah ﷻ will allow that door to be opened.

Haqiqatut Tayy and the Folding of Time and Space

From the teachings of *awliyaullah* (saints), from the *haqqaiq* and the reality of *Haqiqatut Tayy* and the folding of space and time. From Holy Qur'an, Surat al-Anbiya, verse 104.

يَوْمَ نَطْوِي السَّمَاءَ كَطَيِّ السِّجِلِّ لِلْكُتُبِ ۚ كَمَا بَدَأْنَا أَوَّلَ خَلْقٍ نُّعِيدُهُ ۚ وَعْدًا عَلَيْنَا ۚ إِنَّا كُنَّا فَاعِلِينَ ﴿١٠٤﴾

21:104 – "Yawma natwee asSama a katayyi assijelli lilKutubi, kama bada anaa awwala khalqin nu'iduhu, wa'dan 'alayna, inna kunna fa'ileen." (Surat Al-Anbiya)

"The Day when We will fold/roll up the heaven like the folding/scroll rolled up of sheets of book (completed). We produced the first creation, so shall We produce a new one: a promise We have undertaken: truly shall We fulfil it." (The Prophets, 21:104)

Sadaq Allahul azheem. That Allah ﷻ is taking from that verse, it's reality. That Allah ﷻ describes, 'The Day that We roll up the Heaven like a scroll, like a *sijjeel*, like a Book. They roll it up and complete. And even as We produced the first Creation, so shall We produce a new one.'

Our Existence is a Series of Pages Within a Book

From that understanding and from the secret of the *tayy* and the folding that they want us to understand from their *haqqaiq* (realities) that our existence are like pages within a book. Every moment is a page within a book. It's nothing lost. It means it's there. The moment it happens, it's in a book of Allah ﷻ. Every moment is put into a book and our existence from the beginning of time to *akhir zaman* and the end of time are just a series of pages within a book that Allah ﷻ has brought on for our existence.

$$ إِنَّا نَحْنُ نُحْيِي الْمَوْتَىٰ وَنَكْتُبُ مَا قَدَّمُوا وَآثَارَهُمْ ۚ وَكُلَّ شَيْءٍ أَحْصَيْنَاهُ فِي إِمَامٍ مُّبِينٍ ﴿١٢﴾ $$

36:12 – "Inna nahnu nuhyil mawta wa naktubu ma qaddamo wa atharahum, wa kulla shayin ahsaynahu fee imamin mubeen." (Surat YaSeen)

"Indeed it is We who shall give life to the dead, and We record all their footprint of the past and every step they take in the future, and of all things We have taken account in a Perfected Clear Imam (leader/Prophet (pbuh))." (YaSeen, 36:12)

That book – at a higher level of life other than the life within the physicality – in the world of light and in the world of realities, that page in life when they open, they can fold. They can fold a page and move from one point to the other point by that reality. Instead of going all the way through: A, B, C, D, they fold A and Z connect and immediately they connect into the realm of Z and they move through space and time. That can be through their body, through their soul, through their entirety, but most commonly through their tongue.

Awliya are Given Power of Haqiqatut Tayy ul Lisan and Moving Through Space

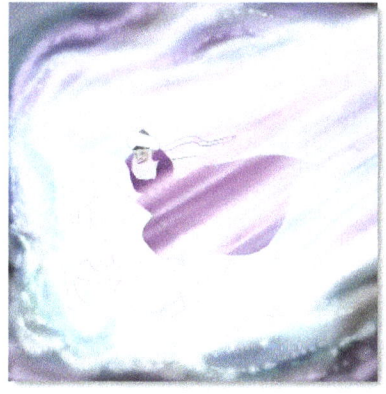

Allah ﷻ opens for them *Haqiqatut Tayy* (Reality of Folding Time and Space) from *lisan*. That through their tongues, their recitations are able to be increased in which to support the energy that Allah ﷻ is dressing on them. Their *zikr* not like regular *zikr* of people saying, *"Allah, Allah, Allah."* That, at a high performance level, the *zikr* within their heart is at a much higher speed and they can connect their tongue into a point which allows their heart to move at a tremendous speed.

That *tayy*, and then the movement of the physical *tayy* means they can move with *Bismillahir Rahmanir Raheem* and they step. They can be on a location that wherever Allah ﷻ wants to send them, wherever Prophet ﷺ wants to send them. We said before, in other talks, that that *adab* of physical movement is no longer necessary because of the mobile phone and people capturing the images of these *awliyaullah* appearing in multiple places.

They have the ability to appear from 12,000 to 24,000 locations at the same time. That their light as you see it as a particle, is more powerful in its wave format. Its wave can be in any direction, in any dimension that Allah ﷻ and Prophet ﷺ give them permission to move. They can manifest in that reality. Through their teachings and what Prophet ﷺ wants, they don't interfere with that dimension, that time, and they alter nothing from Allah's ﷻ Will because there is an *adab* (manner) and a respect.

Jinns and Devils are Moving Through Time and Space

When these days of deceit are open, Allah ﷻ is granting these *shayateen* (devils) a permission. That permission is that they are already moving within these dimensions. These dimensions are locked. Allah ﷻ locked the ability to alter them and to manipulate with them, but Allah ﷻ now unlocked. So, a great deceit is now moving onto Earth. That with these spiritual beings that Prophet ﷺ brought for us an understanding of the *jinn*. The bad *jinns* whose intentions are not good and the *shayateen* who absolutely have incorrect intentions and very negative and deceitful intentions, who are the workers for the *dajjal*. That, that permission granted for them to manipulate time and space.

Allah ﷻ Gave Permission for Devils to Manipulate Time

What happens as a great deceit begins to enter into this *dunya* (material world) is that for us to understand it, is that if somebody travels back into time and manipulates a point in time. Let's say they go back to 1940 because the *jinn* are moving through space and time. They're not limited and bound by the physical realm, but they were not given permission to alter. When

Allah ﷻ opened, because the days of *fitna* have to come, the *zuhoor* and presence of Sayyidina Mahdi ﷺ has to be present.

From Allah ﷻ, because *'bi izzatullah, bi izzatur Rasul wa izzatu mu'mineen'* shaitan is operating. It means that Allah ﷻ had to have given permission, Prophet ﷺ gave permission, and all the *mu'mineen*, who are *ulul amr* and are in charge, they are aware of what *shaitan* was given as a permission. It means that ability to begin to alter. So, what happens is that when these *shayteen*, they go back into 1940 and they alter something. We don't know and we are not aware of it, but something in this life now changed that hadn't been changed before.

﴾٨﴿ وَلِلَّهِ الْعِزَّةُ وَلِرَسُولِهِ وَلِلْمُؤْمِنِينَ وَلَكِنَّ الْمُنَافِقِينَ لَا يَعْلَمُونَ

63:8 – "…Wa Lillahil 'izzatu wa li Rasooli hi wa lil Mumineena wa lakinnal munafiqeena la y'alamoon.."(Surat Al-Munafiqoon)

"…And to Allah belongs [all] honor, and to His messenger, and to the believers, but the hypocrites do not know." (The Hypocrites, 63:8)

Realities Depicted in Sci-Fi Movies Give an Understanding of What's Coming

If you can imagine that everything you watch of scary movies, every sci-fi

movie that you watch, it's in existence. It is a thought within a brain that Allah ﷻ created. That brain can't think of something that Allah ﷻ hasn't. You don't open your computer and what a programmer did not put in there, all of a sudden there is a new software. Whatever the programmer put into that computer, that software is there. Whatever thought people have, Allah ﷻ put that thought.

Whatever concept they have or whatever understanding they have, Allah ﷻ put that. It means it is in existence. Then these sci-fi movies, and all these things that we talk about are trying to give us an understanding of these realities that are coming into this *dunya*.

The Mandela Effect Proves Jinns and Devils' Manipulation

It means if somebody is altering the timeline, goes back and begins to manipulate, something will change in this dimension and now they are seeing. They go and what they want is the attention of people, so they took iconic images, iconic movies, iconic sounds. Everything that was a symbol of our existence on this material *dunya* and they began to play with it. So many people are beginning to become aware that particular movie titles have changed from what we understood the title was. Particular shows, particular cartoons, particular items, their names have changed and things have changed. This is the sign of the great deceit that begins to enter onto this *dunya*.

Shaitans Go Back in Time and Change Holy Books

"But those enemies of mine who did not want me to be king over them- bring them here and kill them in front of me" Luke 19:27

They say there are verses of the Bible that everybody knows the 'Lord's prayer'. That, 'Forgive us our trespassing as we forgive those who trespass and come against us.' Now anybody who Googles the Bible now, it changed. It became from 'trespassing' to 'debt'. 'Forgive us our debt and we forgive our debtors' as if the bank wrote it. It means many of these issues. [Matthew 6:12]

There are verses now coming out, I think they called it Luke, their 19:27, book 19, verse 27 of their book. They say, 'Who didn't believe in me, bring him in front of me and slay him in front of me.' Why would Sayyidina 'Isa (Jesus) عليه السلام speak like that? But the *shaitans* would.

They go back and want to manipulate all the texts and manipulate everything in our *dunya* (material world). So that to drive people crazy and mad that they don't understand what is happening.

Holy Qur'an Cannot Be Changed Because It Has Guardians

Allah 🕮 is giving for us the *sifatal-Hafiz* (attribute of guardian). We're not truly understanding what Allah 🕮 has given to us of Holy Qur'an, of Sayyidina Muhammad ﷺ and from *awliyaullah*. It means when we don't understand that *awliyaullah*, they are guardians.

Those who recite Holy Qur'an and given the secret of Holy Qur'an, why did Allah 🕮 call them *hafiz*? Why not He call them 'the memorizers'? Because the day would come, and every time something came, but not like *akhir zaman* (end of time); not like the appearance of *Dajjal* where all holy books will be changed.

These *shaitans* go back in time and begin to manipulate and they open their book and it's changed because it's not a guarded book. Their books are not guarded books, their TV is not guarded TV, their being is not guarded beings. Those whom Allah 🕮 have guarded, *mahfuz*, then they begin to understand what level of reality Allah 🕮 is talking. That when they go to make a deceit within Holy Qur'an, Allah 🕮 says, 'Impossible! That My reciters, they are *hafiz*. They are guardians of the book.' If you move a *nuqt* (dot), it is known by them. You take a *waw* (Arabic letter W), you change anything and Allah's 🕮 *hafiz*, real *hafiz* – those whom guard the book, they know.

The paper may change but the words will never change. It means if verses and papers and books all around the world begin to change, we begin to understand the greatness of what Prophet ﷺ brought for us. Prophet ﷺ named our reciters, 'They are *hafiz*,' it means they are guardians of a day in which everything will come under attack. This is a greatness and '*Izzat* of Allah 🕮, '*izzatul Islam*.

The Lineage of Mahdiyun are Guarded and Cannot Be Manipulated

If you are destined to be with Sayyidina Mahdi ☝ because they give

another example; if there are four of you and the *shaitans* don't want one of you, they go back into your timeline and take that person out. And then all of a sudden, your picture shows there is only three of you in that picture. They took that problem away and now it doesn't exist in this time except whom Allah ☝ have guarded.

It means their entire lineage must be guarded so that *shaitan* can't manipulate and alter that being from appearing. Whom Allah ☝ wants to appear at the end of times and to be with Sayyidina Mahdi ☝, their entire lineage must be guarded from the beginning of time to the end of time. Like a file in the computer that you don't have access to. Then we understand again *'Izzatullah* and what Allah ☝ is establishing for protection for *insan* (mankind).

An Unimaginable Deceit is Going to Fill the Earth

It means many difficulties coming that are beyond imagination. When Mawlana Shaykh ق keeps saying that, 'Many things are going and many

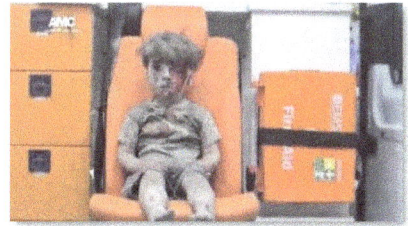

things are coming.' We can't understand the extent of what things are being manipulated, what things are being changed. If we talk too much about it, people would think that you are crazy because they are not waking up to see what is happening. They are arguing and worrying about *wudu* (ablution) and how much water to have for the *wudu*, but

315

yet they are not looking. They are not guarding and understanding their heart. They are not seeking out the knowledge and realities of what is happening within this *dunya*.

What Prophet ﷺ brought for us and taught for us that, 'Great deceit would fill the Earth that a child of seven, his hair would turn gray.'

فَكَيْفَ تَتَّقُونَ إِن كَفَرْتُمْ يَوْمًا يَجْعَلُ الْوِلْدَانَ شِيبًا ﴿١٧﴾

73:17 – "Fakaifa tattaqoona in kafartum yawmany yaj'alul wildaana sheeba" (Surat Al-Muzzammil)

"Then how can you fear, if you disbelieve, a Day that will make the children white-haired?" (The Enshrouded One, 73:17)

It is not going to turn gray from backbiting. When you talk about *fitna*, *fitna* is not backbiting. The *fitna* (confusion) that Prophet ﷺ and *awliyaullah* are fearful of is the *fitna* that *shaitan* now is moving through space and time. And taking his followers through all of this and making an entire *fitna* through all the dimensions so that everything on this Earth will be flipped upside down. Everyday something will be different and not what we thought it to be and become something different. Locations, places and things; all of it will be under his manipulation.

We pray that Allah ﷻ protects us and that Allah ﷻ keeps us under the

nazar of Sayyidina Muhammad ﷺ. When we say '*nazar*' (gaze), we are not really understanding. The *nazar* of *awliyaullah* because under their *nazar*, their watchful eye from the reality of their soul, not the *nazar* (gaze) of their physical eye. But the soul that we don't understand its reality.

That its watchful eye is in these days that are coming. What deceit is being planned by *shaitan* and how their *nazar* is watching it and guarding what Allah 🕉 wants to be guarded. Allah 🕉, *inshaAllah*, count us to be amongst those to be guarded, our family to be guarded, our communities to be guarded, *inshaAllah*.

Subhana rabbika rabbal 'izzati 'amma yasifoon, wa salaamun 'alal mursaleen, walhamdulillahi rabbil 'aalameen. Bi hurmati Muhammad al-Mustafa wa bi siri Surat al-Fatiha.

Sit in the Halaqa e Zikr –
Gardens of Paradise on Earth

Ignorant People are Angry and Distant From God

When we understand portals, now read Qur'an to understand the science of Qur'an. Then you understand how much Allah ﷻ loves you. He's guiding you. When Allah's ﷻ love is not that strong for you, you're like in a dark hole. You're ignorant. As a result of your ignorance, you're actually very angry. As a result of your anger, you're like on fire. Then you know you're distant from God because you're a fiery person.

It means you're not knowledgeable. Ignorant people, they're distant from the Divine. What they've done, how they act, what are the circumstances of their existence creates them to be ignorant. That which is ignorant as if in the law of opposites, it turned its direction from moving towards the sun and the warmth and the light, it moves away from it. As a 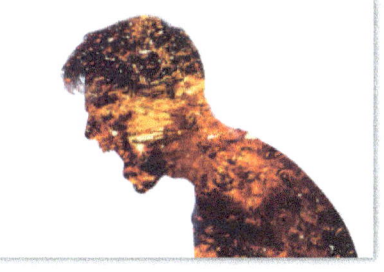 result of its ignorance, becomes very angry because all is darkness, doesn't understand anything. Anyone in darkness bump their head, they get angry; a couple times, three times, four times, very angry, very fiery people.

Move Towards the Light of Your Creator to Become Illuminated

But once you move towards the light, you're no longer ignorant. The light illuminates your soul through its dreams, through its hearings, through these channels, through these teachings. It's a food and a nourishment for the soul. As a result of these lights and enlightenment, they become content. They have good character. As a result, the fire of ignorance within them begins to diminish and the knowledge has power and illuminates.

They call themselves 'Illuminati,' but they're actually naughty. They're doing bad things. But the truly illuminated ones, they move towards the light and the light of the Creator. They study the books and the teachings of the Creator through the reality of the prophets ﷺ and as a result, God enlightens their soul, their eyes, and their entire being.

Seek Refuge in Allah ﷻ From the Dark Energies Released on Earth

Our life is to understand all of the blessings and grace that God has given to us to find these portals. To live within these portals and to go from portal to portal. Because for some reason, people understand the scientific term. They're astonished, 'Wow!

320

You think, really things are going to open like that? I saw this in this movie.' They're seeing now weird, coloured lights in the sky that open up and something happens.

Oh, it's going to be a lot more than that. The hydrogen colliders are all that. They're igniting those things and crazy things happen upon this Earth. They're not telling people. But Mawlana Shaykh ق was very disturbed by their activities, acknowledging what they're doing is very satanic. The bringing of these energies in this dimension when Allah جل جلاله gave to us, *"Qul a'odhu bi Rabbil falaq."* 'Seek refuge in Allah جل جلاله, the Lord of this dark matter.' Because what they're going to bring from this matter upon this Earth was not meant.

قُلْ أَعُوذُ بِرَبِّ الْفَلَقِ ﴿١﴾

113:1 – "Qul a'odhu bi Rabbil falaq." (Surat Al-Falaq)

"Say, I seek refuge in the Lord of daybreak." (The Daybreak, 113:1)

What Did They Give in Exchange for Technology?

This ignorance is not meant. This demonic reality is not meant but these

shaitans want to come and eat everything and everyone. They have no interest in enlightening people. They gave a little bit of technology and ate hundreds of thousands of people as a result. There's a show coming out. There was a man who came to President Eisenhower, this Thor something and they made a commitment that, 'We want to come onto this Earth. We want to do things with people.' And they gave them technologies. They had advisors that came give technologies.

That's how they made these star tracks with these mobile phones. All these things, in exchange for what? To eat people. 'Don't worry about what we want to do with the people and the population. Here's some technology. Sell it, advance yourselves.' So, they have no interest in humanity, definitely not interested in illuminating people. It's *dajjal* (man of deceit) and *dajjal* is a *jinn* and he's coming to spread ignorance. He's coming to create a great deceit.

We Enter Dajjal's Portal Through Backbiting and Become Walking Dead

Allah ﷻ gave to us through Islam and the greatness of Sayyidina Muhammad ﷺ all these realities and we call them paradise. These are pockets of paradise emanating upon this Earth. If you can live by it, be in it, eat and drink from it, you should be truly successful in your life and your journey upon this Earth. If you lived and died by it, your return back to heaven should be of a paradise reality.

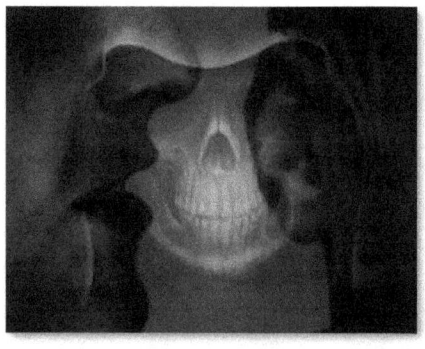

But if you got sucked into *dajjal's* portal, then the means will be difficult. That's what's happening upon this Earth. People are running away from the paradise portals and ending up being sucked into *dajjal's* portals where they're so lost from paradise. They're sort of emptied of any light, of any sound, of any vibration that like zombies walking upon the Earth and flesh eaters. Why Prophet ﷺ described the people whom backbite, they are flesh eaters? They eat the flesh of one another when they backbite.

عَنْ عَبْدِ اللَّهِ إِبْنِ مَسْعُودٍ رَضِيَ اللَّهُ عَنْهُ قَالَ: كُنَّا جُلُوسًا عِنْدَ النَّبِيِّ ﷺ، فَقَامَ رَجُلٌ فَوَقَعَ فِيهِ رَجُلٌ مِنْ بَعْدِهِ.

فَقَالَ النَّبِيُّ ﷺ :" تَخَلَّلْ ." قَالَ :وَمَا أَتَخَلَّلُ يَا رَسُولَ اللَّهِ أَكَلْتُ لَحْمًا ؟ قَالَ ﷺ :" إِنَّكَ أَكَلْتَ لَحْمَ أَخِيْكَ ."

[اَلْطَبَرَانِي، اَلْمُعْجَمُ الْكَبِيرْ ٩٩٥١]

'An 'Abdullah ibn Mas'ud (ra) qala: Kunna jolusan 'inda anNabiyi ﷺ, faqama rajolon, fawqa'a fihi rajolon min ba'dihi.

Faqala anNabiyo ﷺ: "takhallal". Qala: wa ma atakhallalo ya Rasulallahi, akalto lahman? Qala ﷺ: "innaka akalta lahma akhika."
[Al Tabarani, al Mu'jam al Kabir, 9951]

Abdullah ibn Mas'ud (ra) said: We were sitting with the Prophet (pbuh) when a man stood to leave, then another man spoke badly about him after he left. The Prophet (pbuh) said, "Pick your teeth." The man said, "O Messenger of Allah, why should I pick my teeth, when I have not eaten meat?" The Prophet (pbuh) said: "You have eaten the flesh of your brother."
[By Al Tabarani, in the book of Al Mu'jam al Kabir 9951]

That's all you see on television and movies and every entertainment and every YouTube is somebody backbiting somebody. So, this is now the

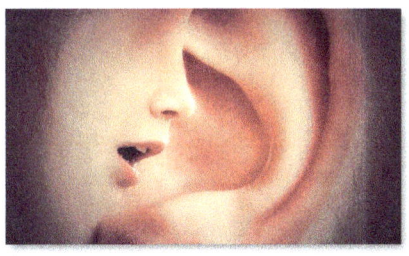

land of the walking dead, flesh eaters. That's what the grossness of 'The Walking Dead' movies. They run after you and then all of a sudden, grab to bite your shoulder and your fingers and your ears.

Prophet ﷺ told, 'This is what I told you.' These are what people are doing. They say hello to you and they eat your ear by backbiting you. They're eating your flesh by attacking you. Even you don't know it but this Earth has become land of the walking dead.

Circles of Zikr are Meadows of Paradise on Earth

So, now what Prophet ﷺ – that's why we said go back now and begin to research in your Islam. Every reference to paradise and how Prophet ﷺ was teaching us that those circles, those portals are right here. Live in them. Graze in them. When you pass the meadows and streams of paradise, sit and graze. One *Hadith* even Prophet ﷺ is describing, 'Graze, eat and drink in them.' Said, 'What are those meadows of paradise?' *Riyad Saliheen* (Meadows of the Righteous). These are the *halaqas* (circles) of *zikr* (Divine remembrance), the associations of remembrance.

عَنْ أَنَسِ بْنِ مَالِكٍ رَضِيَ اللَّهُ عَنْهُ أَنَّ رَسُولَ اللَّهِ ﷺ قَالَ: " إِذَا مَرَرْتُمْ بِرِيَاضِ الْجَنَّةِ فَارْتَعُوا." قَالُوا وَمَا رِيَاضُ الْجَنَّةِ؟ قَالَ: "حِلَقُ الذِّكْرِ." [سُنَنُ التِّرْمِذِي ٣٥١٠]

'An Anasi ibni Malikin (ra) anna Rasulallahi ﷺ qala: "Izaa marartum beriyadil jannati, farta'u." Qalu: wa ma riyadul jannati? Qala ﷺ: "Hilaquz Zikri [Sunan at-Tirmidhi 3510]

Anas ibn Malik (ra) reported: The Messenger of Allah (pbuh) said, "When you pass by the gardens of Paradise, then feast/indulge (in their blessings)." They said, "What are the gardens of Paradise?" The Prophet (pbuh) said, "The circles of Divine remembrance." [Sunan al-Tirmidhi 3510]

Angels Roam on Earth to Find Halaqa e Zikr (Circles of Remembrance)

Let's read the *Hadith al Qudsi* (Holy Hadith). This is the 14th of 40 *Hadith* from Imam Nawawi ق and this is a *Hadith al Qudsi*. It means in its category is right next to Qur'an. Holy Qur'an is Allah's ﷻ Speech and that which Allah ﷻ revealed to Prophet ﷺ, that would have made it to be Qur'an but they categorized it as *Hadith al Qudsi. Bismillah.*

عَنْ أَبِي هُرَيْرَةَ رَضِيَ اللهُ عَنْهُ عَنِ النَّبِيِّ ﷺ قَالَ: إِنَّ لِلهِ تَبَارَكَ وَتَعَالَى مَلَائِكَةً سَيَّارَةً فُضْلًا يَتَبَّعُونَ مَجَالِسَ الذِّكْرِ. فَإِذَا وَجَدُوا مَجْلِسًا فِيهِ ذِكْرٌ، قَعَدُوا مَعَهُمْ، وَحَفَّ بَعْضُهُمْ بَعْضًا بِأَجْنِحَتِهِمْ، حَتَّى يَمْلَئُوا مَا بَيْنَهُمْ وَبَيْنَ السَّمَاءِ الدُّنْيَا. فَإِذَا تَفَرَّقُوا عَرَجُوا وَصَعِدُوا إِلَى السَّمَاءِ.

قَالَ: فَيَسْأَلُهُمُ اللهُ عَزَّ وَجَلَّ وَهُوَ أَعْلَمُ بِهِمْ: "مِنْ أَيْنَ جِئْتُمْ؟" فَيَقُولُونَ: "جِئْنَا مِنْ عِنْدِ عِبَادٍ لَكَ فِي الْأَرْضِ، يُسَبِّحُونَكَ وَيُكَبِّرُونَكَ وَيُهَلِّلُونَكَ وَيَحْمَدُونَكَ وَيَسْأَلُونَكَ." قَالَ فَيَقُولُ: "قَدْ غَفَرْتُ لَهُمْ فَأَعْطَيْتُهُمْ مَا سَأَلُوا وَأَجَرْتُهُمْ مِمَّا اسْتَجَارُوا."

فَيَقُولُونَ: "رَبِّ فِيهِمْ فُلَانٌ عَبْدٌ خَطَّاءٌ، إِنَّمَا مَرَّ فَجَلَسَ مَعَهُمْ." قَالَ: "وَلَهُ غَفَرْتُ هُمُ الْقَوْمُ لَا يَشْقَى بِهِمْ جَلِيسُهُمْ."

[حَدِيثُ الْقُدْسِي، صَحِيحُ الْبُخَارِي ٦٤٠٨ صَحِيحُ مُسْلِم ٢٦٨٩]

'An Abi Hurayra (ra) 'an an Nabiyi ﷺ *qala: "Inna lillahi tabaraka wa ta'ala Malaayikatan sayyaratan fudulan, yatabba'una majaalisaz zikri. Fa iza wajadu majlisan fihi zikrun, qa'adu ma'ahum, wa haffa ba'dohum ba'dan bi ajnihatihim, hatta yamla'oo ma baynahum wa baynas samayid dunya.*

Fa iza tafarraqu 'arajoo wa sa'idu ilas samaa.

Qala: Fayas aluhum Allah 'azza wa jalla, wa huwa a'lamu bihim: "Min ayna jeytum?"

Fayaquluna: "Jeyna min 'ind 'ibadin laka fil ardi, yusabbihunaka, wa yukabbirunaka, wa yuhallilunaka, wa yahmadunaka wa yas alunaka."

325

Qala: fayaqulu: "Qad ghafartu lahum fa a'ataytohum maa sa'aloo, wa ajartohum mimma astajaroo."

Fayaquluna: "Rabbi fihim fulanon 'abdun khatta'un, innama marra fa jalasa ma'ahum." Qala: "Wa lahu ghafartu hum al qawmu la yashqa bihim jalisohum."
[Hadith Qudsi, Sahih al Bukhari 6408, Sahih Muslim 2689]

Abu Hurairah (ra) narrated: The Prophet (pbuh) said, "Verily, Allah, the Owner of blessings and Exalted, Has angels who roam the earth, seeking gatherings of Divinely remembrance. When they find such gatherings in which there is remembrance (of Allah (AJ)), they join them and form a circle with their wings around the gathering that extends all the way to the first heaven.

When the people disperse, they ascend to the heavens. Allah Almighty and Sublime asks them, although He Knows everything: "From where have you come?" They respond: "We came from Your servants on earth, who glorify You, proclaim Your Greatness and Oneness, praise You, and ask from You".

Allah (AJ) says: "I have forgiven them and granted them what they have asked for, and I have given them protection from what they sought safety from."

They say: "Our Lord, there is one among them, a servant who made mistakes. He happened to pass by and sat with them." Allah (AJ) says: "And for him, I have granted forgiveness as well. Those people (of zikr) are such that anyone who sits with them shall not be deprived of blessings."
[Hadith Qudsi – Authentic by al Bukhari 6408, and Muslim 2689]

Open Your Eyes and Ears to See the Blessings of the Halaqa ul Zikr

MashaAllah wa sadaqah Rasulul Kareem (The Most Generous Messenger). Whatever Prophet ﷺ brought for us, it's not something that even can be questioned, the immensity. But we have ears that don't hear and eyes that definitely don't see.

وَلَقَدْ ذَرَأْنَا لِجَهَنَّمَ كَثِيرًا مِّنَ الْجِنِّ وَالْإِنسِ ۖ لَهُمْ قُلُوبٌ لَّا يَفْقَهُونَ بِهَا وَلَهُمْ أَعْيُنٌ لَّا يُبْصِرُونَ بِهَا وَلَهُمْ آذَانٌ لَّا يَسْمَعُونَ بِهَا ۚ أُولَٰئِكَ كَالْأَنْعَامِ بَلْ هُمْ أَضَلُّ ۚ أُولَٰئِكَ هُمُ الْغَافِلُونَ ﴿١٧٩﴾

7:179 – "Wa laqad zara'naa li jahannama kaseeram minal Jinni wal Insi lahum quloobul laa yafqahoona bihaa, wa lahum a'yunul laa yubisiroona bihaa, wa lahum aazaanul laa yasma'oona bihaa; Olaayika kal an'aami bal hum adhal; Olaayika humul ghaafiloon."
(Surat Al-A'raf)

"Many from the Jinns and human beings, We have created for hell: They have hearts with which they don't understand, they have eyes with which they don't see, and they have ears with which they don't hear. They are like cattle, nay they are more misguided. They are heedless (of warning)."
(The Heights, 7:179)

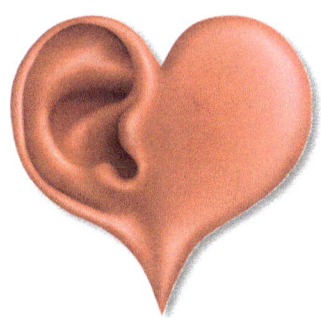

The shaykh's responsibility is to bring you back to a state that, 'Open your ears from what you heard. And open your eyes.' Not your physical eyes that lost in the material world but open the eyes of your heart and your soul and understand what Prophet ﷺ is telling us. That there are angels circumambulating the *zikrs* (Divine remembrance).

It means a *majlis* (association) and a center (Naqshbandi Center in Vancouver) in which 12 years of recitation is a complete portal. The angels are not looking for us. They occupy the space. They circumambulate the energy of this space. Doing what? Taking the requests of the space up to the throne of Allah ﷻ. The burdens of the association, God's grace and forgiveness dressing and blessing them. In every food and water and drink, you are doing it in a circle of paradise, if you have belief. You begin to understand, you entered into paradise, and anyone who enters into paradise can never leave paradise. It means then there's a reality of your light must always be in this association. It must always be dressed from these realities, must always be blessed from these realities. Every action and dress is upon that soul. Every difficulty and *mushkilat* is being taken by these angels and these are immense powerful portals of the Divinely presence.

Dajjal Doesn't Want Us to Have the Blessings of Zikr

All who enter into these circles of paradise are dressed, if they have ears to hear and eyes to see (Holy Qur'an, 7:179). Otherwise, they deem this, 'Huh, what else, whatever.' But they missed it. They missed the reality and as a result, when they miss it, they don't understand what they have access to. They don't respect what they have access to. They're definitely not living their life based on that reality. As a result of the difficulty of Earth, they're being sucked into different places and that's all that *dajjal* (man deceit) wants. That's why the *dajjal* is so busy in teaching in *masjids* that, 'There are no *zikrs*,' to get them out of the circle of Allah ﷻ, out of the mercy of Allah ﷻ. Then playing their music, jumping, dancing and levitating towards his cave in which he plans to eat everyone.

Sayyidina Yahya ☉ Approached the Green Throne of Sayyidina Muhammad ☉

It means the immensity of the cave. Then they came and now teach that if you sit in your home, play the *zikr*, these same angels will appear in your home. They'll circumambulate your living room because you made the intention of *majlis* of the *zikr*, *majlis of salli alan Nabi* ☉. That you're conducting a *Milad* (celebration of the birthday of Prophet ☉) in your home, praising upon the king of the entire created universe in which God created this entire kingdom for the reality of Sayyidina Muhammad ☉.

He's in the book of revelation, the emerald throne in which Sayyidina Yahya, John ☉ , approached the throne. Say, 'I see the king and he's not God and seated next to him is the lamb, Sayyidina Isa (Jesus) ☉.' It's not a coincidence Madina's green. It was for them to read emerald throne, emerald turban, green Dome of Madina. They've ears but they don't hear and eyes that they don't see (Holy Qur'an, 7:179).

Create a Heavenly Portal in Your Home Where Angels Will Come to Bless You

These are the portals that Allah ☉ has given to the nation. That if you want safety, enter these portals. Immediately the *zikr* starts, turn your living room into that portal. Play the *salawats* (praises upon Prophet Muhammad ☉) within the house so that the energy, the angels are coming, pushing away every negativity. You put your food and water, salt, whatever you need as a *shifa* and healing and it will be dressed and blessed by that. The *khatms* and the *zikrs* with the shaykhs, then they are being dressed with that, blessed with that.

We have teas that are here under this building (Rumi Rose Garden) like paradise that drink from them. They're a *shifa* and a healing. The *ta'weezs* (prayer for protection); all of these things were meant for a difficulty that's coming upon this Earth. Thousands of *ta'weezs* are being distributed. Who did that before? Nobody. Everybody cares about their own chair. They don't care about anything. They don't even give an *awrad* (daily practice) for anyone to do. They claim how great they are and go about their way.

When You Fast, Seven Gates of Paradise Open for You

But the responsibility of guidance is you should have these items from the kingdom because the kingdom of God is coming and it's not a tailgate party. It's a community who fasts, wash and clean. Who does that? You think God's kingdom is a tailgate party, drinking, screaming, yelling? Or it's a kingdom washed and clean? Cleanliness is nearness to God.

Then Prophet ﷺ described, 'The one whom fasts immediately enters into paradise and the seven gates.' So many *Hadiths* on these realities. As soon as the servant fasts, seven gates of paradise are open for them – another portal.

عَنْ سَهْلٍ رَضِيَ اللهُ عَنْهُ، عَنِ النَّبِيِّ ﷺ قَالَ: إِنَّ فِي الْجَنَّةِ بَابًا يُقَالُ لَهُ اَلرَّيَّانُ، يَدْخُلُ مِنْهُ اَلصَّائِمُونَ يَوْمَ الْقِيَامَةِ. لَا يَدْخُلُ مِنْهُ أَحَدٌ غَيْرُهُمْ. يُقَالُ: أَيْنَ الصَّائِمُونَ؟ فَيَقُومُونَ، لَا يَدْخُلُ مِنْهُ أَحَدٌ غَيْرُهُمْ. فَإِذَا دَخَلُوا أُغْلِقَ، فَلَمْ يَدْخُلْ مِنْهُ أَحَدٌ.
[صَحِيحُ اَلْبُخَارِي ١٨٩٦، صَحِيحُ مُسْلِم ١١٥٢]

'An Sahli (ra), 'an anNabiyi ﷺ qala: "Inna fil jannati baban yuqalou lahu ar rayyanu, yadkhulu minhu as sayimuna yawmal qiyamati. La yadkhulu minhu ahadun ghayrohum. Yuqalu: "Ayna as sayimuna?" Fayaqumuna, la yadkhulu minhu ahadun ghayruhum. Fa izaa dakhalu ughliqa, falam yadkhul minhu ahadun."
[Sahih al-Bukhari 1896, Sahih Muslim 1152]

Sahl (ra) narrated: the Prophet (pbuh) said, "Verily, there is a gate in Paradise called arRayyan, through which only those who fasted will enter on the Day of Resurrection. No one else will enter through it other than them. It will be said: "Where are those who fasted?" They will stand up, no one will enter it except them. When they enter it, it will be closed and no one else will go through it."
[Authentic by al-Bukhari 1896 & Muslim 1152]

Anyone in difficulty, fast that day. Things are not opening for you, fast that day. Even if you can fast intermittent fasting. That you wake up, have only water, make intention, *'Ya Rabbi*, I'm asking to enter into this portal of *rahmah* (mercy), to the gates of paradise.' As soon as the servant begins the *siyam* (fasting), not only Ramadan. At any time the servant fasts, seven gates of paradise open for them.

Fasting is Your Portal of Protection Against Demonic Energies

Now go back and start reading everything Prophet ﷺ gave to us. Because people are thinking, 'Oh, paradise when I die.' Say, 'No, no, it will open now.' Because when you start to see the *dajjal* openings and you'll be astonished, 'Wow! How is he doing that? How these things happening? Oh, look at these  ships or creatures are coming through these things.' It requires people to have a bane, 'No, the shaykhs taught us. Prophet ﷺ brought all of that for us.' You're not a people without. Allah ﷻ gave the bounty of paradises and heavens to this nation. Fast and open your portal. Immediately when you feel a danger, begin fasting.

As soon as you fast, a portal is opening. What happens if a demonic energy is coming to attack you and you enter into a portal from paradise? It's your protection. If at any time you're in difficulty and distressed, begin *siyam* and fasting. Prophet ﷺ gave to us, 'If you're in difficulty and distress and things are not opening, open your portal of paradise.'

Paradise Portals Exist Here, Why Don't You Eat From Them?

Immediately, put the *zikr* and the *khatm* in the house. Sit with the *zikr* and the *khatm* playing. The angels have no time. They don't say, 'Oh, we only accept this at 8:00 at night.' Anytime you feel the difficulty, put the YouTube and the *khatm* and immediately, the *majlis* and all the angels and the energy is moving, blessing and dressing; anytime the servant feels that the satanic energy is overwhelming.

Allah ﷻ says, 'I gave you all these portals. Why you don't believe in them?' If you call it paradise, you keep thinking it's for your death. Talking about paradise now. The streams and the meadows of paradise now that are available for us and that eat from them, Prophet ﷺ described.

عَنْ أَنَسِ بْنِ مَالِكٍ رَضِيَ اللهُ عَنْهُ أَنَّ رَسُولَ اللهِ ﷺ قَالَ: " إِذَا مَرَرْتُمْ بِرِيَاضِ الْجَنَّةِ فَارْتَعُوا. " قَالُوا وَمَا رِيَاضُ الْجَنَّةِ؟ قَالَ: "حِلَقُ الذِّكْرِ." [سُنَنُ التِّرْمِذِي ٣٥١٠]

'An Anasi ibni Malikin (ra) anna Rasulallahi ﷺ qala: "Izaa marartum beriyadil jannati, farta'u." Qalu: wa ma riyadul jannati? Qala ﷺ: "Hilaquz Zikri [Sunan at-Tirmidhi 3510]

Anas ibn Malik (ra) reported: The Messenger of Allah (pbuh) said,
"When you pass by the gardens of Paradise, then feast/indulge (in their
blessings)." They said, "What are the gardens of Paradise?"
The Prophet (pbuh) said, "The circles of Divine remembrance."
[From Traditions of al-Tirmidhi 3510]

Why you have difficulty and you don't eat from here? You're occupied and you are a resident of this community in which there's an entire portal and every food and rice and grain is from Paradise. Yet you choose to go to the merchants of death and buy goods and sustenance from them. Why you don't eat from paradise if you have difficulty? Because your faith is weak. Then you wonder why you have difficulties.

Riyadul Jannah and the Presence of Prophet ﷺ in Madina Sharif is a Portal to Paradise

When the faith is strong, the belief is strong. They make their lives in this reality of this portal. That my life has to be in this portal of energy. '*Ya Rabbi*, that I'm asking to be nourished by that energy, blessed by that energy.'

Then Prophet ﷺ said, 'There is a piece of paradise in *Madinatul Munawwara* (luminous city of Prophet ﷺ)' which all of Madina and all of the presence of Prophet ﷺ is a portal. But even Prophet ﷺ gave, 'Between my house and my *minbar* where the green carpet is paradise.' Again, an immense portal in the presence of the most powerful portal of Allah's ﷻ creation.

333

عَنْ أَبِي هُرَيْرَةَ (رضى الله عنه) عَنِ النَّبِيِّ ﷺ قَالَ: " مَا بَيْنَ بَيْتِي وَمِنْبَرِي رَوْضَةٌ مِنْ رِيَاضِ الْجَنَّةِ، وَمِنْبَرِي عَلَى حَوْضِي ." [صَحِيحُ الْبُخَارِيّ ١١٩٦]

'An Abi Hurayrah (ra) 'anin Nabiyi ﷺ qala: "Ma bayna bayti wa minbari rawdhatun min riyadhil jannati, wa minbari 'ala hawdhi."

The Prophet (pbuh) said, "Between my house and my pulpit there is a garden of the gardens of Paradise, and my pulpit is on my pond of abundance (Kawthar)." [Sahih al Bukhari, Hadith #1196]

Run to the Cave of Sayyidina Muhammad ﷺ to Be Dressed by Rahmah

It means we started with the understanding of a mountain. That Allah ﷻ gave to us these caves. Run to them, be with these mountains. They represent the reality of Sayyidina Muhammad ﷺ. As soon as you love them and enter into them, then you're asking for the dress, what Allah ﷻ, 'We'll dress you from a *rahmah*. Don't worry and we settle your affairs'. It means your things will become settled.

وَإِذِ اعْتَزَلْتُمُوهُمْ وَمَا يَعْبُدُونَ إِلَّا اللَّهَ فَأْوُوا إِلَى الْكَهْفِ يَنشُرْ لَكُمْ رَبُّكُم مِّن رَّحْمَتِهِ وَيُهَيِّئْ لَكُم مِّنْ أَمْرِكُم مِّرْفَقًا ﴿١٦﴾

18:16 – "Wa idhi' tazaltumo hum wa ma ya'budoona illAllaha fawoo ilal kahfi yanshur lakum rabbukum mir rahmatihi wa yuhayyi lakum min amrikum mirfaqa." (Surat Al-Kahf)

"When ye turn away from them and the things they worship other than Allah, betake yourselves to the Cave: Your Lord will shower His mercies on you and disposes of your affair towards comfort and ease."
(The Cave, 18:16)

Strengthen Your Faith to See Allah's ﷻ Blessings in These Gardens

Then you listen to their guidance is eat from that paradise, drink from that paradise. If somebody is doing magic on you, you don't know what that eat and drink has. It is your *shifa*. It's your healing. It's your sustenance. Everything is coming from that paradise reality to relieve your hardship. But people want it to be no longer with faith, but they want it to be like a visual, right? They want to see the shining lights. They want to see the food is glowing and then as a result, then they'll take it for healing. But this is the land of *iman* (faith) and this way is the way of faith. That you have to believe in Allah ﷻ. You have to believe in the *Hadith* of Prophet ﷺ that this is a paradise.

As a result with your belief that I eat and drink from that reality. I pray in that reality. I make *du'a* (supplication) in that reality and *ya Rabbi*, dress me from that reality, bless me from that reality. Anytime I need, I fast and enter into that reality. That everything that's happening then has to do with these things that are opening upon this Earth. We pray that Allah ﷻ give us an understanding of how to enter this.

Busy Yourself in Circles of Zikr, Not in Worldly Distractions

Now we're in Surat Al-Kahf and Surat Al-Kahf is all about the *adab* (manners) of this portal. That seek a life like *Ashab ul Kahf*. Where we ended at the last one about the importance of the mountain looking at you. Verse 28 was thrown in there like a catch-all clause in a contract.

وَاصْبِرْ نَفْسَكَ مَعَ الَّذِينَ يَدْعُونَ رَبَّهُم بِالْغَدَاةِ وَالْعَشِيِّ يُرِيدُونَ وَجْهَهُ ۖ وَلَا تَعْدُ عَيْنَاكَ عَنْهُمْ تُرِيدُ زِينَةَ الْحَيَاةِ الدُّنْيَا ۖ وَلَا تُطِعْ مَنْ أَغْفَلْنَا قَلْبَهُ عَن ذِكْرِنَا وَاتَّبَعَ هَوَاهُ وَكَانَ أَمْرُهُ فُرُطًا ﴿٢٨﴾

18:28 – "Wasbir nafsaka ma'al ladheena yad'ona Rabbahum bilghadati wal'ashiyi yureedona Wajhahu, wa la ta'du 'aynaka 'anhum tureedu zeenatal hayatid dunya, wa laa tuti' man aghfalnaa qalbahoo 'an zikrinaa wattaba'a hawaahu wa kaana amruhoo furutaa."
(Surat Al-Kahf)

"And keep yourself patient [by being] with those who call upon their Lord in the morning and the evening, seeking His Holy Face;. And let not your eyes pass beyond them, desiring adornments/glitter of the worldly life and do not obey one whose heart We have made heedless of Our remembrance and who follows his desire and whose affair is ever [in] neglect. (The Cave, 18:28)

That don't busy yourself with the people of *hayat ad dunya* (life of material world), these big *amirs*. They look like they're doing a lot but they do absolutely a lot of nothing. But the gaze of Prophet ﷺ, by command of Allah ﷻ,

be upon those whom they busy themselves in that cave. They busy themselves in the circles of *zikr*. They busy themselves with their *zikr* asking Allah's ﷻ Holy Face, asking Allah ﷻ forgiveness. It means *Ahle Zikr* (People of Divinely Remembrance).

That the immensity of that reality that you're going to be under that gaze and under that *rahmah*. You'll be under the *nazar* (gaze) of Prophet ﷺ because these are the people of *Ashab ul Kahf*, the people whom ran to the cave of Allah ﷻ. That they're continuously under the dress of angels and *malaika* blessing them, dressing them, taking away every type of difficulty from them.

Subhana rabbika rabbal 'izzati 'amma yasifoon, wa salaamun 'alal mursaleen, walhamdulillahi rabbil 'aalameen. Bi hurmati Muhammad al-Mustafa wa bi siri Surat al-Fatiha.

Circles of Zikr are Portals to Heaven

Seven Categories of Awliya Create Heavenly Portals in Halaqa ul Zikr

By understanding the reality then we understand that these associations are designed as portals. That the minute you enter into their association, you have to distinguish and differentiate yourself from your physicality and the reality of your soul. Your physicality thinks it's sitting there and probably doesn't know why it's sitting there. But at the same time, your soul is free in the association and the two of you are not the same. As soon as it enters into this association, the *madad* (support) of the shaykhs and the authorized representatives, their association is not from here. Their association is from a light and a circle above us from these masters. As soon as the associations begin, their lights are emanating.

As a result of their lights – from *Budala, Nujaba, Nuqaba, Awtad wal Akhyar, jinn* (unseen beings) *wa malaika* (angels) – seven categories of saintly souls. That energy from their presence immediately creates a portal in which all the souls of the attendees are entered into that dimension and into that association. The physical body doesn't even know what's transpiring. The one who has been trained feels it, they feel an energy, they feel a vibration. If they've been trained in their seeing and spiritual seeing, they may see the association. They may feel and witness the energies that are taking place.

Angels Surround the Circles of Zikr All the Way to Heaven

That is what the circles of *zikr* (Divine Remembrance) were described

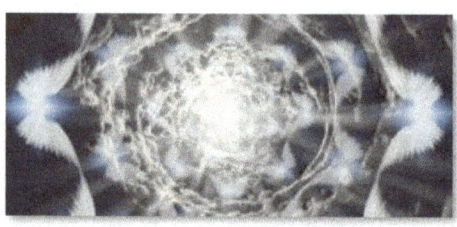

by Prophet ﷺ, described them as portals. If you see a *halaqa* (circle) of *zikr* know that that is a circle from paradise. It was a portal and that portal is encompassed by angels all

the way to *'Arsh ar Rahman* (Throne of the Most Compassionate). It is the *Hadith*.

عَنْ أَبِي هُرَيْرَةَ رَضِيْ الله عَنْهُ، عَن النَّبِيِّ ﷺ قَالَ: إِنَّ لِلَّهِ مَلَائِكَةً سَيَّارَةً فُضْلًا يَتَتَبَّعُونَ مَجَالِسَ الذِّكْرِ. فَإِذَا وَجَدُوا مَجْلِسًا فِيهِ ذِكْرٌ، قَعَدُوا مَعَهُمْ وَحَفَّ بَعْضُهُمْ بَعْضًا بِأَجْنِحَتِهِمْ، حَتَّى يَمْلَئُوا مَا بَيْنَهُمْ وَبَيْنَ السَّمَاءِ الدُّنْيَا. [حَدِيثُ الْقُدْسِي - صَحِيحُ الْبُخَارِي ٦٤٠٨، صَحِيحُ مُسْلِم ٢٦٨٩]

'An Abi Hurayra (ra) 'an an Nabiyi ﷺ qala: "Inna lillahi tabaraka wa ta'ala Malaayikatan sayyaratan fudulan, yatabba'una majaalisaz zikri. Fa iza wajadu majlisan fihi zikrun, qa'adu ma'ahum, wa haffa ba'dohum ba'dan bi ajnihatihim, hatta yamla'oo ma baynahum wa baynas sama'yid dunya.
[Hadith ul Qudsi – Sahih al Bukhari 6408, Sahih Muslim 2689]

Abu Hurairah (ra) narrated: The Prophet (pbuh) said, "Verily, Allah, the Owner of blessings and Exalted, Has angels who roam the earth, seeking gatherings of Divinely remembrance. When they find such gatherings in which there is remembrance (of Allah (AJ)), they gather to join them and form a circle with their wings around the gathering that extends all the way to the first heaven.
[Holy Hadith – Authentic by al Bukhari 6408, and Muslim 2689]

That this is a circle of paradise and the angels circumambulate around that circle all the way to the throne of Allah ﷻ, sending blessings and lifting difficulties. That was a portal. So as soon as they sit in that association, or they turn the video on at home, their home becomes that portal because their home becomes the circle of paradise. As soon as they turn it on, the *tajalli* (manifestations) of these masters come. The *tajalli* of the angels come because they're listening for the *zikr* and immediately, that becomes a portal under *'Arsh ar-Rahman* and all their soul is moving in that reality.

What do you think is transpiring to your soul and how long is that happening? You could be living lifetimes in that circle and you don't even know it. You don't know what time and what has transpired in that reality and in that portal of light. You have no idea what has happened to you, what dress was given to you, what blessings were sent upon you.

Isra wal Mi'raj was Prophet's ﷺ Journey Through a Portal

Prophet ﷺ went for *Isra wal Mi'raj* (Night Journey and Ascension); that the story sounds like it was lifetimes, went to this paradise, went to that paradise. You think it happened in five seconds? No, Allah ﷻ described an entire tour of paradises. Then all of those were finished went into the tour of the Divinely Presence, went to *Sidratul Muntaha* (Lote Tree of the Farthest Boundary), went to every aspect of paradise. It was not five minutes. When you read the *Hadith*, it's making it sound like it  was fast. It was a lifetime that never ends. Then Sitna Aisha ﷺ describes,

'His body came back and his space was still warm.' But that never ended. That *Mir'aj* never ends. That reality and the dress never end.

When You Find Circles of Paradise, Sit in Them

The one who enters into that portal is not going into emptiness. They're going into Allah's ﷻ *rahmah* and mercy. What type of lights dress them, bless them and eternally dress them. As a result, the physicality is receiving all of these rewards, all of these blessings. It doesn't know how it became blessed. It has no idea how it became blessed. It just knows it is blessed because the soul is now moving into these oceans, into these realities. So no doubt, no doubt, the circles, the *khatms*, the presence and the associations, everything is about a portal to paradise. That's why it's asked in last days – all these people who claim to love Allah ﷻ, why they don't come to the circles and the portals of paradise? If it's Allah ﷻ you love, why you're not looking for a circle of paradise? Who promised you that if you prayed, you had a circle of paradise? But Allah ﷻ has given a gift to Prophet ﷺ, 'If you see the *halaqas* of *zikr*, sit. They're a circle from paradise, a portal to paradise.'

حَدِيثُ اِبْنِ عُمَرَرَضِيَ اللّٰهُ عَنْهُ قَالَ، قَالَ رَسُولُ اللّٰهِ ﷺ: "إِذَا مَرَرْتُهُمْ بِرِياضِ الْجَنَّةِ فَارْتَعُوا." قَالُوا: وَمَارِيَاضِ الْجَنَّةِ يَارَسُولِ اللّٰهِ ﷺ؟

قَالَ ﷺ: "حَلَقَ الذِّكْرِ." [جَامِعُ اَلتِّرْمِذِيُّ – جُزْء٦، كتاب ٤٨، حديث٣٥١٠]

342

Ibn 'Umar (ra) qala, qala Rasulullahi 🕌: "Izaa marra rathum beriyadil jannati, fa irta'o. Qalu: wa ma riyadil jannati ya Rasulillah 🕌? Qala🕌: Halaquz Zikri." [Jami' at Tirmidhi, Juz' 6, Kitab 48, Hadith 3510]

The son of 'Umar (ra) reported that the Prophet (pbuh) said: "When you pass by the gardens of Paradise, indulge in/enjoy (their blessings)." The holy Companions asked: "What are the gardens of Paradise, O Messenger of Allah (pbuh)?" He (pbuh) replied: "The circles of zikr (Divine Remembrance)."
[Narrated by Imam Tirmidhi, Volume 6, Book 45, Hadith 3510]

Build Your Love for Prophet 🕌 By Sitting in the Circles of Zikr to Gain Nazar

Then the circles, the *zikrs*, the *khatms*, the *salawats* (praises upon Prophet Muhammad 🕌) is build your relationship and your love with Prophet 🕌. Prophet 🕌 described, 'If you make one *salawat* upon me, I will come like a portal now and begin to dress you with ten *salawats*.'

عَنْ أَنَسِ بْنِ مَالِكٍ رَضِيَ اللهُ عَنْهُ، قَالَ: قَالَ رَسُولُ اللهِ ﷺ: " مَنْ صَلَّى عَلَيَّ صَلَاةً وَاحِدَةً، صَلَّى اللهُ عَلَيْهِ عَشْرَ صَلَوَاتٍ، وَحُطَّتْ عَنْهُ عَشْرُ خَطِيئَاتٍ، وَرُفِعَتْ لَهُ عَشْرُ دَرَجَاتٍ. "

"'An Anasin ibn Malik (ra) qala: Qala Rasulullah 🕌: Man Salla 'alaiya Salatan wahidatan, Sallallahu 'alayhi 'ashra Salawatin, wa Huttat 'anhu 'ashru khaTeatin, wa ruf'at lahu 'ashru darajatin."

Prophet Muhammad (pbuh) said: "Whoever sends blessings [Praises] upon me, God will shower His blessings upon him ten times, and will erase ten of his sins, and elevate [raise] his [spiritual] station ten times."
[Hadith recorded by Nasa'i]

The one whom sits and makes their *salawats* and their *durood* (praising on Prophet Muhammad ﷺ), what's happening for them? They're in the presence of the most powerful portal which is the presence of Sayyidina Muhammad ﷺ. As a result when they want that portal to open, its blessings to open, then it's their good deeds. They go out, they live a life of service, they do all of these good geeds, all these good actions. Why? So that they can get the *nazar*.

The *nazar* means that the gaze of the soul is looking upon you. When that gaze comes, it's an entire protection. The one whom is under the gaze of the All-Merciful, then this is a gaze and a light of immense power and immense protection, *inshaAllah*. Allah ﷻ dress us with its blessings and dresses with its realities, *inshaAllah*.

Subhana rabbika rabbal 'izzati 'amma yasifoon, wa salaamun 'alal mursaleen, walhamdulillahi rabbil 'aalameen. Bi hurmati Muhammad al-Mustafa wa bi siri Surat al-Fatiha.

Tafakkur Opens Divinely Portal for the Soul

The People of the Cave Were Time Travellers

We talked about and if we meditate and contemplate, how much Allah ﷻ is giving of understandings and realities that play an immense role in the last days. In the last days in which so much *fitna* and confusion that fills the Earth. Allah ﷻ is giving for us that these youths that are running from a group of people wishing to harm them, hate them and destroy their faith. That within a short period of time, they entered the cave and Allah ﷻ clarifies they're asking each other as they were awoken, 'How long have we been here?' A day or less than a day? 300 and Allah ﷻ added 9 years has traversed.

وَلَبِثُوا فِي كَهْفِهِمْ ثَلَاثَ مِائَةٍ سِنِينَ وَازْدَادُوا تِسْعًا ﴿٢٥﴾

18:25 – "Wa labisoo fee kahfihim salaasa mi'atin sineena wazdaadoo tis'aa" (Surat Al-Kahf)

"And they remained in their cave for three hundred years and exceeded by nine." (The Cave, 18:25)

It means they left one dimension in which people hate them. They were awoken into a group of people who loved them because as soon as they went to the marketplace, people were astonished by their reality and argued what to build over their site. That it is of an immense miracle for the people. So one – the miracle for the actual sleepers, that they traversed through time and space. They moved in 309 years and for them it was but a moment, a day and they said, 'No, less than a day.'

وَكَذٰلِكَ بَعَثْنَاهُمْ لِيَتَسَاءَلُوا بَيْنَهُمْ ۚ قَالَ قَائِلٌ مِنْهُمْ كَمْ لَبِثْتُمْ ۚ قَالُوا لَبِثْنَا يَوْمًا أَوْ بَعْضَ يَوْمٍ ۚ قَالُوا رَبُّكُمْ أَعْلَمُ بِمَا لَبِثْتُمْ فَابْعَثُوا أَحَدَكُمْ بِوَرِقِكُمْ هٰذِهِ إِلَى الْمَدِينَةِ فَلْيَنْظُرْ أَيُّهَا أَزْكَىٰ طَعَامًا فَلْيَأْتِكُمْ بِرِزْقٍ مِنْهُ وَلْيَتَلَطَّفْ وَلَا يُشْعِرَنَّ بِكُمْ أَحَدًا ﴿١٩﴾

18:19 – "Wa kazaalika ba'asnaahum liyatasaaa'aloo bainahum; qaala qaaa'ilum minhum kam labistum qaaloo labisnaa yawman aw ba'da yawm; qaaloo Rabbukum a'lamu bimaa labistum fab'asooo ahadakum biwariqikum haazihee ilal madeenati falyanzur ayyuhaaa azkaa ta'aaman falyaatikum birizqim minhu walyatalattaf wa laa yush'iranna bikum ahadaa" (Surat Al-Kahf)

"And similarly, We awakened them that they might question one another. Said a speaker from among them, "How long have you remained [here]?" They said, "We have remained a day or part of a day." They said, "Your Lord is most knowing of how long you remained. So send one of you with this silver coin of yours to the city and let him look to which is the best of food and bring you provision from it and let him be cautious. And let no one be aware of you."
(The Cave, 18:19)

346

The Sleepers of the Cave Were Preserved for 309 Years

Allah ﷻ is giving and Prophet ﷺ is expanding the immensity of this

understanding of time travel and the movement through the world of light and these realities. That Allah ﷻ is free to open anything Allah ﷻ wants to open. That they ran from a difficulty and Allah ﷻ dressed them within a cave, awoken them. For them, they

had moved in time in the exact same location has moved 309 years (Holy Qur'an, 18:25). They came out to a community that loved them, that were astonished by them and thought of their presence as a miracle. That, you are time travelers. They were from this era and they had coins from that era. As a result, they came as proof that people can move through space and time and preserved through space and time.

For Allah ﷻ to give that in Holy Qur'an, it becomes immensely relevant in last days when *fitna* (confusion) of *dajjal* (man of deceit). Because people were asking, 'Why Prophet ﷺ drew our attention to reciting Surat Al-Kahf for the arrival of *dajjal* and protection against the deceitful one?' We see that the holy *surah* (chapter) has all of these realities within it, preparing the believers that time travel and the reality of light is something that can't be understood.

عَنْ أَبِي الدَّرْدَاءِ رَضِيَ اللَّهُ عَنْهُ، أَنَّ رَسُولَ اللَّهِ ﷺ قَالَ: "مَنْ حَفِظَ عَشْرَ آيَاتٍ مِنْ أَوَّلِ سُورَةِ الْكَهْفِ، عُصِمَ مِنَ الدَّجَّالِ."
[صَحِيحْ مُسْلِمٌ، رِيَاضُ الصَّالِحِينْ ١٠٢١]

*'An Abi ad Darda (ra), anna Rasulallahi ﷺ qala: "Man hafizha
'ashra aayatin min awwali Suratil Kahf, 'usima minad Dajjal."
(Sahih Muslim, Riyad as Salihin 1021)*

Abu al Darda' (ra) reported the Messenger of Allah (pbuh) said: "Whoever memorizes the first ten verses of Suratil Kahf, will be safe/protected from (the trial of) the Man of Deceit (Antichrist)." [Authentic by Muslim, Riyad as Salihin 1021]

There is No Time in the World of Light

Allah ﷻ gives to us an understanding that in this world of light, the time is not the way we're calculating from the world of physicality. *Alhamdulillah,* in other talks we've talked about, light is a constant and anybody moving at the speed of light, time stops for them. There is no time in that world of light. That, that time stops. Prophet ﷺ, through holy *Hadith,* described the ones whom they make a *tafakkur* and contemplation, it's as if 70 years of worshipness. Because all of these are  now drawing our attention to time travel and the existence of a portal and a movement of energy and interruption of an energy field.

قَالَ رَسُولُ اللهِ ﷺ: تَفَكُّرْ سَاعَةٍ خَيْرٌ مِنْ عِبَادَةِ سَبْعِينْ سَنَةً

Qala Rasulullahi ﷺ: "Tafakkur saa'atin khairun min 'ibadati sab'yeen sanatan."

The Messenger of Allah (pbuh) said: "One hour of contemplation is more valuable than seventy years of worship."

Tap Into Your Immense Power Through Meditation and Contemplation

It means that anything from a paradise reality that enters into this *dunya*, (material world) because we're talking from the heavenly, that has the

ability to move people through space and time. That what's important is the one whom sits and understands *tafakkur* and opens for themselves in their space of meditation a Divinely portal, opening a frequency of energy. We described before that if each cell carries 1.4 volts and the scientists came out and said, 'There's 70 trillion cells. That's about 90 trillion volts of energy.'

So immense, immense power *insan* (mankind) has. Prophet ﷺ was directing us the one whom makes their *tafakkur* means they understood the *muraqabah* (spiritual connection). They left the physical plane and they seek inside their heart to enter into their hearts and they seek a way of inner contemplation and reflection. Once they begin to train in that reality, they understand all the breathing and *qudra* (power) and energizing all of the perfections.

'Who knows himself will know his lord.' It means who knows himself will know that which governs him. It means who knows himself will know that which governs him. If he understands that which

governs him from negativity and brings and diminishes it. And that which governs him from his positivity and empowers the positive and

diminish the negative. Well then he has access to 90 trillion volts of energy from what these scientists and people are understanding. But the energy of the soul has no limit in its capacity. It's enough to bring about an energy that from paradise and opens a *kahf*, opens a cave. As a result of that cave, a *tajalli* (manifestation) can come upon the servant

قَالَ رَسُولُ اللَّهِ ﷺ: " مَنْ عَرَفَ نَفْسَهُ فَقَدْ عَرَفَ رَبَّهُ. "

Qala Rasulullahi ﷺ: *"Man 'arafa nafsahu faqad 'arafa Rabbahu."*

The Messenger of Allah (pbuh) said: "Who knows himself, knows his Lord."

Control the Ears to Let the Soul Enter into a Portal of Timeless Reality

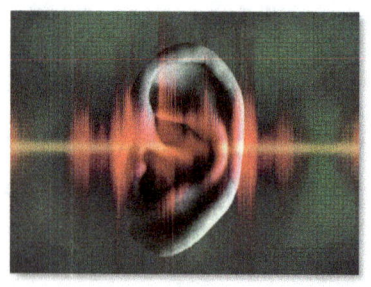

Allah ﷻ says, 'We put a seal upon their ear.' So then again, that's why when you look at the Naqshbandi practices of *tafakkur* (contemplation), as soon as they sit and contemplate, the most important focus is their ears. Don't let *shaitan* (satan) keep whispering to the ear. So, there must be a seal upon the ear because Allah ﷻ gave that, 'We put a seal upon their hearing and then they entered into their reality of the sleepers.'

فَضَرَبْنَا عَلَىٰ آذَانِهِمْ فِي الْكَهْفِ سِنِينَ عَدَدًا ﴿١١﴾

18:11 – "Fadarabnaa 'alaa aazanihim fil Kahfi seneena 'adadaa" (Surat Al-Kahf)

"Then We draw (a veil) over their ears, for a number of years, in the Cave, (so that they heard not)." (The Cave, 18:11)

It means it had a tremendous importance that when we understood that, entered the cave, understood to put the *salawats* (praises upon Prophet Muhammad ﷺ) upon the hearing. To put that which is holy upon the

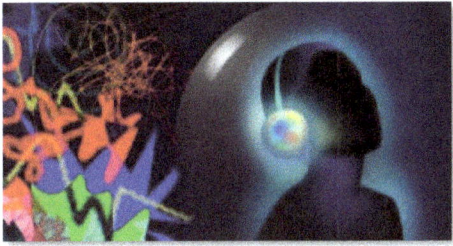

hearing so that it seals the hearing from the satanic influence and brings the heavenly *tajallis* and heavenly energies that empower the power of the soul. As a result of that, the freedom of the soul to begin its movement out of the physical plane. If the soul begins to come out from its physical confinement like a bird being released from its cage, then that soul is a body of energy. It's connecting with the energy of the *madad* (support) and the energies that we've been training. Therefore, enters now into a portal and a timeless reality.

A Timeless Reality: One Hour of Contemplation is like 70 Years of Worship

That's what's important is that we leave the negativity. And in an instant of *tafakkur* and contemplation, they begin to contemplate and that *tajalli* for *Ummat e Muhammad* ﷺ (nation of Prophet Muhammad ﷺ), that they trained and they bring that *tajalli*. They immediately enter into a timeless reality in which Prophet ﷺ describing like 70 years of worship.

قَالَ رَسُولُ اللهِ ﷺ: تَفَكُّرْ سَاعَةٍ خَيْرٌ مِنْ عِبَادَةِ سَبْعِينْ سَنَةً

Qala Rasulullahi ﷺ: "Tafakkur saa'atin khairun min 'ibadati sab'yeen sanatan."

The Messenger of Allah (pbuh) said: "One hour of contemplation is more valuable than seventy years of worship."

That's why Einstein's theory of relativity, and all these understandings that the scientists were coming, that if you moved at the speed of light and came back to the Earth as if 60 to 70 years had passed but for you could have been but a moment. This was given by Prophet ﷺ for us to understand the world of light.

Retreat From the Crowd to Perfect Yourself

Qur'an is coming with all of its *daleels* and proofs because it's a book of truth with complete guidance. That's the reality that Allah ﷻ is giving for *Ashab ul Kahf* (companions of the cave) for us to understand that, that in these times of difficulty, the state of isolation is most important. Miracles happen when you isolate.

If you plan on being amongst the crowd in a time of difficulty, then you are under the umbrella of that crowd and whatever difficulty coming upon them. Those whom train themselves to isolate and take yourself away from the crowd because we don't know whom Allah ﷻ is planning on punishing. So, if you stand there while Allah ﷻ is going to be throwing rocks upon people, you're most likely going to get hit with a rock.

Build Your Cave With Love & Stay Firm on Your Path

So Allah ﷻ, Prophet ﷺ is training for us – live a life in which you continuously retreat from crowds of people. Seek a path in which to build your cave with all these elements, this love, this *ishq*, these good manners. That my cave is the love of Prophet ﷺ. I am the dog and that my life is all about being tested and having good character. To have good character until the day Allah ﷻ raises me to speak so that I have a *yaqeen* and a certainty that, 'I will not give up and my *istiqam* and my firmness upon my path.' At that time the companions of the cave understood that, 'This dog is sincere and he's not going to eat us and he's going to be dressed by a *tajalli* from Allah ﷻ to be of service and *khidmat*.'

وَأَن لَّوِ اسْتَقَامُوا عَلَى الطَّرِيقَةِ لَأَسْقَيْنَاهُم مَّاءً غَدَقًا ﴿١٦﴾

72:16 – "Wa allawis taqaamoo 'alat tareeqati la asqaynaahum maa'an ghadaqaa" (Surat Al-Jinn)

"And [Allah revealed] that: "If they had only remained firm on their tariqa (straight path), We would have bestowed on them Rain/water in abundance." (The Jinn, 72:16)

353

Allah ﷻ Commanded to Build a Masjid Over the Ashab ul Kahf

So much is transpiring within these few *surahs* of what Allah ﷻ is giving us of a reality that enter into this world of light. They *(Ashab ul Kahf)*

ran from hatred and blink of an eye, half a day or less, the portal opened. They were in a dimension in same location but 309 years of time had passed. Now Allah ﷻ brought them into a group of people who want to build a *masjid* over them.

That's in this Holy Qur'an, in this *ayah kareem* (generous verse of Holy Qur'an). Allah ﷻ is even describing that anything holy, anything related to spiritual activity, build a *masjid* over it.

...فِيهَا إِذْ يَتَنَازَعُونَ بَيْنَهُمْ أَمْرَهُمْ ۖ فَقَالُوا ابْنُوا عَلَيْهِم بُنْيَانًا ۖ رَّبُّهُمْ أَعْلَمُ بِهِمْ ۚ قَالَ الَّذِينَ غَلَبُوا عَلَىٰ أَمْرِهِمْ لَنَتَّخِذَنَّ عَلَيْهِم مَّسْجِدًا ﴿٢١﴾

18:21 – "...Feehaa iz yatanaaza'oona bainahum amrahum faqaalub noo 'alaihim bunyaanaa; Rabbuhum a'lamu bihim; qaalal lazeena ghalaboo 'alaaa amrihim lanat takhizanna 'alaihim masjidaa." (Surat Al-Kahf)

"... Behold, they dispute among themselves as to their affair. (Some) said, 'Construct a building over them:' Their Lord knows best about them: those who prevailed over their affair said, 'Let us surely build a place of worship over them.'" (The Cave, 18:21)

So when people come and say, 'Why? Why you people have *masjids* over graves. Why you have *masjids*? Why you do these things? Because that's what Allah ﷻ is giving in Surat Al-Kahf. That because of what they accomplished in the world of light in that station and that *maqam* and that cave, Allah ﷻ gives the word, 'Build over them a *masjid*.' (Holy Qur'an, 18:21)

The Lights of Holy Souls Eternally Stays in Their Maqams Like Portals

It means what they have accomplished, the *tajalli*, it stays there eternally. Because once you open the realm of light, that light is continuously in that environment and in that space. Then Allah ﷻ said, 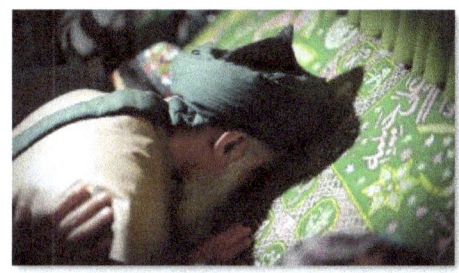 'Build a *masjid* over.' It means that you should keep your *'ibadah* and your worshipness in these holy places. They are portals. They are not things that vanish and go away.

These are portals to paradise. That's the only reason why *hizbul shaitan* (party of satan) is always fighting that, 'Why you're going into these holy places?' They want to destroy these portals on Earth. They want to build satanic portals and destroy the portals of heavens, where any *'ibadah* and worship that was done by a holy person becomes a portal towards paradise.

If their souls are buried there, it's a immense power. As soon as you enter into that *maqam*, into the mausoleum or into the grave vicinity of where a holy and a pious person has passed away, their soul is emanating in that area. Their soul is in paradise in the presence and the Muhammadan light of their reality is shining there.

Believe in These Powers Because They are Signs of Allah's Greatness

It means that this power and this reality of *malakut* (heavenly realm), it's in the reality of, *"Yaaa aiyuhal lazeena aamanoo, aaminoo."*

يَا أَيُّهَا الَّذِينَ آمَنُوا آمِنُو ﴿١٣٦﴾

4:136 – Yaaa aiyuhal lazeena aamanoo aaminoo." (Surat An-Nisa)

"O ye who believe! Believe." (The Women, 4:136)

Oh, you who have entered Islam, *alhamdulillah*. But Allah is asking us again, 'Oh, you who believe, believe.' That at every moment, open the horizon of your belief. Because when we say, *"Allahu Akbar"* (Allah is the Greatest), the greatness of Allah can't be contained, can't be understood, can't be condensed to – 'No, it's not possible.' Then you don't believe in *Allahu Akbar*. When we say *"Allahu Akbar,"* it means Allah is great beyond anything you can comprehend. Allah's greatness is not comprehensible. In the world of light and *malakut*, immense. Throughout Qur'an is giving for us all of these expressions of light.

Shaitan Makes Mechanisms to Disrupt Our Energy Field

That the one whom has knowledge of the book moving with the speed of thought. That speed of thought is more powerful to go back in time and forward in time. Only through their *tafakkur* and their contemplation, they don't need a vehicle. They don't need a mechanical mechanism to artificially simulate and disrupt an energy field. That's the difference between the *shaitan* (satan) and *Rahman* (The Most Compassionate). *Shaitan* has to make a mechanism in which to disrupt an energy field. So, you see on those movies and stargates. It's like a fabric that they're trying to disrupt the fabric and either bring something in or take somebody through.

Heavenly System is to Build Spiritual Connection to a Living Shaykh's Portal

Allah ﷻ gives this to the believers and this is the system being taught by the *muraqabah*. That your only mechanism that you need to build is the connection with those whom are in the heavens and those whom live upon this Earth and they are walking from their paradise reality. It means the living shaykh, whom has that reality and dressed from those realities, they are one foot in paradise, one foot on this Earth. They've been trained by their reality.

When you learn the process of *madad* (support), you're bringing a tremendous energy force. That's why the system is built, that there must be a connection with the living shaykhs. Those who call themself Qadiri think that they can connect to Sayyidina Abdul Qadir Jilani ق – without a living guide is not possible. The way of Prophet ﷺ is *itiba'* (obedience). That you follow *Sahabi* (Holy Companions of Prophet ﷺ), you follow *tabi'yeen* (followers of the holy companions), you follow *Tabi'et Tabi'yeen* (followers of the followers). It means you have the law of *itiba'* and to follow. There must be living shaykhs. 124,000 portals on this Earth. Not all of them are open for traversing but the ones whom teaching, they are definitely of that reality.

The First Step of Tafakkur is to Veil Your Ears

As a result, they're teaching how to connect, how to bring that energy. As soon as you learn how to make your *madad* and your connection, you're bringing their reality, their soul. Their soul coming with their shaykh, with their shaykh, with their shaykh, with their shaykh all the way to the presence of Sayyidina Muhammad ﷺ. So, you bring an immense Muhammadan doorway. Its vibration is so powerful and so strong.

As soon as the servant sits in that presence, they are authorized by Allah ﷻ to take the servant into a state of death. It means as soon as they begin to meditate with how they described is put the veil upon your ear. So as soon as they learn, they're going to meditate, they're going to play their *salawats* because they need to deflect. The *salawat* is a protection from *shaitan*. It needs to protect the ears.

Recognize Your Falsehood and Seek Madad From the Truth

They learn how to make the connection. The energy and the reflection of these souls begin to vibrate and their vibration is very powerful from a heavenly vibration. *"Qul jaa alhaqq wa zahaqal baatil."*

وَ قُلْ جَآءَالْحَقُّ وَزَهَقَ الْبَطِلُ، إِنَّ الْبَطِلَ كَانَ زَهُوقًا ﴿٨١﴾

17:81 – "Wa qul jaa alhaqqu wa zahaqal baatil, innal batila kana zahoqa." (Surat Al-Isra)

"And say, Truth has come, and falsehood has perished. Indeed falsehood, [by its nature], is ever perishing/ bound to perish."
(The Night Journey, 17:81)

It means 'Say to the truth, when the truth comes, the falsehood is perishing.' Why? Because the falsehood within us that's blocking us from that dimension. If you sit by yourself, your falsehood doesn't leave. Because Allah ﷻ said, *"Qul"*

– 'Call, call to the truth.' Say, oh to the truth. If you recognize yourself as the *zalim* (oppressor). *Ana abdukal 'ajeez, wa dayeef, wa miskin, wa zhalim, wa jahl* (I am your servant who is helpless, weak, poor, oppressor and ignorant). I am the *zalim* (oppressor). How I'm going to call myself to relieve myself? Allah ﷻ say, *'Qul*; say to the truth.' It means is a *madad*.

Meditation Eliminates Falsehood to Build Your Frequency and Light

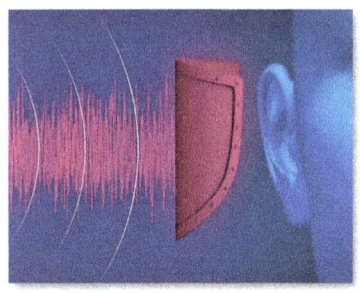

All of the Surat Al-Kahf is about a *madad*. Go and enter, seal your ears. As soon as you enter into that *madad*, you're calling for that support. When you call for that support, that energy and that vibration is now appearing. As the vibration is coming, it's beginning to disrupt and change everything within the soul of that person.

All the falsehood that they bring into that presence is running from the

light that coming now in that meditation. But people don't have an eye to see. Had they had eyes to see – if you could make it like a graphic movie – as soon as they meditate, immense lights are lighting up and illuminating the room. When those illuminations come, all the falsehoods within them run. Everything falls in the room, runs. That's why they asked, 'Make a cave and isolate.' You can't do that in the middle of a mall, but everybody should have a cave, a space in which is sacred and clean to them. If they have and they don't then put a *pardeh* (veil) over your head and make the cave for yourself.

As soon as you make the *madad* (support), that energy comes, the soul comes. The most powerful energy comes which is the soul of the believer. As that vibration comes with an immense amount of energy, it begins to shake every type of falsehood. As a result of shaking and destroying, *"Zahoqan."* The falsehood has no bearing to stand in the presence of that light. It has no power. It's like dust in the presence of wind. Dust is not given any ability to withhold or withstand the wind.

One Hour of Tafakkur With Awliya Dresses Us From 70 Years of Worship

As a result of that energy, it begins to shatter every type of falsehood and immediately build up based on its frequency and its light, the light and energy of that individual. As soon as that soul is dressing the soul of that person, Prophet ﷺ is giving to them now *isharah* (sign) – you're now travelling in their light.

One hour if you sit in that light, it will be as if 70 years has gone but for you, it's just a second. 'What happened?' You come out, oh it was maybe 10, 20, 30 minutes. If you did the whole hour or something, it's an hour. But Allah ﷻ, Prophet ﷺ is describing, 'No.' If you made *madad* with these shaykhs, they are that reality that Prophet ﷺ is describing. That one hour of *madad* with them will dress you 70 years of worship. 70 years you've been taken into their presence and dressed with that worshipness and with that light.

قَالَ رَسُولُ اللهِ ﷺ: تَفَكُّرْ سَاعَةٍ خَيْرٌ مِنْ عِبَادَةِ سَبْعِينْ سَنَةً.

Qala Rasulullahi ﷺ: "Tafakkur saa'atin khairun min 'ibadati sab'yeen sanatan."

The Messenger of Allah (pbuh) said: "One hour of contemplation is more valuable than seventy years of worship."

Be Present and Do Not Be Distracted With the Past and the Future

It means immense realities Surat Al-Kahf brings about. "*Subhana man huwa 'Alimul Hakim.*" That these Divinely knowledges and wisdoms is the entry into the cave of the heart of Prophet ﷺ in which is an immense timeless reality.

سُبْحَانَ الْعَلِيْمُ الْحَكِيْمُ

"Subhanal 'Alimul Hakim"

"Glory be to the All-Knowing, the Wise"

361

The one whom opens timelessness upon their soul, the knowledge of whatever was passed can come to them. The knowledge of whatever has already been written, what they call the future can come to them. All of that exists within the plane of being present. All of this is only existing in the present because there's no past to worry about. There's no future to be scared about.

When the person dies to every fear and apprehension because these are two ropes that *shaitan* putting upon them – to be scared of the future and regretful of the past. When they cut what *shaitan* did from the past, the past is the past. It's spilt milk. Don't think about it. It's already finished. There's nothing to fear of the future, but to open that reality now.

So, they live in meditation. Anything they need, they go and isolate and begin to contemplate. All that's important for them is that moment. In that moment, all knowledges and energies that come to give a tranquility to the heart. That becomes guidance and lights and the nourishment of their soul.

Subhana rabbika rabbal 'izzati 'amma yasifoon, wa salaamun 'alal mursaleen, walhamdulillahi rabbil 'aalameen. Bi hurmati Muhammad al-Mustafa wa bi siri Surat al-Fatiha.

Proofs of Portals and Time Travel in the Holy Qur'an

Sayyidina Sulaiman عليه السلام Wanted Something From Another Dimension

So much of what Allah عز وجل and Holy Qur'an is giving to us – don't be such a timed person in which you're all about your brain and physicality. You will have lost the entire miracle of Holy Qur'an. Sayyidina Sulaiman عليه السلام comes and begins to teach for us in the next month (Rabbi'ul Awwal, 3rd lunar month) in Surat An-Naml, the Ant, about the power of these two powers. That when Sayyidina Sulaiman عليه السلام wanted something from another dimension, he asked, 'I want the throne of Sheba to be brought to me.' The power of the *ifrit* (powerful demon) and the *jinn* (unseen beings) powers, they said, 'We'll bring it, it will take some time.' They were planning on stealing it.

363

قَالَ يَا أَيُّهَا الْمَلَأُ أَيُّكُمْ يَأْتِينِي بِعَرْشِهَا قَبْلَ أَن يَأْتُونِي مُسْلِمِينَ ﴿٣٨﴾ قَالَ عِفْرِيتٌ مِّنَ الْجِنِّ أَنَا آتِيكَ بِهِ قَبْلَ أَن تَقُومَ مِن مَّقَامِكَ ۖ وَإِنِّي عَلَيْهِ لَقَوِيٌّ أَمِينٌ ﴿٣٩﴾

27:38-39 – "Qala ya ayyuha almalao ayyukum yateenee bi'arshiha qabla an yatoonee muslimeen. (38) Qala 'ifreetun mina aljinni ana ateeka bihi qabla an taqooma min maqamika wa inni 'alayhi laqawiyyun ameen. (39)" (Surat An-Naml)

"[Solomon] said (to his own men), "O Chiefs! which of you can bring me her throne before they come to me in submission? (38) Said An 'Ifrit, of the Jinns, I will bring it to you before you rise from your place/council, and indeed, I am for this (purpose/task) strong and trustworthy (39)" (The Ant, 27:38-39)

The Throne of Sheba Was Brought Faster Than the Speed of Light

The one whom Allah ﷻ gave knowledge of the book means *awliya* (saints), that's a completely different power. They said, 'By the time your eye blinks, we will have replicated it,' and he presented it into the presence of Sayyidina Sulaiman ﷺ.

قَالَ الَّذِي عِندَهُ عِلْمٌ مِّنَ الْكِتَابِ أَنَا آتِيكَ بِهِ قَبْلَ أَن يَرْتَدَّ إِلَيْكَ طَرْفُكَ ۚ فَلَمَّا رَآهُ مُسْتَقِرًّا عِندَهُ قَالَ هَٰذَا مِن فَضْلِ رَبِّي ... ﴿٤٠﴾

27:40 – "Qala alladhee 'indahu 'ilmun minal kitabi ana ateeka bihi qabla an yartadda ilayka Tarfuka, falamma raahu mustaqirran 'indahu qala hadha min fadli rabbi..." (Surat An-Naml)

"Said one who had knowledge of the book: "I will bring it to you within the twinkling of an eye!" Then when (Solomon) saw it placed firmly before him, he said: "This is by the Grace of my Lord!..." (The Ant, 27:40)

They Can Move at the Speed of Thought in the Powerful Portals

So, now you have the power of light and the speed of light. These people

are trying to travel at a speed. When they bring a power of light, and if the portal has a power of light, they can move within a constant. They say that, 'Oh, we can go forward in time, but there's no way to go back in time.' But Allah ﷻ is giving a *daleel* (proof) in the story of Surat Al-Sulaiman عليه السلام. No, there's a power much faster than the speed of light and that's the speed of thought and the ones whom have knowledge of the book. Because now the book of Allah ﷻ is Prophet ﷺ.

All of those were imitated realities. The power of Sayyidina Sulaiman عليه السلام is like a drop in the power of the reality from Prophet ﷺ. He took from Prophet ﷺ a ring. By the blessings of the ring, he was given a key into that power. But the one whom owns the power and doesn't need a ring is Sayyidina Muhammad ﷺ.

By virtue of that knowledge of the book he said, 'By the time you think about it, we have replicated because prophets don't steal. We replicated the throne of Sheba, of Bilqis عليها السلام.' So much so that she thought, 'It looks and appears like my throne.' Knowing that, 'No, I know you didn't steal my throne but you did a nice simulation.'

Recite Names of Pious Souls to Bring the Immense Portal in Your Home

Another good example is that Sayyidina Abbas Khidr ☪ , he's a walking portal. Allah ☪ has given to his reality, that he is in the *shajarah* (spiritual lineage) of *Naqshbandiya tul 'Aliya* (Most Distinguished Naqshbandi Order). He's in the chain for an immense *barakah* and blessings of the chain. He's here to bless the chain of *Naqshbandiya tul 'Aliya.*

Because he's a shaykh in the *tariqah* (spiritual path), then his *nazar* (gaze) is continuously upon the *tariqah* students. When they try to meditate and contemplate, he is a great support to facilitate that *madad.*

That's why when we say that when you want to meditate, you want to make your *madad* (support), that recite the *madad*. Recite the recitation and the names of these holy shaykhs because they come with an immense power. Anybody who wants to have that energy of that portal in their home, recite the *madad*. Continuously recite the *madad* in your home calling the chain of *Naqshbandiya tul 'Aliya.*

Sayyidina Khidr ☪ Facilitates an Interdimensional Connection

Then Mawlana Sayyidina Abbas Khidr ☪ then has an important role in an inter-dimensional connection. It means the one whom is on Earth and trying to connect into the realities of *barzakh* (purgatory), then he plays that role to facilitate their connection and to facilitate the conveyance of knowledges reaching towards the Divinely knowledges. That's why Allah ☪ gave that example of Sayyidina Khidr ☪ coming up in Surat Al-Kahf.

The reality of Surat Al-Kahf, why it was so difficult for Sayyidina Musa ؏ is because he was not seen. Sayyidina Khidr ؏ was not seen so all of the transpiring understanding of Sayyidina Musa ؏ and meeting with Sayyidina Khidr ؏ and then passing. How you could pass if you saw somebody standing there? He's unseen and the only way to understand that Sayyidina Khidr ؏ was there, that there were signs of the revival. That he had the power to revive the dead. So when Yashua ؏ put his fish and they passed, he said, 'What happened to our lunch?' 'Oh, I forgot. I put the fish down to prepare for lunch and it was *ajeeb* (strange). The fish came to life and jumped into the river.'

فَلَمَّا جَاوَزَا قَالَ لِفَتَاهُ آتِنَا غَدَاءَنَا لَقَدْ لَقِينَا مِن سَفَرِنَا هَٰذَا نَصَبًا ﴿٦٢﴾ قَالَ أَرَأَيْتَ إِذْ أَوَيْنَا إِلَى الصَّخْرَةِ فَإِنِّي نَسِيتُ الْحُوتَ وَمَا أَنسَانِيهُ إِلَّا الشَّيْطَانُ أَنْ أَذْكُرَهُ ۚ وَاتَّخَذَ سَبِيلَهُ فِي الْبَحْرِ عَجَبًا ﴿٦٣﴾

18:62-63 – "Falammaa jaawazaa qaala lifataahu aatinaa ghadaaa'anaa laqad laqeena min safarinaa haazaa nasabaa. (62) Qaala ara'ayta iz awainaaa ilas sakhrati fa innee naseetul hoota wa maaa ansaaneehu illash Shaitaanu an azkurah; wattakhaza sabeelahoo fil bahri'ajabaa (63)" (Surat Al-Kahf)

"So when they had passed beyond it, [Moses] said to his boy, "Bring us our morning meal. We have certainly suffered in this, our journey, [much] fatigue. (62) He said, "Did you see when we retired to the rock? Indeed, I forgot [there] the fish. And none made me forget it except Satan – that I should mention it. And it took its course into the sea amazingly (63)". (The Cave, 18:62-63)

So his meeting with the unseen shaykh, he realized, 'That was the sign I was looking for; the one who can bring the dead to life. Let's retrace our tracks.' The whole event with Sayyidina Khidr عليه السلام was unseen by anyone. That's why Nabi Musa عليه السلام had a difficult time. Everything that was happening, nobody could see Sayyidina Khidr عليه السلام.

Sayyidina Khidr عليه السلام is also of that reality now. That if the student has good character and that they have their meditation and sincerity, they should be able to connect with the reality of Sayyidina Abbas Khidr عليه السلام. That his purpose is to facilitate the connection into that realm and facilitate the conveyance of knowledge. So, it's a great portal under the *Muhammadan haqqaiqs* (realities), *inshaAllah*.

The Holy Qur'an and Bible are Books of Rhythm and Sound

InshaAllah, that you have questions related to sound. The hearing is very deep that for people to hear and try their best to meditate and contemplate on this subject so that you can go deeper into that understanding. It is the secret of all spirituality. It's the secret of the last days and why the book of Sayyidina Isa عليه السلام was *Injil*. It was a spoken book and the reality of Holy Qur'an is a recited book.

It means these last books, two books from the last days, are based on sound and that they're recited in *qira'ats*, (recitations) in rhythms and sound vibrations for the protection of *insan* (mankind). So, it's not a coincidence. There's no coincidences by this world. Everything is in a design so to have an immense important, immense reality. The one whom can grasp the understanding of energy and sound then they can reach to these realities.

Companions of the Cave Moved Through 309 Years and Felt Like a Day

We described before these are stories of portals upon this Earth. The Earth is filled with portals. All of Holy Qur'an has many, many examples of portals. These are manifestations of energies upon this Earth in which are meant to through move space and time. We're in the month of *Ashab ul Kahf*, [Safar, 2nd lunar month], the companions of the cave in which they entered a cave and the synopsis is they thought it was a day or less and 309 years have transpired. It means in a blink of an eye, they moved 309 years in time. When they ran from an oppressor, when they came out of the cave, they were loved by people.

وَلَبِثُوا فِي كَهْفِهِمْ ثَلَاثَ مِائَةٍ سِنِينَ وَازْدَادُوا تِسْعًا ﴿٢٥﴾

18:25 – "Wa labisoo fee kahfihim salaasa mi'atin sineena wazdaadoo tis'aa" (Surat Al-Kahf)

"And they remained in their cave for three hundred years and exceeded by nine." (The Cave, 18:25)

Nabi Musa ﷺ Saw the Fire of a Portal to The Divine Presence

Nabi Musa ﷺ walked in a desert, saw the fire of the portal, entered in. Allah ﷻ describes, 'He entered into a space and told take your shoes off. This is a Divinely Presence.' It appeared; Allah ﷻ made that portal to appear and Nabi Musa ﷺ went into that,

received what he needed to receive from the Divine and then he was
sent back.

فَلَمَّا أَتَاهَا نُودِيَ يَا مُوسَىٰ ﴿١١﴾ إِنِّي أَنَا رَبُّكَ فَاخْلَعْ نَعْلَيْكَ ۖ إِنَّكَ بِالْوَادِ الْمُقَدَّسِ
طُوًى ﴿١٢﴾

*20:11-12 – "Falammaa ataahaa noodiya yaa Moosaa (11) Innee Ana
Rabbuka fakhla' na'laika innaka bilwaadil muqaddasi Tuwaa (12)"
(Surat Taha)*

*"But when he came to the fire, he was called: O Moses! (11) Verily I am
your Lord! therefore (in My presence) remove your sandals/shoes: you are
in the sacred valley Tuwa. (12)" (Taha, 20:11)*

Sitna Maryam ☉ Was Provided Sustenance From Paradise

That's what was the example Allah ☉ gave for us in Sitna Maryam
(Mary) ☉. In all of the Jewish temple, the prayer of the Prophet
Zakariya ☉ was not accepted. It was the holiest temple for all of Judaism
and for 99 years, this prayer was not answered.

So, inside of their temple was a holy
woman. Holy because she's very special
to the presence of Sayyidina
Muhammad ﷺ. In her portal, what
Allah ☉ called the niche, she was being
provided sustenance from paradise.
Angels weren't going out into the field
and bringing her vegetables. Her
sustenance was coming from paradise,
from other dimensions into that portal.

...كُلَّمَا دَخَلَ عَلَيْهَا زَكَرِيَّا الْمِحْرَابَ وَجَدَ عِنْدَهَا رِزْقًا قَالَ يَا مَرْيَمُ أَنَّىٰ لَكِ هَٰذَا
قَالَتْ هُوَ مِنْ عِنْدِ اللَّهِ إِنَّ اللَّهَ يَرْزُقُ مَن يَشَاءُ بِغَيْرِ حِسَابٍ ﴿٣٧﴾

3:37 – "...Kullama dakhala 'alayha Zakariyya almihraba wajada
'indaha rizqan, qala ya Maryamu anna laki hadha? qalat huwa min
'indi Allahi innAllaha yarzuqu man yashao bighayri hisab."
(Surat Ali 'Imran)

"...Every time Zakariyya entered upon her in the niche/prayer chamber,
he found with her provision. He said, "O Mary, from where is this
[coming] to you?" She said, "It is from Allah. Indeed, Allah provides for
whom He wills without account." (Family of Imran, 3:37)

Sayyidina Zakariya's ﷺ Prayers Were Only Answered in Sitna Maryam's ﷺ Portal

As a result, when Sayyidina Zakariya ﷺ entered and his heart witnessed what he needed to witness, he realized in all of this temple, my prayer was not asked, was not given. But in this portal, in this dimension of what she has created and what Allah ﷻ has dressed her with from her worshipness, immediately he made a prayer. Sayyidina Jibreel ﷺ appeared to him and says, 'Your prayer is accepted.' It means his presence was already in that dimension and the prayer was completely accepted.

هُنَالِكَ دَعَا زَكَرِيَّا رَبَّهُ ۖ قَالَ رَبِّ هَبْ لِي مِن لَّدُنكَ ذُرِّيَّةً طَيِّبَةً ۖ إِنَّكَ سَمِيعُ الدُّعَاءِ
﴿٣٨﴾ فَنَادَتْهُ الْمَلَائِكَةُ وَهُوَ قَائِمٌ يُصَلِّي فِي الْمِحْرَابِ أَنَّ اللَّهَ يُبَشِّرُكَ بِيَحْيَىٰ مُصَدِّقًا
بِكَلِمَةٍ مِّنَ اللَّهِ وَسَيِّدًا وَحَصُورًا وَنَبِيًّا مِّنَ الصَّالِحِينَ ﴿٣٩﴾

*3:38-39 — "Hunalika da'a zakariyya Rabbahu, qala rabbi hab lee min
ladunka dhurriyyatan tayyibatan, innaka samee'ud du'a. (38) Fanadat
hu almalaikatu wa huwa qaaimun yusallee fil mihrabi annAllaha
yubashshiruka bi Yahya musaddiqan bikalimatin minAllahi wa
sayyidan wa hasooran wa Nabiyyan minas saliheen. (39)"*
(Surat Ali 'Imran)

*"At that, Zakariyya called upon his Lord, saying, "My Lord, grant me
from Yourself a good offspring. Indeed, You are the Hearer of
supplication. (38) While he was standing in prayer in the chamber, the
angels called unto him: "Indeed, Allah gives you good tidings of Yahya
(John), witnessing the truth of a Word from Allah, and (be besides)
noble, chaste, and a prophet,- of the (goodly) company of the righteous."*
(Family of Imran, 3:38-39)

Sayyidina Zakariya ؏ Recognized the Blessing of Sitna Maryam's ؏ Portal

So, Qur'an has many *qissah* (stories), many examples. Sayyidina Zakariya ؏ went into the niche of Sitna Maryam ؏ and saw that this is a portal that's supplying sustenance; not from this time, not from this season and could understand that this was extraordinary. At that time, he made *du'a* (supplication) within that portal and his *du'a* was accepted and Allah ﷻ granted him Sayyidina Yahya ؏ [Holy Qur'an, 3:37-39]. So filled with Qur'an examples.

This Life is Made Up of Different Layers From Infinite Dimensions

Now when you see the *shaitan* trying to make these portals by spinning; what we said, this Earth and our existence is a fabric of energy. They want to spin the atoms at a very high rate of speed, breaking something within the fabric.

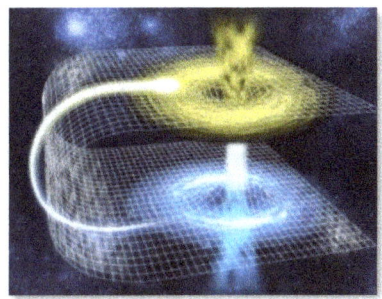

Our life is like an Adobe software. Anybody who's dealt with Adobe, you draw in layers. You draw something, you put a layer. You draw another layer, you put another layer. When you put all these layers together, we look like this – like we're one dimension. It's not one dimension; infinite dimensions within this space and time. There are other creatures standing and sitting here, living here above us, below us and all around us. It's all designed in layers.

They Manipulate the Energy to Summon Demons

So, they understood this layering and they begin to manipulate the energy. When you manipulate the energy and now NASA is putting out videos on portals. That they manipulate the energy to tear the fabric of this reality and move through it or summon something from it. Considering they're not benevolent people, they're most likely calling *shaitans* through it that summoning. And all of that industry was based on this practice. When they wanted to make rockets, they went out into the desert and summons, summons, summons. When they summon, they summon these *ifrit* (powerful demon) that taught them how to make those rockets. Their whole science is based on that understanding. So their portals are designed for bringing very negative energies into this dimension.

Awliyaullah are the Most Powerful Portals Upon the Earth

Allah ﷻ has that in Qur'an, that there are portals. The strongest and most powerful of these portals are 124,000 *awliyaullah* (saints) upon this Earth. That their souls and the reality of their presence vibrate at the power of the

soul. As a result of their presence and being in the presence of their soul, the vibration in which they're emanating is creating a Divinely door. They don't have to tear anything. They don't have to make any device. It's by virtue of their soul and the presence and companionship of the soul. As a result of making and learning how to make the *madad* (support) and to accompany that reality, that energy comes to be present. The energy of the soul and the power of the soul is not something that can be comprehended. But because *shaitan* doesn't have that, he has to use power from the *ifrit*.

The Throne of Sheba Was Replicated Using a Portal of Time

So, when Sayyidina Sulaiman ﷺ, was asking 'Who can bring me the throne of Sheba?' The *ifrit* said, who were forced under command of Sayyidina Sulaiman ﷺ, 'We'll bring it. It takes time.' But the one whom had *Ahlul Kitab* (people of the book), the knowledge of the book said, 'By the time you blink, you thought about it,' he reproduced the entire throne of Sheba in his presence.

قَالَ يَا أَيُّهَا الْمَلَأُ أَيُّكُمْ يَأْتِينِي بِعَرْشِهَا قَبْلَ أَن يَأْتُونِي مُسْلِمِينَ ﴿٣٨﴾ قَالَ عِفْرِيتٌ مِّنَ الْجِنِّ أَنَا آتِيكَ بِهِ قَبْلَ أَن تَقُومَ مِن مَّقَامِكَ ۖ وَإِنِّي عَلَيْهِ لَقَوِيٌّ أَمِينٌ ﴿٣٩﴾ قَالَ الَّذِي عِندَهُ عِلْمٌ مِّنَ الْكِتَابِ أَنَا آتِيكَ بِهِ قَبْلَ أَن يَرْتَدَّ إِلَيْكَ طَرْفُكَ ۚ فَلَمَّا رَآهُ مُسْتَقِرًّا عِندَهُ قَالَ هَٰذَا مِن فَضْلِ رَبِّي ... ﴿٤٠﴾

27:38-40 – "Qala ya ayyuha almalao ayyukum yateenee bi'arshiha qabla an yatoonee muslimeen. (38) Qala 'ifreetun mina aljinni ana ateeka bihi qabla an taqooma min maqamika wa inni 'alayhi laqawiyyun ameen. (39) Qala alladhee 'indahu 'ilmun minal kitabi ana ateeka bihi qabla an yartadda ilayka Tarfuka, falamma raahu mustaqirran 'indahu qala hadha min fadli rabbi...(40)"
(Surat An-Naml)

"[Solomon] said (to his own men), "O Chiefs! which of you can bring me her throne before they come to me in submission? (38) Said An 'Ifrit, of the Jinns, I will bring it to you before you rise from your place/council, and indeed, I am for this (purpose/task) strong and trustworthy. (39) Said one who had knowledge of the book: "I will bring it to you within the twinkling of an eye!" Then when (Solomon) saw it placed firmly before him, he said: "This is by the Grace of my Lord!...(40)"
(The Ant, 27:38-40)

It means the knowledge of the book was far more powerful than the energy of the *ifrit*. So, *shaitan* uses the reality of the *ifrit* and *Ar-Rahman* (The Most Compassionate) uses knowledge of the *kitab* (book).

Madad is Soul-to-Soul Connection Into a Timeless Reality

So, it means that the power of the *kitab* and these *awliyaullah* whom their souls resonate at this energy and these vibrations. As soon as people learn how to make their *madad*, their connection, the vibration of that soul is coming and begins to create for them an eternal portal, something from paradise realities. As soon as they make *madad* and make their connection, their soul is making a soul-to-soul connection and entering into a timeless reality.

Prophet ﷺ Described Tafakkur is Like a Portal of 70 Years Worship

That's why we described last night, Prophet ﷺ described, 'The one whom can make *tafakkur* versus the one who doesn't make *tafakkur* is like 70 years of worshipness.' The one who enters into his *tafakkur*, his one hour of contemplation is like 70 years of worshipness.

قَالَ رَسُولُ اللهِ ﷺ: تَفَكُّرُ سَاعَةٍ خَيْرٌ مِنْ عِبَادَةِ سَبْعِينْ سَنَةً.

Qala Rasulullahi ﷺ: "Tafakkur saa'atin khairun min 'ibadati sab'yeen sanatan."

The Messenger of Allah (pbuh) said: "One hour of contemplation is more valuable than seventy years of worship."

Well, that was Einstein's theory, that if you moved at this speed of light and came back, 70 years would have transpired. So immense, immense realities for us to think and contemplate that what Allah ﷻ is granting of realities and are we able to dress ourselves from these realities to prepare for the difficulty that's always upon this Earth and that's opening upon this Earth, *inshaAllah*.

Holy Qu'ran Contains Timeless Realities

So much amazing realities in Qur'an and this why it's the guidance, immense guidance for the last days. When things will happen and people

will look to their books and nothing written there. They say, 'No, it doesn't. These things don't happen.' Allah ﷻ wrote everything in Qur'an. That no, no He ﷻ has already written and the nation has the information and the Holy Qur'an. Anything big or small is all within the Qur'an's reality. It brings its reality out for the time that's necessary and the understanding that's necessary for that time. That's the miraculous nature of the reality of the heart of Prophet ﷺ, that bringing out all the beatific speech of Allah ﷻ, *inshaAllah*.

Subhana rabbika rabbal 'izzati 'amma yasifoon, wa salaamun 'alal mursaleen, walhamdulillahi rabbil 'aalameen. Bi hurmati Muhammad al-Mustafa wa bi siri Surat al-Fatiha.

Sixth Power

Haqiqatul Irshad

Reality of Guidance

The Six Powers of the Heart
Used for Guidance

Anyone Can Be Given Permission for Zikr

Alhamdulillah, sharing always for myself and if anyone take any benefit. In the oceans of reality and in the oceans of guidance and understanding, the opening of the heart and the levels of the heart. There are many common terms and many people using various terms and may have a different understanding for these terms. To be given *ijazah* (permission) for the *zikr* (Divine remembrance) is something very easy. Anybody who comes to the shaykh, they will give you *ijazah* for *zikr* because they want the *zikr* to spread throughout the world. Especially if you are somebody already doing a *zikr* and you come and say, 'Can I have *ijazah* for the Naqshbandi *zikr*?' *Alhamdulillah*, they give that because the *hikmah* and the wisdom of that *ijazah*, that *khatm* and that style of *zikr* to spread.

1. Haqiqatul Juzba (The Reality of Attraction)

The understanding of the levels of the heart and the guidance of the heart then is a completely different ocean of reality. That from the *haqqaiq* (reality) and the training that they're going to train that servant and that student, the servant of Allah ﷻ, becoming their student. That Mawlana Shaykh's ق training was to bring down all the bad characteristics, to bring down all the wild desires. One of the first *haqqaiqs* (realities) that has to be developed is the reality of *juzba*, the reality of attraction. That can only be achieved through *tafakkur* and contemplation. The reality of *Haqiqatul Juzba* (Reality of Attraction) means the magnetic character. That you have a magnetic character, magnanimous, they call in English, that people are attracted to you.

Fight Your Bad Characteristics Through Contemplation

That has to do – we don't go into each one too long – each one is its own oceans and books of reality. That it's for us to understand when some people use these comments and they talk very lightly about it, but the Naqshbandiya way and Naqshbandiya Haqqani, from Sultanul Awliya Mawlana Shaykh Muhammad Nazim Haqqani ق, and under his hand and guidance of Mawlana Shaykh ق; our understanding and the way that we've been taught in these realities and trained in these realities, is that the first step of the seeker is to know himself is to know his Lord.

قَالَ رَسُولَ اللَّهِ ﷺ: "مَنْ عَرَفَ نَفْسَهُ فَقَدْ عَرَفَ رَبَّهُ."

Qala Rasulullahi ﷺ: *"Man 'arafa nafsahu faqad 'arafa Rabbahu."*

The Messenger of Allah (pbuh) said: "Who knows himself, knows his Lord."

He takes a way of extreme *tafakkur* (contemplation). That the time you're spending with the shaykh, in company of the shaykh, is to take away the bad characteristics because the light that emanates from the shaykh and the characteristic – sort of the uprightness of the characteristic of the shaykh – brings out all of the character defects. So, you're bringing out all of those and trying to attack them, trying to attack them. But the essential element in that formula is the way of *tafakkur* (contemplation).

Tafakkur is the Essential Element of Knowing the Self

The way of *tafakkur* and contemplation means that that servant is trained for hours a day to constantly keep to themselves, constantly go within themselves, begin the practices of *tafakkur* and meditation. That meditate, meditate, meditate upon yourself, your bad characteristics, asking constantly to be nothing, to be nothing, to be nothing.

From there, they begin to teach you that you keep the *muhabbat* of the shaykh, the love because they are the *Nurul Muhammadi* ﷺ (Light of Prophet Muhammad ﷺ) that are dressing us and blessing us. So, we train to keep that love. You keep their presence. The love and the presence with *tafakkur* opens annihilation because you're talking about the world of light. You're not talking about the physicality. This guidance that they're talking about is from *malakut* (heavenly realm). That if they want to open real guidance, it's not the guidance of the body. The body will be used at the last stage when it's prepared. What they want is to develop the soul.

So, when they begin to develop the soul is that go back into the *malakut*. That meet us there, keep your dress there, keep your association there. Keep asking Allah ﷻ that you don't want from this *dunya* (material world). You don't want nothing but Divinely Knowledges and Allah's ﷻ Satisfaction. So, it's based on the deep practices of *tafakkur*, to be nothing, to be nothing, to be nothing and begin to be dressed by their lights, blessed by their lights.

We Must Purify the Iron in Our Body

One of the secrets of it is that they'll begin to train that the iron on your body that is holding your energy has to be purified. That iron that Allah ﷻ gives to your body that makes your blood to be red is because of the iron, *hadid*; *hadid* in Arabic. It's not from Earth. They say it's from the heavens to be found on Earth.

وَأَنزَلْنَا الْحَدِيدَ فِيهِ بَأْسٌ شَدِيدٌ وَمَنَافِعُ لِلنَّاسِ وَلِيَعْلَمَ اللَّـهُ مَن يَنصُرُهُ وَرُسُلَهُ بِالْغَيْبِ ۚ إِنَّ اللَّـهَ قَوِيٌّ عَزِيزٌ ﴿٢٥﴾

57:25 – "...Wa anzalnal hadeeda feehi baasun shadeedun wa manaafi'u linnaasi wa liya'lam Allahu man yansuruhu wa Rusulahu bilghaib; innAllaha Qawiyun 'Aziz." (Surat Al-Hadid)

"...And We sent down iron, in which is (material for) great military might as well as many benefits for mankind, and so that Allah may test/make evident who will support him and His messengers from the unseen world. Indeed, Allah is Powerful and Exalted in Might."
(The Iron, 57:25)

It means very holy metal, that Allah ﷻ put that metal within the body to be purified by *zikr* (Divine remembrance), by all these practices. That metal to be purified. That metal is what contains and carries the energy. That when you begin to develop yourself and you have purified your blood and the shaykh's training on how to purify yourself, purify yourself, bring good characteristics, you begin to keep the dress and the light of the energy that Allah ﷻ wants to dress you from. The shaykh is the container of that dress.

It means the Muhammadan lights that is within the shaykh begins to dress. If your iron is not correct and not clean and you're not using from your soul, this energy dresses and goes. It's not something the student is able to contain, to keep and to begin to nourish that energy, begin to build that energy.

Build Your Energy to Become Excess Positive

When they're trained on how to build that energy from the *haqqaiq* of *juzba* (attraction), it means then they begin to have an excessive amount of energy. The same we did in school and we've explained before. That when you're in school, they give you an iron rod and they teach you how to magnetize iron. You have to put two charges on iron, a positive and negative charge.

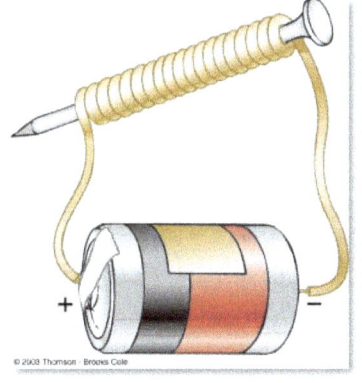

You've now brought a charge onto this iron. You magnetized it. The charge that Allah ﷻ teaching us is that this emanation, this *Nurul*

Muhammadi ﷺ (Light of Prophet Muhammad ﷺ), that the shaykh is the container of that light.

When you bring that *qudra* (power) and you bring that light and practice, you be nothing and bring that energy, bring that light. It begins to magnetize the iron within your body. Once you magnetize the iron, it becomes excessive positive. When it becomes excessive positive, the emanation and the energy that emanating from you becomes magnetic. It means it is able to attract other people. The energy that they're deficient on, the energy that their souls are in need of, they feel attracted to that individual. It can be here and it can be 10,000 kilometres away, it doesn't matter. Later, we talk about how that's happening. It means that they've trained on how to bring the energy system within their body. That's why you eat *halal* (permissible) because Prophet ﷺ described, 'The *shaitan* (satan) runs through the blood.' It means all the training, all the *Hadith* of Prophet ﷺ is to bring about these perfections.

عَنْ أَنَسٍ قَالَ، قَالَ رَسُولُ اللهِ ﷺ: "إِنَّ الشَّيْطَانَ يَجْرِي مِنَ الْإِنْسَانِ مَجْرَى اَلدَّمِ." [المَصْدَرْ: صَحِيحْ مُسْلِمْ ٢١٧٤]

'An Anasin Qala Rasulallahi ﷺ*: "Innash Shaitana yajri minal Insani majra addami." [Sahih Muslim 2174]*

Narrated by 'An Anas (ra) that the Messenger of Allah (pbuh) said, "Satan circulates/flows through the human being as blood circulates/flow in the body." [Authentic by Muslim 2174]

2. Haqiqatul Faiz
(Reality of Downpouring Emanation)

When you begin to bring about the perfection and cleansing and bring the energy, the iron becomes charged. The individual becomes excessively positive. Then the *haqqaiq* of *faiz* (downpouring blessings) begins to dress that servant. It means that they're excessively positive in their training. In their soul's reality, they begin to attract Allah's ﷻ downpourings.

It means from the *haqqaiq* of *faiz* is that when they're excessively positive, they have a tremendous amount of *himmah* (zeal) because now their *'amal* (action) is becoming more real, more real. They're attracting Allah's ﷻ *faiz*. Allah's ﷻ *rida* and satisfaction means many lights, many emanations; many realities begin to pour upon them, pour upon their soul, pour upon their soul. They attract the *faiz* of the shaykh. They attract the *faiz* of Prophet ﷺ and from whatever Allah ﷻ wants to begin of downpouring. It means then that is the reality of that *haqqaiq* but because of their *tafakkur* and contemplation and the charge upon their soul, they're attracting these realities like a satellite dish.

3. Haqiqatut Tawajjuh
(Reality of Directing to Divinely Face)

It means then they begin to teach from that reality, the *haqqaiq* of *tawajjuh* (focusing). It means that in their *tafakkur* and in their contemplation, they're opening for them that what you're seeking is the source of all power. It means these *haqqaiqs* of guidance – why they want us to understand is because somebody throws out a comment about guidance as if it's something so simple. But these are lifetime trainings of how they train. That when they train you, that in your *tafakkur*, in your *tafakkur* and in your contemplation, Allah ﷻ describes, 'Everything perishes but the Holy Face.'

$$\text{...}كُلُّ شَيْءٍ هَالِكٌ إِلَّا وَجْهَهُ ۚ ...﴿٨٨﴾$$

28:88 – "...Kullu shayin halikun illa wajha..." (Surat Al-Qasas)

"...Everything (that exists) will perish except His holy Face..."
(The Stories, 28:88)

Sayyidina Ibrahim ؏ Sought the Holy Face

So, they begin to teach you that seek nothing in life but the Holy Face. That everything else is going to be a distraction. Even in Holy Qur'an, Sayyidina Ibrahim ؏, in his ascension into the heavens, he sought the reality of the stars, the reality of the moon, the reality of the sun.

$$فَلَمَّا جَنَّ عَلَيْهِ اللَّيْلُ رَأَىٰ كَوْكَبًا ۖ قَالَ هَٰذَا رَبِّي ۖ فَلَمَّا أَفَلَ قَالَ لَا أُحِبُّ الْآفِلِينَ ﴿٧٦﴾$$

6:76 – "Falamma janna 'alayhil laylu raa kawkaban, qala hadha Rabbi, falamma afala qala la uhibbul afileen." (Surat Al-An'am)

"So when the night covered him [with darkness], he saw a star. He said, "This is my lord." But when it set, he said, I like not those that disappear." (The Cattle, 6:76)

It means the stars were the *awliya* (saints), the *diwan al awliya* (association of saints) because Prophet ﷺ said, 'Follow my Companions. Any of them, they are like stars on a dark night.'

أَصْحَابِيْ كَالنُّجُـــومْ بِأَيِّهِمْ اَقْتَدَيْتِمْ اَهْتَدَيْتِمْ

"Ashabi kan Nujoom, bi ayyihim aqta daytum ahta daytum."

"My companions are like stars. Whoever among them you follow, you will be rightly guided." Prophet Muhammad (pbuh)

He left that *diwan*, he went to the *maqam* (station) of the moon which means is the *Ghawth* because that is the strongest of all of those realities.

فَلَمَّا رَأَى الْقَمَرَ بَازِغًا قَالَ هَذَا رَبِّي
فَلَمَّا أَفَلَ قَالَ لَئِن لَّمْ يَهْدِنِي رَبِّي

لَأَكُونَنَّ مِنَ الْقَوْمِ الضَّالِّينَ ﴿٧٧﴾

6:77 – "Falamma raa alQamara bazighan qala hadha Rabbi, falamma afala qala la in lam yahdinee rabbi laakonanna minal qawmid dalleen." (Surat Al-An'am)

"And when he saw the moon rising, he said, "This is my lord." But when it set, he said, Unless my Lord guides me, I will surely be among the people gone astray." (The Cattle, 6:77)

Seek Refuge From Everything Except the Holy Face

He sought even above that to the reality of the sun, *Ayat al-Akbar* (the Great Sign). It means these are all from the realities. *Ayat al-Akbar* means something great of realities and Sayyidina Ibrahim عليه السلام even wanted beyond that and that becomes that *haqqaiq*. Of the *tawajjuh*, it means that seek everything. That seek that which will not perish and they begin to train you on how to seek the Holy Face, *Wajhi hil Karim* (The Holy Face of the Most Generous). That's why in the *du'as* (supplications), they say, '*A'uzu bi Wajhi hil Karim*. 'I seek refuge from everything except that Holy Face.' It becomes the training on how to reach the source of power.

389

Du'a of Wajhi hil Karim (The Holy Face of the Most Generous)

[1] "أَعُوذُ بِوَجْهِ اللهِ الْكَرِيمِ وَبِكَلِمَاتِ اللهِ التَّامَّاتِ اَللَّاتِي لَا يُجَاوِزُهُنَّ بَرٌّ وَلَا فَاجِرٌ، مِنْ شَرِّ مَا يَنْزِلُ مِنَ السَّمَاءِ وَشَرِّ مَا يَعْرُجُ فِيهَا. وَشَرِّ مَا ذَرَأَ فِي الْأَرْضِ وَشَرِّ مَا يَخْرُجُ مِنْهَا وَمِنْ فِتَنِ اللَّيْلِ وَالنَّهَارِ وَمِنْ طَوَارِقِ اللَّيْلِ وَالنَّهَارِ إِلَّا طَارِقًا يَطْرُقُ بِخَيْرٍ يَا رَحْمَنُ " [مُوَطَّأُ إِمَامُ مَالِكٍ، كِتَابٌ ٥١، عَدَدٌ ٥١.٤.١٠]

"A'udhu bi wajhillahil Karim wa bi kalimatillahil tammati allati la yujawizu hunna barrun wa la faajirun min sharri ma yanzilu minas samayi wa sharri ma ya'roju fiha wa sharri ma zhara 'a fil ardi, wa sharri ma yakhruju minha wa min fitanil layli wan nahari. Wa min tawariqal layli wan nahari, illa taariqan yatruqu bi khayrin ya Rahman." [Muwatta' Imam Malik - Kitab 51 – 'adad 51.4.10]

I seek refuge with the Noble Face of Allah and with the perfect holy words of Allah (AJ), which neither the righteous nor the wicked/corrupt can exceed, from the evil of what descends from the sky and the evil of what ascends in it. And from the evil of what is created/spread in the earth and the evil of what emerges/comes out of it what emerges from it. And from the trials of the night and day, and from the difficulties/visitations of the night and day, except for a difficulty that strikes with goodness. O the Most Compassionate!
[Source: Malik Muwatta, Book 51, Number 51.4.10]

――――――――――――

[1] عَنْ يَحْيَى بْنِ سَعِيدٍ، أَنَّهُ قَالَ أُسْرِيَ بِرَسُولِ اللهِ ﷺ فَرَأَى عِفْرِيتًا مِنَ الْجِنِّ يَطْلُبُهُ بِشُعْلَةٍ مِنْ نَارٍ كُلَّمَا الْتَفَتَ رَسُولُ اللهِ ﷺ رَآهُ . فَقَالَ لَهُ جِبْرِيلُ (عَلَيْهِ السَّلَامُ): أَفَلَا أُعَلِّمُكَ كَلِمَاتٍ تَقُولُهُنَّ إِذَا قُلْتَهُنَّ طَفِئَتْ شُعْلَتُهُ وَخَرَّ لِفِيهِ؟ فَقَالَ رَسُولُ اللهِ ﷺ " بَلَى." فَقَالَ جِبْرِيلُ (عَلَيْهِ السَّلَامُ): فَقُلْ

'An Yahya ibn Sa'yid (ra) annahu qala: "Usriya bi Rasulillahi ﷺ, fa ra'a 'ifritan minal jinni yatlubuhu bi shu'latin min narin, kullama iltafata ltafata Rasulullahi ﷺ ra'aahu. Faqala lahu Jibrilu (as): 'Afala u'allimuka kalimatin taquluhunna, izaa qultahunna tafi'at shu'latuhu, wa kharra lifihi?' Faqala Rasulullahi ﷺ: "Bala." Faqala Jibrilu (as) faqul:

Yahya ibn Sa'yid (ra) said, "When the Messenger of Allah (pbuh) was taken on the Night Journey, he saw an evil jinn seeking him with a torch of fire. Whenever the Messenger of Allah (pubh), turned, he (pbuh) saw him. Jibril (as) said to him, 'Shall I teach you some words to say? When you say them, his torch will be put out and will fall from him.'

The Messenger of Allah (pbuh) said, 'Yes.' Jibril said, 'Say:

Receive Training From the World of Souls

That when that Holy Face begins to open in the world of souls, that Holy Face they begin to train you not on the highest level, but from *Ulul Amr* (saints). *"Atiullaha wa atiur Rasul wa Ulil amre minkum."* It means you've been trained now in the world of souls where in the world of souls, when you're training and training and training, they begin to teach you that when you are connecting with this energy, keep asking Allah ﷻ there's all that you want is the Holy Face. All that you want is the Holy Face.

...أَطِيعُوا اللَّهَ وَأَطِيعُوا الرَّسُولَ وَأُولِي الْأَمْرِ مِنْكُمْ... ﴿٥٩﴾

4:59 – "...Atiullaha wa atiur Rasula wa Ulil amre minkum..." (Surat An-Nisa)

"... Obey Allah, Obey the Messenger, and those in authority among you..." (The Women, 4:59)

The face of these souls is the hardest to reach. Not the physical face of seeing their picture on the wall, closing your eyes and seeing their picture, but seeing their *arwah* (soul) and being in the world of souls to see their picture and to be asked to be dressed by their face, dressed by their face.

Divinely Attributes Dress the Seven Holy Openings of the Face

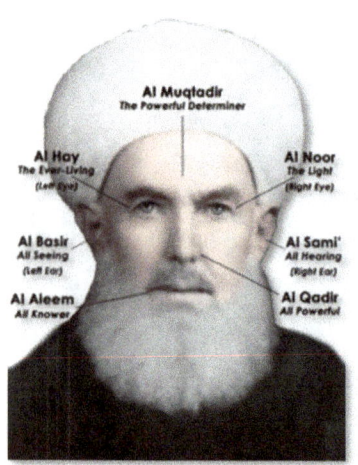

It means the seven holy openings of the face and these are from Divine Essences out of *Ismullah* (Name of Allah ﷻ). These are the essences of creation that dress the holy openings – the two that open onto the ears, the two eyes, the two nostrils and then the light that opens upon the tongue. They be dressed by that hearing. They be dressed by the seeing. They be dressed by the *qudra* of breath. They be dressed by the Divinely Speeches, *Lisan as Siddiq* (the Tongue of Truth) that they inherit from Prophet ﷺ. From that Holy Face, they train that keep your soul always seeking that reality. That we're dressing you from that reality, dressing you from reality. This is all from the *malakut* (heavenly realm), dressing you from that reality.

4. Haqiqatut Tawassul (Reality of Conveyance)

Then *Haqqaiq al Tawassul* (Reality of Conveyance) begins to open that when you've been trained to the company of that face, you begin to ask only that presence. That's why they have the *haqqaiq* of *tawassul*. How they can convey the burdens and the needs of people is because through their soul, they've been trained. As soon as they need to efface themself and begin their practices, they're

seeking that which is real. In the presence of that which is real from *"Atiullah,"* their station may be in Divinely Presence. From *"Atiur Rasul,"* maybe in the Prophetic presence, *"wa Ulil amre minkum"* – maybe amongst the *Ulul Amr* (saints).

Either way, when they make their *du'a* (supplication), when they make the *tawassul*, it means when they convey what you wanted them to convey, they merely connect their hearts and they convey to the face that Allah ﷻ authorized them because there are three authorizations. If they're able to rise above that *Ulul Amr*, they will take them to the presence of Prophet ﷺ, in *Alam al-Arwah* and the world of souls that convey what they have to convey to the reality of what Prophet ﷺ wants to show them of realities.

Awliya's Conveyance is Real-Time

So, their conveyance is real-time. The difference in their *du'a* (supplication) and other people's *du'a* is that other people are like throwing arrows at a target. They may recite many different things, ten different things – recite them and let's see…whoop! Maybe with some *barakah* (blessing), one of them got there. It's different because the one making *du'a* is blind and the one asking is blind.

But *Ahlul Basirah* (the people whose hearts are opened), how he's blind? He's conveying exactly to his *Ulul Amr* (saints). That *Ulul Amr* that you see, my shaykh, you don't see him like we see him. They don't

see him like somebody else sees him, it's even different. You say, 'No, I see him through the physicality.' But if you're trained from the soul, that's a completely different reality. See, even their request is going to be different than the other *muridin* (devoted disciples) because if the *muridin* are only seeing the physicality because this was always the situation even in Cyprus. The forty people who were sleeping in Cyprus, they thought they were the forty *khalifas* (representatives) of Sayyidina Mahdi ﷺ. They only saw the external face of their shaykh. No, there are people who trained with the internal reality and that's why Allah ﷻ says, 'Go into every home through the correct door.'

وَلَيْسَ الْبِرُّ بِأَن تَأْتُوا الْبُيُوتَ مِن ظُهُورِهَا وَلَٰكِنَّ الْبِرَّ مَنِ اتَّقَىٰ ۗ وَأْتُوا الْبُيُوتَ مِنْ أَبْوَابِهَا ۚ وَاتَّقُوا اللَّـهَ لَعَلَّكُمْ تُفْلِحُونَ ﴿١٨٩﴾

2:189 – "...Wa laysal birru bi-an tatol buyoota min zuhooriha wa lakinnal birra manit taqa, wa' tol buyoota min abwabiha, wat taqollaha la'allakum tuflihoon." (Surat Al-Baqarah)

"...And it is not righteousness to enter houses from the back, but righteousness is [in] one who fears Allah. And enter houses from their doors. And be Conscious of Allah that you may succeed."
(The Cow, 2:189)

Haqiqatut Tawassul is From the Heart

What's the correct door for Allah ﷻ? That which is eternal, the soul. It

means if you are making your entrance only to the physicality, that's going to perish. But if your training was from *malakut* (heavenly realm) and from the light and from the world of souls, their connection is real. So, that's the *tawassul* (conveyance). When they begin to make their conveyance, they don't have to talk very much. They merely convey their heart. They say *Fatiha* [opening chapter of Holy Qur'an], they can recite the names of the shaykhs. It's their responsibility to take that *du'a* (supplication) to the presence of Prophet ﷺ. From the presence of Prophet ﷺ, then Prophet ﷺ does what he wants with that *du'a*, that it be conveyed to Allah ﷻ or be resolved at that level. That is the reality of the *haqqaiq*.

5. Haqiqatut Tayy
(Reality of Folding Time and Space)

From that reality, it means they begin now to train from the *haqqaiq* of *tayy* (Folding Time and Space) and the moving between space and time, that we are bound by space and time. The *haqqaiq* of *tayy*, the first levels that have to open is on the

tongue. It means what they're going to train through *khalwah* and seclusions is that the soul power of your tongue begin to recite at a speed far beyond what we understand.

It means their recitation like their breath, in and breath out, and they achieve *zikr* in hundreds of thousands. It means the *tayy* and the movement of space and time, first for the tongue. Then for the body but for the understanding of the body because in the time of *dajjal* (man/system of deceit) now, they don't give permission for the body to be in many places at the same time. Because of the advent of mobile phones, ten people will take a picture of you, place it on Facebook and show that you've been in many places at the same time. You be confused with *dajjal*.

Training at the Soul Level is to Strive for Good Character

But this reality is the reality of the soul. That when Allah ﷻ is training at your soul level, merely they make *tafakkur* (contemplation) and their soul can be many places at the same time. They can enter any environment that Allah ﷻ wants them. This is the world of light. Now this is different than the world of *jinn* (unseen beings). The people who don't have this reality and they play with *jinn*. They ask the *jinn* to take them to go and look into someone's home. They be punished on the Day of Judgement for that or they be punished in this *dunya* (material world). This is not from that reality. This is from what Allah ﷻ opens from their soul under the obedience of good characteristics.

That they are trained with such a characteristic that they don't look at anything that Allah ﷻ don't want them to look at. They don't constantly stare at people with bad character. They don't. They train their eyes. They train their heart to be of the best of character so that these realities open. When these realities open, their soul can move anywhere, can be many places, can enter any environment and pray in that environment, and pray that Allah ﷻ take difficulty away from that environment.

They're trained by Allah ﷻ not to look to the *surah* (face) of people. Don't look to their form.

Shaykhs' Souls Visit Mureeds

It means that *tayy* is a very powerful reality of the soul. For that reason, they visit many of the homes of their students because that one visit enough for them to place one light, one atom of their being in that presence. The one atom of their being is enough to keep praying in that environment, praying and blessing that environment, and convey everything that happening in that environment to the soul of that guide. Because you have to think from the world of light and the power of light, that the atoms of the light all have power. One atom can hear, can see, it can speak; doesn't make a difference whether it's the many or just one. It means wherever they are, their atoms are conveying everything to their soul. Now whether the physicality wants all that information or it's not necessary for the physicality to have the information, but the soul has it.

Importance of Visiting Rauza e Sharif and Holy Maqams

That's why they visit many holy places. Think that if you go to *Rauza e Sharif* (holy burial chamber), into the presence of Sayyidina Muhammad ﷺ, you don't think that a part of your soul will stay with Prophet ﷺ? Is there a way to go to paradise and leave? It's impossible!

That's why Prophet ﷺ being humble, didn't say that, 'I'm the owner of paradise. Come to me.' But, 'My *mihrab* is a piece of paradise.' What *mihrab*? The presence of Sayyidina Muhammad ﷺ; he's the owner of paradises. If not for the reality of Prophet ﷺ, there is no paradise. Allah ﷻ didn't create it. All of it is for Prophet ﷺ.

عَنْ أَبِي هُرَيْرَةَ رَضِيّ اللهُ عَنْهُ عَنِ النَّبِيِّ ﷺ قَالَ : " مَا بَيْنَ بَيْتِي وَمِنْبَرِي رَوْضَةٌ مِنْ رِيَاضِ الْجَنَّةِ، وَمِنْبَرِي عَلَى حَوْضِي ." [صَحِيحُ الْبُخَارِيِّ ١١٩٦]

'An Abi Hurairah (ra) 'anin Nabiyi ﷺ qala: 'Ma bayna bayti wa minbari rawdhatun min riyadhil jannati, wa minbari 'ala hawdhi.'"

Narrated by Abu Hurairah (ra) that the Prophet (pbuh) said, "Between my house and my pulpit there is a garden of the gardens of Paradise, and my pulpit is on my pond of abundance (Kawthar)."
[Sahih al Bukhari, Hadith #1196]

So, when you go and visit *Rauza e Sharif* and visit holy *maqams*, part of your light is staying there, being dressed by their light, blessed by their light, under their *nazar* (gaze). From their *nazar*, they're sending it back to you. If they open *Haqiqatut Tayy* (Reality of Folding Time and Space), then you are receiving these real-times. On holy nights, what Allah ﷻ dressing the soul of Prophet ﷺ, Prophet ﷺ dressing their *arwah* (souls), dressing their atoms. What their shaykh been dressed by, the shaykh is dressing their *arwah*, dressing their atoms because they are from the people of the world of light.

6. Haqiqatul Irshad (Reality of Guidance)

At that time, a permission comes from Allah ﷻ, from Prophet ﷺ to the *Murshid* (authorized spiritual guide) that, give them now *ijazah* (permission) for guidance. The manifestation of the *ijazah* for guidance in *Naqshbandiya tul 'Aliya* (The Most Distinguished Naqshbandi Order) is based on all these realities, that you have to have been a person trained in the world of light. The world of light signed off on all of these realities. You've been trained in these realities and they are infinite in their *darajat* (spiritual rank). The shaykhs above have infinite more capacity because the world of light can't be limited. What Allah ﷻ gives can never be understood and limited so each one much more powerful.

But the basic minimum of understanding that for that guidance to come, it means they were heavily trained in the world of light. If your soul has been trained and they begin to open the connection with your physicality, that's where the physicality comes in because they trained all of your realities upon your soul. Allah ﷻ begins to give the permission that, 'Give that person permission to guide' because they're

guiding with all of these faculties. They have the *juzba* and magnetism to attract. They have all the realities of these lights blessing them. They are connected to the Holy Face. Their *du'as* (supplications) are reaching towards that holy reality. At the same time, their soul is moving in directions wherever Allah 🕮 wants their soul to move. That becomes the oceans of guidance and the oceans of reality.

When they celebrate holy nights, it's not like other people celebrating. They're being dressed from these realities, blessed from these realities, and they freely dress anybody who's around like the sun that gives its rays to anybody who is sitting on that beach. It means that becomes the understanding of these realities and these lights and these blessings, *inshaAllah*.

Subhana rabbika rabbal 'izzati 'amma yasifoon, wa salaamun 'alal mursaleen, walhamdulillahi rabbil 'aalameen. Bi hurmati Muhammad al-Mustafa wa bi siri Surat al-Fatiha.

Get Your
Very Own
Signed Copy!

A Timeless Reality

Ancient Wisdoms of the Soul & Meditation

ABOUT THE BOOK

Meditation, known as *tafakkur* (contemplation), serves to nourish the spirit, acquire the essence of sincere knowledge, and open powerful secrets for the soul to achieve inner peace. In times of global upheaval, it's essential to face challenges with strengthened spiritual reflection and resolve. This unique compilation teaches how to slow life down, detach from the physical realm, and awaken the soul's connection to the world of light – the Divine's ancient timeless reality.

Speaking from 26 years of spiritual training and many seclusions, Shaykh Nurjan Mirahmadi conveys ancient wisdoms for the soul that will cultivate a higher consciousness of the Divine. As a Certified Shaykh in this field of meditation, he provides inspirational guidance supported with full-colour visuals, allowing the student to understand, reflect, and progress in their spiritual development.

Presented in a question and answer format, this book guides the reader in practicing meditation, connecting the heart to a guide, benefiting from daily spiritual practices, understanding the effects of positive and negative energy on the body, mind, and soul, and applying the concepts of contemplation towards building good character. *A Timeless Reality* will transform every aspect of your life as you embark on a life-changing quest for the Divine.

Available at
amazon

**ORDER YOUR
COPY TODAY!**

FIVE STAR REVIEWS

By Amazon Reviewers

⭐⭐⭐⭐⭐

A Treasure Trove for the Seeker
"The knowledge and guidance provided in this book is immeasurable. Anyone seeking to know themselves by way of truth must read this book! The chapters, Q&A compilation and graphics are thoughtfully arranged to shepherd the reader through deep realities of the soul while inspiring the importance of self purification. A true treasure trove of knowledge on subjects of meditation, energy practices, divine love and character building.

There is something for everyone from the novice to the seasoned meditator. Beautiful color illustrations and heavenly cover. Recommend to any Sufi aspirant or Seeker of Spiritual Knowledge."

Limitless Oceans That Keep Giving to the Soul
"Blessed and heavenly knowledges that have been compiled into an easily readable and digestable format. This question and answer format will make you feel you're right in front of the Shaykh getting direct guidance at a place and time convenient for you. If you're on a journey to find yourself and are seeking Divine's satisfaction, this is the book for you!"

Essential for Mental Health & Wellness
"Feels nurturing, empowering, and soul-lifting! Definitely worth the time and attention including putting into practice the meditation techniques."

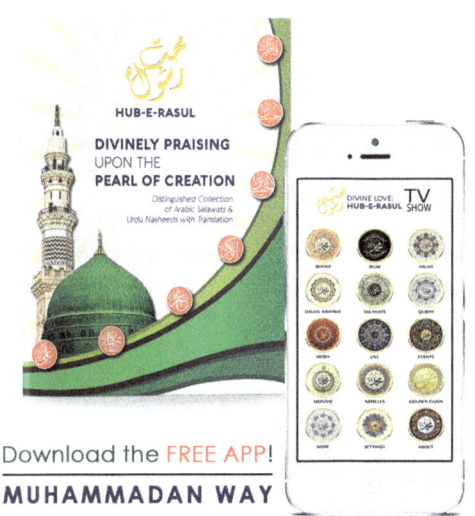

Download the **FREE APP!**

MUHAMMADAN WAY

HUB-E-RASUL

DIVINELY PRAISING
UPON THE
PEARL OF CREATION

FIVE STAR REVIEWS
By Amazon Reviewers

ABOUT THE BOOK

Divinely Praising Upon the Pearl of Creation is a distinguished collection of supplications and praisings upon the Prophet Muhammad (peace be upon him).

By sending salutations the reciter builds a tremendous light and energy within their heart and soul while increasing love and gratitude for all Prophets and the Divine. Salawats carry an immense power and provide healing and relief from ailments and difficulties.

This book features well-known Arabic Salawats and Urdu Nasheeds. Praisings are presented in an easy-to-read format with original language script, full English transliteration and in-depth translation. This compilation of invocations comes from authentic Arabic and Urdu sources which have been recited for centuries.

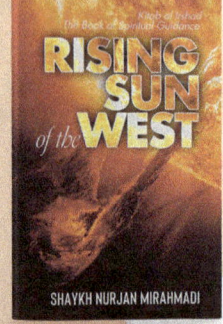
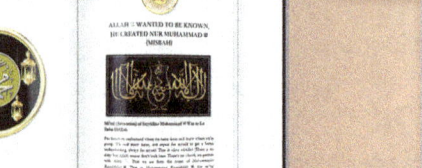

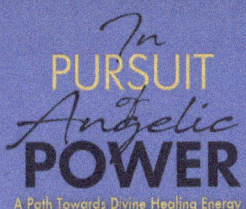

In PURSUIT Angelic POWER

A Path Towards Divine Healing Energy

Now Available in Urdu!

ABOUT THE BOOK

As heavenly beings, our souls are eternally in pursuit of healing energy through Divine and Angelic Power. By understanding the origins of energy through light and sound, the seeker learns to attune to the guides of heavenly knowledge and discovers essential techniques to acquire and increase positive energy within our beings.

FIVE-STAR REVIEWS

By Amazon Reviewers ⭐⭐⭐⭐⭐

"This invigorating book broadens and promotes a knowledge of the affinity and interactions between Angels and Humans."

"A must have in every home!
"In Pursuit of Angelic Power" serves to mankind an introduction and insight to our illuminating friends."

YASEEN

PROPHET ﷺ IS THE WALKING QURAN

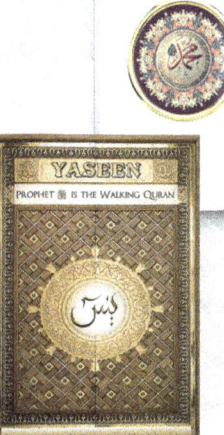

ABOUT THE BOOK

Prophet Muhammad ﷺ has been granted the highest of stations by Allah ﷻ (the Divine) and nowhere is it clearer than in the heart of the Holy Qur'an, Surat YaSeen. It is through Prophet Muhammad's ﷺ light that all of creation came into existence and it is through his heart that the Holy Qur'an was revealed. As the chief of all Prophets, he is the literal Walking Qur'an, conveying the sublime realities of Allah's ﷻ Holy Speech to all.

FIVE-STAR REVIEWS

By Amazon Reviewers ⭐⭐⭐⭐⭐

"This is yet another amazing book from Shaykh Nurjan. His knowledge is without limit and his delivery is digestible to the well versed and the initiate. Illustrations are beautiful and fill this book from the first page to the last."

"Author's heavenly knowledge touches the heart and feeds the soul. If knowledge is power, then can you imagine what heavenly knowledge is? Empower your soul and buy this book."

Available at

ORDER YOUR COPY TODAY!

LEVELS OF THE HEART
LATAIF AL QALB

SECRET REALITIES
OF HAJJ

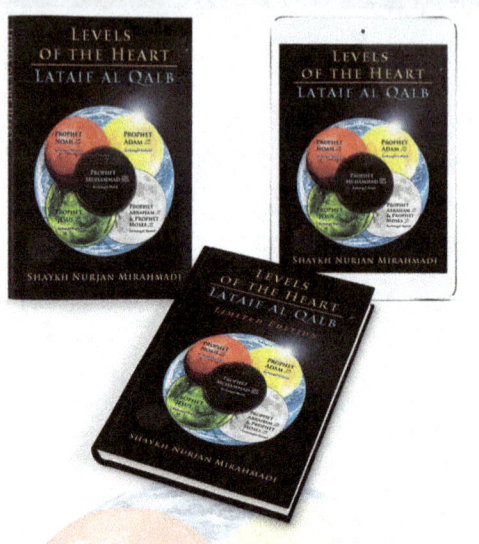

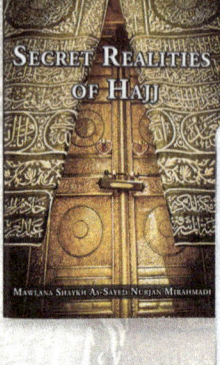

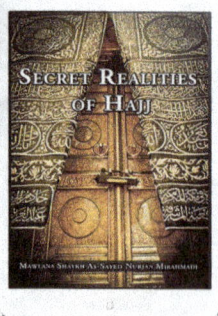

ABOUT THE BOOK

There are subtle energies and realities that are dressing the heart – these are the Levels of the Heart (Lataif al Qalb). Shaykh Nurjan has composed an exceptional work on the map of the heart, intertwining the teachings of its spiritual attributes and how they affect every aspect of a seeker's path.

ABOUT THE BOOK

Secret Realities of Hajj features invaluable teachings and spiritual insight into the Islamic holy pilgrimage of Hajj. From the historical references of holy prophets to the remarkable scientific explanations of the circumambulation, this book provides a deeper understanding of this important pillar of faith.

FIVE-STAR REVIEWS
BY AMAZON REVIEWERS ★★★★★

"I've learned more about Islam in 6 months than in 20 years reading Shaykh Nurjan's books, reading the articles on his app and watching his YouTube channel videos. His teachings transcend the worldly divisions we've created and helps unveil our deeper spiritual and universal realities within."

"To finally have all this information in one book is simply incredible. It is an ocean of spiritual knowledge."

FIVE-STAR REVIEWS
By Amazon Reviewers ★★★★★

"Amazing! A rare jewel filled with illuminating knowledge. Highly recommended for non-Muslims and Muslims equally, as the secrets referred to are, in reality, secrets related to creation itself, and the inner reality of the human heart."

"A must-read for people interested in the spirtitual dimensions and secrets of the Hajj. The author has intimate knowledge of the topic from a long lineage of Sufi Masters. Pick up and enjoy, I did."

Available at
amazon

**ORDER YOUR
COPY TODAY!**

CHECK US OUT ON SOCIAL MEDIA!

Shaykh Nurjan
Mirahmadi

The Muhammadan Way

shaykhnurjanmirahmadi

Shaykh Nurjan
Mirahmadi

The Muhammadan Way

WhatsApp

The Muhammadan Way

SMC MERCHANDISE

SMC

SUFI SUNNAH APPAREL
ISLAMIC CALLIGRAPHY WEAR

ACCESSORIES
UNIQUE ITEMS WITH
ORIGINAL CALLIGRAPHIC
DESIGN

SUFI ESSENTIALS
TAWEEZ / PRAYER BEADS
STICKERS AND MORE

BAKHOOR AND PERFUMES
BLESSED SUFI SCENTS
FEATURING
PREMIERE ARABIAN BRANDS

WELLNESS TEAS
CUSTOM-BLENDS WITH
HEALING PROPERTIES

LIMITED EDITION PRODUCTS!

VIEW THE FULL SELECTION OF ITEMS AT

SMCMERCH.COM

WWW.SMCMERCH.COM

Discover the renowned SMC collection showcasing the remarkable Phoenix emblem and exquisite Islamic calligraphy

GIVE THE PERFECT GIFT!

SHOP ONLINE TODAY!

"Give charity without delay, for it stands in the way of calamity." ~ Prophet Muhammad ﷺ

Sponsor a Well

Donate to install a water well or give towards repair work of current wells.

Please add a special note for dedication or any prayer requests you have.

Sadaqah

Please add a note on which Sadaqah the payment is for and prayer (du'a) requests.

Sadaqah Nafilah
Sadaqah Wajibah

Zakat

Fulfilling your Zakat is an act of faith that purifies wealth while also serving humanity.

Your payment offers recipients much-needed help, hope and a chance to improve lives!

Use the zakat calculator to determine your personal amount for the year.

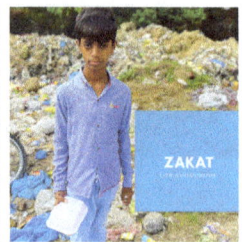

Orphan Support

Dedicated to looking after the welfare of orphaned children around the world with the goal to reshape the lives of these children for the better.

Ongoing programs: orphanage repairs, providing nutritious meals, clothing, health and wellness support, pediatric care, and education supplies.

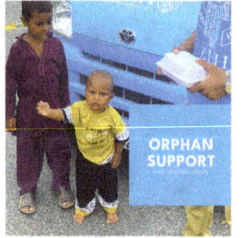

Milad an-Nabi ﷺ

Donations go towards Mawlid Events such as the Annual Grand Milad un Nabi ﷺ.

These are special programs to commemorate the life and times of our Holy Prophet Muhammad ﷺ.

Mobile Relief

Food rescue and redistribution throughtout Vancouver, Los Angeles, Chicago, and Pakistan.

Supporting local communities on a weekly basis to help reduce hunger.

Qurban Support

Preparation and distribution of thousands of pounds of fresh meat to deprived communities around the world.

Please add note for dedication or any dua requests you have.

New Masjid Support

The mosque is the heart of a community, a key necessity for people to feel connected, and a center for knowledge for all.

Help spread the light and love of Islam.

Dawah

Knowledge propagation to present Islamic spiritual teachings to the general public.

Donations go towards:

- Book Publishing
- Computer Equipment
- App Development
- Social Media Marketing
- Website Maintenance
- Hosting Servers
- Graphic Design
- Film, TV Show, Media

Give a Gift

Shaykh Nurjan is authorized to teach, guide, and counsel religious students around the world to Islamic Spirituality.

Show your love and appreciation with a generous contribution.